the greatest trade ever

The Behind-the-Scenes Story of How John Paulson
Defied Wall Street and Made Financial History

the
greatest
trade ever

gregory zuckerman

CROWN
BUSINESS
NEW YORK

Copyright © 2009, 2010 by Gregory Zuckerman

Published in the United States by Crown Business, an imprint of
the Crown Publishing Group, a division of Random House, Inc., New York.
www.crownpublishing.com

CROWN BUSINESS is a trademark and CROWN and the Rising Sun colophon
are registered trademarks of Random House, Inc.

Originally published in hardcover in slightly different form in the United States
by Broadway Books, an imprint of the Crown Publishing Group, a division of
Random House, Inc., New York, in 2009.

Crown Business books are available at special discounts for bulk purchases for sales
promotions or corporate use. Special editions, including personalized covers,
excerpts of existing books, or books with corporate logos, can be created in
large quantities for special needs. For more information, contact Premium Sales at
(212) 572-2232 or e-mail specialmarkets@randomhouse.com.

Library of Congress Cataloging-in-Publication Data
Zuckerman, Gregory.
    The greatest trade ever: the behind-the-scenes story of how John Paulson
defied Wall Street and made financial history / Gregory Zuckerman. — 1st ed.
        p. cm.
    1. Paulson, John Alfred, 1955–   2. Hedge funds—United States.
3. Hedging (Finance)   I. Title.
HG4930.Z83 2009
332.64'5092—dc22
[B]   2009033255

ISBN 978-0-385-52994-5

Printed in the United States of America

Design by Ralph Fowler / rlfdesign

Frontispiece: John Paulson (Mike McGregor / Contour by Getty Images)

10 9 8 7 6 5 4 3 2 1

First Paperback Edition

TO DAD AND TO MOM,

MY TEACHERS, MY FOUNDATION

TO MICHELLE, GABRIEL, AND ELIJAH,

MY JOY, MY INSPIRATION

the greatest trade ever

introduction

The tip was intriguing. It was the fall of 2007, financial markets were collapsing, and Wall Street firms were losing massive amounts of money, as if they were trying to give back a decade's worth of profits in a few brutal months. But as I sat at my desk at *The Wall Street Journal* tallying the pain, a top hedge-fund manager called to rave about an investor named John Paulson who somehow was scoring huge profits. My contact, speaking with equal parts envy and respect, grabbed me with this: "Paulson's not even a housing or mortgage guy. . . . And until this trade, he was run-of-the-mill, nothing special."

There had been chatter that a few little-known investors had anticipated the housing troubles and purchased obscure investments that now were paying off. But few details had emerged and my sources were too busy keeping their firms afloat and their careers alive to offer very much. I began piecing together Paulson's trade, a welcome respite from the gory details of the latest banking fiasco. Cracking Paulson's moves seemed at least as instructive as the endless mistakes of the financial titans.

Riding the bus home one evening through the gritty New Jersey streets of Newark and East Orange, I did some quick math. Paulson hadn't simply met with success—he had rung up the biggest financial coup in history, the greatest trade ever recorded. All from a rank outsider in the world of real estate investing—could it be?

The more I learned about Paulson and the obstacles he overcame, the more intrigued I became, especially when I discovered he wasn't alone—a group of gutsy, colorful investors, all well outside Wall Street's establishment, was close on his heels. These traders had become concerned about an era of loose money and financial chicanery, and had placed billions of dollars of investments to prepare for a meltdown they were certain was imminent.

Some made huge profits and won't have to work another day of their lives. But others squandered an early lead on Paulson and stumbled at the finish line, a historic prize just out of reach.

Paulson's winnings were so enormous they seemed unreal, even cartoonish. His firm, Paulson & Co., made $15 billion in 2007, a figure that topped the gross domestic products of Bolivia, Honduras, and Paraguay, South American nations with more than twelve million residents. Paulson's personal cut was nearly $4 billion, or more than $10 million *a day*. That was more than the combined earnings of J. K. Rowling, Oprah Winfrey, and Tiger Woods. At one point in late 2007, a broker called to remind Paulson of a personal account worth $5 million, a sum now so insignificant it had slipped his mind. Just as impressive, Paulson managed to transform his trade in 2008 and early 2009 in dramatic form, scoring $5 billion more for his firm and clients, as well as $2 billion for himself. The moves put Paulson alongside Warren Buffett, George Soros, Bernard Baruch, and Jesse Livermore in Wall Street's pantheon of traders. They also made him one of the richest people in the world, wealthier than Steven Spielberg, Mark Zuckerberg, and David Rockefeller Sr.

Even Paulson and the other bearish investors didn't foresee the degree of pain that would result from the housing tsunami and its related global ripples. By early 2009, losses by global banks and other firms were nearing $3 trillion while stock-market investors had lost more than $30 trillion. A financial storm that began in risky home mortgages left the worst global economic crisis since the Great Depression in its wake. Over a stunning two-week period in September 2008, the U.S. government was forced to take over mortgage-lending giants Fannie Mae and Freddie Mac, along with huge insurer American International Group. Investors watched helplessly as onetime Wall Street power Lehman Brothers filed for bankruptcy, wounded brokerage giant Merrill Lynch rushed into the arms of Bank of America, and federal regulators seized Washington Mutual in the largest bank failure in the nation's history. At one point in the crisis, panicked investors offered to buy U.S. Treasury bills without asking for any return on their investment, hoping to find somewhere safe to hide their money.

By the middle of 2009, a record one in ten Americans was delinquent or in foreclosure on their mortgages. During the teeth of the crisis, even celebrities such as Ed McMahon and Evander Holyfield fought to keep their homes. U.S. housing prices fell more than 30 percent from their 2006 peak. In cities such as Miami, Phoenix, and Las Vegas, real-estate values dropped more than 40 percent. Several million people lost their homes. And more than 30 percent of U.S. home owners held mortgages that were underwater, or greater than the value of their houses, the highest level in seventy-five years.

John Paulson and a small group of underdog investors were among the few who triumphed over the hubris and failures of Wall Street and the financial sector.

But how did a group of unsung investors predict a meltdown that blindsided the experts? Why was it John Paulson, a relative amateur in real estate, and not a celebrated mortgage, bond, or housing specialist like Bill Gross or Mike Vranos, who pulled off the greatest trade in history? How did Paulson anticipate Wall Street's troubles, even as Hank Paulson, the former Goldman Sachs chief who ran the Treasury Department and shared his surname, missed them? Short sellers kicked themselves for dismissing signs of trouble. Even Warren Buffett overlooked the trade, and George Soros phoned Paulson for a tutorial.

Did the investment banks and financial pros truly believe that housing was in an inexorable climb, or were there other reasons they ignored or continued to inflate the bubble? And why did the very bankers who created the toxic mortgages that undermined the financial system get hurt most by them?

This book, based on more than two hundred hours of interviews with key participants in the daring trade, aims to answer some of these questions, and perhaps provide lessons and insights for future financial manias.

prologue

John Paulson seemed to live an ambitious man's dream. At the age of forty-nine, Paulson managed more than $2 billion for his investors, as well as $100 million of his own wealth. The office of his Midtown Manhattan hedge fund, located in a trendy building on 57th and Madison, was decorated with dozens of Alexander Calder watercolors. Paulson and his wife, Jenny, a pretty brunette, split their time between an upscale town house on New York's fashionable Upper East Side and a multimillion-dollar seaside home in the Hamptons, a playground of the affluent where Paulson was active on the social circuit. Trim and fit, with close-cropped dark hair that was beginning to thin at the top, Paulson didn't enjoy exceptional looks. But his warm brown eyes and impish smile made him seem approachable, even friendly, and Paulson's unlined face suggested someone several years younger.

The window of Paulson's corner office offered a dazzling view of Central Park and the Wollman skating rink. This morning, however, he had little interest in grand views. Paulson sat at his desk staring at an array of numbers flashing on computer screens before him, grimacing.

"This is crazy," he said to Paolo Pellegrini, one of his analysts, as Pellegrini walked into his office.

It was late spring of 2005. The economy was on a roll, housing and financial markets were booming, and the hedge-fund era was in full swing. But Paulson couldn't make much sense of the market. And he wasn't making much money, at least compared with his rivals. He had been eclipsed by a group of much younger hedge-fund managers who had amassed huge fortunes over the last few years—and were spending their winnings in over-the-top ways.

Paulson knew he didn't fit into that world. He was a solid investor, careful and decidedly unspectacular. But such a description was almost an insult in a world where investors chased the hottest hand, and traders could recall the investment returns of their competitors as easily as they could their children's birthdays.

Even Paulson's style of investing, featuring long hours devoted to intensive research, seemed outmoded. The biggest traders employed high-powered computer models to dictate their moves. These investors accounted for a majority of the activity on the New York Stock Exchange and a growing share of Wall Street's wealth. Other gutsy hedge-fund managers borrowed large sums to make risky investments, or grabbed positions in the shares of public companies and bullied executives to take steps to send their stocks flying. Paulson's tried-and-true methods were viewed as quaint.

It should have been Paulson atop Wall Street, his friends thought. Paulson had grown up in a firmly middle-class neighborhood in Queens, New York. He received early insight into the world of finance from his grandfather, a businessman who lost a fortune in the Great Depression. Paulson graduated atop his class at both New York University and Harvard Business School. He then learned at the knees of some of the market's top investors and bankers, before launching his own hedge fund in 1994. Pensive and deeply intelligent, Paulson's forte was investing in corporate mergers that he viewed as the most likely to be completed, among the safest forms of investing.

When the soft-spoken Paulson met with clients, they sometimes were surprised by his limp handshake and restrained manner, unusual in an industry full of bluster. His ability to explain complex trades in straightforward terms left some wondering if his strategies were routine, even simple. Younger hedge-fund traders went tieless and dressed casually, feeling confident in their abilities thanks to their soaring profits and growing stature. Paulson stuck with dark suits and muted ties.

Paulson's lifestyle once had been much flashier. A bachelor well into his forties, Paulson, known as J.P. among friends, was a tireless womanizer who chased the glamour and beauty of young models, like so many others on Wall Street. But unlike his peers, Paulson employed an unusually modest strategy with women, much as he did with stocks. He was kind, charming, witty, and gentlemanly, and he met with frequent success.

In 2000, though, Paulson grew tired of the chase and, at the age of forty-four, married his assistant, a native of Romania. They had settled into a quiet domestic life. Paulson cut his ties with wilder friends and spent weekends doting on his two young daughters.

By 2005, Paulson had reached his twilight years in accelerated Wall Street–career time. He still was at it, though, still hungry for a big trade that might prove his mettle. It was the fourth year of a spectacular surge in housing prices, the likes of which the nation never had seen. Home owners felt flush, enjoying the soaring values of their homes, and buyers bid up prices to previously unheard-of levels. Real estate was the talk of every cocktail party, soccer match, and family barbecue. Financial behemoths such as Citigroup and AIG, New Century and Bear Stearns, were scoring big profits. The economy was roaring. Everyone seemed to be making money hand over fist. Everyone but John Paulson, that is.

To many, Paulson seemed badly out of touch. Months earlier, he had been ridiculed at a party in Southampton by a dashing German investor incredulous at Paulson's meager returns and his resistance to housing's allures. Paulson's own friend, Jeffrey Greene, had amassed a collection of prime Los Angeles real estate properties valued at more than $500 million, along with a coterie of celebrity friends, including Mike Tyson, Oliver Stone, and Paris Hilton.

But beneath the market's placid surface, the tectonic plates were quietly shifting. A financial earthquake was about to shake the world. Paulson thought he heard far-off rumblings—rumblings that the hedge-fund heroes and frenzied home buyers were ignoring.

Paulson dumped his fund's riskier investments and began laying bets against auto suppliers, financial companies, anything likely to go down in bad times. He also bought investments that served as cheap insurance in case things went wrong. But the economy chugged ever higher, and Paulson & Co. endured one of the most difficult periods.

Even bonds of Delphi, a bankrupt auto supplier that Paulson assumed would tumble, suddenly surged in price, rising 50 percent over several days.

"This [market] is like a casino," he insisted to one trader at his firm, with unusual irritation.

He challenged Pellegrini and his other analysts: "Is there a bubble we can short?"

PAOLO PELLEGRINI felt his own mounting pressures. A year earlier, the tall, stylish analyst, a native of Italy, had called Paulson, looking for a job. Despite his amiable nature and razor-sharp intellect, Pellegrini had been a failure as an investment banker and flamed out at a series of other businesses. He'd been lucky to get a foot in the door at Paulson's hedge fund—there had been an opening only because a junior analyst left for business school. Paulson, an old friend, agreed to take him on.

Now, Pellegrini, just a year younger than Paulson, was competing with a group of hungry twenty-year-olds—kids the same age as his own children. His early work for Paulson had been pedestrian, he realized, and Pellegrini felt his short leash at the firm growing tighter. Somehow, he had to find a way to keep his job and jump-start his career.

Analyzing reams of housing data into the night, hunched over a desk in his small cubicle, Pellegrini began to discover proof that the real estate market had reached untenable levels. He told Paulson that trouble was imminent.

Reading the evidence, Paulson was immediately convinced Pellegrini was right. The question was, how could they profit from the discovery? Daunting obstacles confronted them. Paulson was no housing expert, and he never had traded real estate investments. Even if he was right, Paulson knew, he could lose his entire investment if he was too early anticipating a bursting of what he saw as a real estate bubble, or if he didn't implement the trade properly. Any number of legendary investors, from Jesse Livermore in the 1930s to Julian Robertson and George Soros in the 1990s, had failed to successfully navigate financial bubbles, costing them dearly.

Paulson's challenges were even more imposing. It was impossible to directly bet against the price of a home. Just as important, a robust infrastructure had grown to support real estate, as a network of low-cost lenders, home appraisers, brokers, and bankers worked to keep the money spigot flowing. On a national basis, home prices never had fallen over an extended period. Some rivals already had been burned trying to anticipate an end of housing's bull market.

Moreover, unbeknownst to Paulson, competitors were well ahead of him, threatening any potential windfall. In San Jose, California, three thousand miles away, Dr. Michael Burry, a doctor-turned-hedge-fund manager, was busy trying to place his own massive trades to profit from a real estate collapse. In New York, a brash trader named Greg Lippmann soon would begin to make bearish trades, while teaching hundreds of Paulson's competitors how to wager against housing.

Experts redirected Paulson, pointing out that he had no background in housing or subprime mortgages. But Wall Street had underestimated him. Paulson was no singles hitter, afraid of risk. A part of him had been waiting for the perfect trade, one that could prove Paulson to be among the greatest investors of all. Anticipating a housing collapse—and all that it meant—was Paulson's chance to hit the ball out of the park and win the acclaim he deserved. It might be his last chance. He just had to find a way to pull off the trade.

And chase the frothy bubbles,
While the world is full of troubles.
—William Butler Yeats

A GLIMPSE OF WALL STREET'S TRADING FLOORS AND INVESTMENT
offices in 2005 would reveal a group of revelers enjoying
a raging, multiyear party. In one corner, making a whole
lot of noise, were the hedge-fund managers, a particularly exuberant
bunch, some with well-cut, tailored suits and designer shoes, but others
a bit tipsy, with ugly lampshades on their heads.

Hedge funds gained public consciousness in the new millennium
with an unusual mystique and outsized swagger. But hedge funds actually had been around since 1949, when Alfred Winslow Jones, an
Australian-born writer for *Fortune Magazine* researching an article
about innovative strategies, decided to take a stab at running his own
partnership. Months before the magazine had a chance to publish his
piece, Jones and four friends raised $100,000 and borrowed money on
top of that to create a big investment pool.

Rather than simply own stocks and be exposed to the whims of the
market, though, Jones tried to "hedge," or protect, his portfolio by betting against some shares while holding others. If the market tumbled,
Jones figured, his bearish investments would help insulate his portfolio

and he could still profit. If Jones got excited about the outlook of General Motors, for example, he might buy 100 shares of the automaker, and offset them with a negative stance against 100 shares of rival Ford Motor. Jones entered his bearish investments by borrowing shares from brokers and selling them, hoping they fell in price and could be replaced at a lower level, a tactic called a short sale. Borrow and sell 100 shares of Ford at $20, pocket $2,000. Then watch Ford drop to $15, buy 100 shares for $1,500, and hand the stock back to your broker to replace the shares you'd borrowed. The $500 difference is your profit.

By both borrowing money and selling short, Jones married two speculative tools to create a potentially conservative portfolio. And by limiting himself to fewer than one hundred investors and accepting only wealthy clients, Jones avoided having to register with the government as an investment company. He charged clients a hefty 20 percent of any gains he produced, something mutual-fund managers couldn't easily do because of legal restrictions.

The hedge-fund concept slowly caught on; Warren Buffett started one a few years later, though he shuttered it in 1969, wary of a looming bear market. In the early 1990s, a group of bold investors, including George Soros, Michael Steinhardt, and Julian Robertson, scored huge gains, highlighted by Soros's 1992 wager that the value of the British pound would tumble, a move that earned $1 billion for his Quantum hedge fund. Like Jones, these investors accepted only wealthy clients, including pension plans, endowments, charities, and individuals. That enabled the funds to skirt various legal requirements, such as submitting to regular examinations by regulators. The hedge-fund honchos disclosed very little of what they were up to, even to their own clients, creating an air of mystery about them.

Each of the legendary hedge-fund managers suffered deep losses in the late 1990s or in 2000, however, much as Hall of Fame ballplayers often stumble in the latter years of their playing days, sending a message that even the "stars" couldn't best the market forever. The 1998 collapse of mega–hedge fund Long-Term Capital Management, which lost 90 percent of its value over a matter of months, also put a damper on the industry, while cratering global markets. By the end of the 1990s, there were just 515 hedge funds in existence, managing less than $500 billion, a pittance of the trillions managed by traditional investment managers.

It took the bursting of the high-technology bubble in late 2000, and the resulting devastation suffered by investors who stuck with a conventional mix of stocks and bonds, to raise the popularity and profile of hedge funds. The stock market plunged between March 2000 and October 2002, led by the technology and Internet stocks that investors had become enamored with, as the Standard & Poor's 500 fell 38 percent. The tech-laden Nasdaq Composite Index dropped a full 75 percent. But hedge funds overall managed to lose only 1 percent, thanks to bets against high-flying stocks and holdings of more resilient and exotic investments that others were wary of, such as Eastern European shares, convertible bonds, and troubled debt. By protecting their portfolios, and zigging as the market zagged, the funds seemed to have discovered the holy grail of investing: ample returns in any kind of market. Falling interest rates provided an added boost, making the money they borrowed—known in the business as leverage, or gearing—inexpensive. That enabled funds to boost the size of their holdings and amplify their gains.

Money rushed into hedge funds after 2002 as a rebound in global growth left pension plans, endowments, and individuals flush, eager to both multiply and retain their wealth. Leveraged-buyout firms, which borrowed their own money to make acquisitions, also became beneficiaries of an emerging era of easy money. Hedge funds charged clients steep fees, usually 2 percent or so of the value of their accounts and 20 percent or more of any gains achieved. But like an exclusive club in an upscale part of town, they found they could levy heavy fees and even turn away most potential customers, and still more investors came pounding on their doors, eager to hand over fistfuls of cash.

There were good reasons that hedge funds caught on. Just as Winston Churchill said democracy is the worst form of government except for all the others, hedge funds, for all their faults, beat the pants off of the competition. Mutual funds and most other traditional investment vehicles were decimated in the 2000–2002 period, some losing half or more of their value. Some mutual funds bought into the prevailing wisdom that technology shares were worth the rich valuations. Others were unable to bet against stocks or head to the sidelines as hedge funds did. Most mutual funds considered it a good year if they simply beat the market, even if it meant losing a third of their investors' money, rather than half.

Reams of academic data demonstrated that few mutual funds could best the market over the long haul. And while index funds were a cheaper and better-performing alternative, these investment vehicles only did well if the market rose. Once, Peter Lynch, Jeffrey Vinik, Mario Gabelli, and other savvy investors were content to manage mutual funds. But the hefty pay and flexible guidelines of the hedge-fund business allowed it to drain much of the talent from the mutual-fund pool by the early years of the new millennium—another reason for investors with the financial wherewithal to turn to hedge funds.

For years, it had been vaguely geeky for young people to obsess over complex investment strategies. Sure, big-money types always got the girls. But they didn't really want to hear how you made it all. After 2000, however, running a hedge fund and spouting off about interest-only securities, capital-structure arbitrage, and attractive tracts of timberland became downright sexy. James Cramer, Suze Orman, and other financial commentators with a passion for money and markets emerged as matinee idols, while glossy magazines like *Trader Monthly* chronicled, and even deified, the exploits of Wall Street's most successful investors.

Starting a hedge fund became the clear career choice of top college and business-school graduates. In close second place: working for a fund, at least long enough to gain enough experience to launch one's own. Many snickered at joining investment banks and consulting firms, let alone businesses that actually made things, preferring to produce profits with computer keystrokes and brief, impassioned phone calls.

By the end of 2005, more than 2,200 hedge funds around the globe managed almost $1.5 trillion, surpassing even Internet companies as the signature vehicle for amassing fortune in modern times. Because many funds traded in a rapid-fire style, and borrowed money to expand their portfolios, they accounted for more than 20 percent of the trading of U.S. stocks, and 80 percent of some important bond and derivative markets.[1]

The impressive gains and huge fees helped usher in a Gilded Age 2.0 as funds racked up outsized profits, even by the standards of the investment business. Edward Lampert, a hedge-fund investor who gained control of retailer Kmart and then gobbled up even larger Sears, Roebuck, made $1 billion in 2004, dwarfing the combined $43 million that chief executives of Goldman Sachs, Microsoft, and General Electric made that year.[2]

The most successful hedge-fund managers enjoyed celebrity-billion-aire status, shaking up the worlds of art, politics, and philanthropy. Kenneth Griffin married another hedge-fund trader, Anne Dias, at the Palace of Versailles and held a postceremony party at the Louvre, following a rehearsal dinner at the Musée d'Orsay. Steven Cohen spent $8 million for a preserved shark by Damien Hirst, part of a $1 billion art collection assembled in four years that included work from Keith Haring, Jackson Pollock, van Gogh, Gauguin, Andy Warhol, and Roy Lichtenstein. Whiz kid Eric Mindich, a thirty-something hotshot, raised millions for Democratic politicians and was a member of presidential candidate John Kerry's inner circle.

Hedge-fund pros, a particularly philanthropic group that wasn't shy about sharing that fact, established innovative charities, including the Robin Hood Foundation, notable for black-tie fund-raisers attracting celebrities like Gwyneth Paltrow and Harvey Weinstein, and for creative efforts to revamp inner-city schools.

The hedge-fund ascension was part of a historic expansion in the financial sector. Markets became bigger and more vibrant, and companies found it more inexpensive to raise capital, resulting in a burst of growth around the globe, surging home ownership, and an improved quality of life.

But by 2005, a financial industry based on creating, trading, and managing shares and debts of businesses was growing at a faster pace than the economy itself, as if a kind of financial alchemy was at work. Finance companies earned about 15 percent of all U.S. profits in the

1970s and 1980s, a figure that surged past 25 percent by 2005. By the mid-2000s, more than 20 percent of Harvard University undergraduates entered the finance business, up from less than 5 percent in the 1960s.

One of the hottest businesses for financial firms: trading with hedge funds, lending them money, and helping even young, inexperienced investors like Michael Burry get into the game.

MICHAEL BURRY had graduated medical school and was almost finished with his residency at Stanford University Medical School in 2000 when he got the hedge-fund bug. Though he had no formal financial education and started his firm in the living room of his boyhood home in suburban San Jose, investment banks eagerly courted him.

Alison Sanger, a broker at Bank of America, flew to meet Burry and sat with him on a living-room couch, near an imposing drum set, as she described what her bank could offer his new firm. Red shag carpeting served as Burry's trading floor. A worn, yellowing chart on a nearby closet door tracked the progressive heights of Burry and his brothers in their youth, rather than any commodity or stock price. Burry, wearing jeans and a T-shirt, asked Sanger if she could recommend a good book about how to run a hedge fund, betraying his obvious ignorance. Despite that, Sanger signed him up as a client.

"Our model at the time was to embrace start-up funds, and it was clear he was a really smart guy," she explains.

Hedge funds became part of the public consciousness. In an episode of the soap opera *All My Children*, Ryan told Kendall, "Love isn't like a hedge fund, you know . . . you can't have all your money in one investment, and if it looks a little shaky, you can't just buy something that looks a little safer." (Perhaps it was another sign of the times that the show's hedge-fund reference was the only snippet of the overwrought dialogue that made much sense.) Designer Kenneth Cole even offered a leather loafer called the Hedge Fund, available in black or brown at $119.98.[3]

Things soon turned a bit giddy, as investors threw money at traders with impressive credentials. When Eric Mindich left Goldman Sachs to start a hedge fund in late 2004, he shared few details of how he would operate, acknowledged that he hadn't actually managed money for several years, and said investors would have to fork over a minimum of $5 million and tie up their cash for as long as four and a half years to gain access to his fund. He raised more than $3 billion in a matter of months, leaving a trail of investors frustrated that they couldn't get in.[4]

Both Mindich and Burry scored results that topped the market, and the industry powered ahead. But traders with more questionable abilities soon got into the game, and they seemed to enjoy the lifestyle as much as the inherent investment possibilities of operating a hedge fund. In 2004, Bret Grebow, a twenty-eight-year-old fund manager, bought a new $160,000 Lamborghini Gallardo as a treat and regularly traveled with his girlfriend between his New York office and a home in Highland Beach, Florida, on a private jet, paying as much as $10,000 for the three-hour flight.

"It's fantastic," Mr. Grebow said at the time, on the heels of a year of 40 percent gains. "They've got my favorite cereal, Cookie Crisp, waiting for me, and Jack Daniel's on ice.[5] (Grebow eventually pled guilty to defrauding investors of more than $7 million while helping to operate a Ponzi scheme that bilked clients without actually trading on their behalf.)

A 2006 survey of almost three hundred hedge-fund professionals found they on average had spent $376,000 on jewelry, $271,000 on watches, and $124,000 on "traditional" spa services over the previous twelve months. The term *traditional* was used to distinguish between full-body massages, mud baths, seaweed wraps and the like, and more exotic treatments. The survey reported anecdotal evidence that some hedge-fund managers were shelling out tens of thousands of dollars to professionals to guide them through the Play of Seven Knives, an elaborate exercise starting with a long, luxuriant bath, graduating to a full massage with a variety of rare oils, and escalating to a series of cuts inflicted by a sharp, specialized knife aimed at eliciting extraordinary sexual and painful sensations.[6]

Not only could hedge funds charge their clients more than most businesses, but their claim of 20 percent of trading gains was treated as capital gains income by the U.S. government and taxed at a rate of 15 percent, the same rate paid on wage income by Americans earning less than $31,850.

For the hedge-fund honchos, it really wasn't about the money and the resulting delights. Well, not entirely. For the men running hedge funds and private-equity firms—and they almost always were men—the money became something of a measuring stick. All day and into the night, computer screens an arms-length away provided minute-by-minute accounts of their performance, a referendum on their value as investors, and affirmation of their very self-worth.

A S THE HEDGE-FUND celebrations grew more intense in 2005, the revelers hardly noticed forty-nine-year-old John Paulson, alone in the corner, amused and a bit befuddled by the festivities. Paulson had a respectable track record and a blue-chip pedigree. But it was little wonder that he found himself an afterthought in this overcharged world.

Born in December 1955, Paulson was the offspring of a group of risk-takers, some of whom had met their share of disappointment.

Paulson's great-grandfather Percy Thorn Paulsen was a Norwegian captain of a Dutch merchant ship in the late 1890s that ran aground one summer off Guayaquil, Ecuador, on its way up the coast of South America. Reaching land, Paulsen and his crew waited several weeks for the ship to be repaired, using the time to explore the growing expatriate community in the port city. There, he met the daughter of the French ambassador to Ecuador, fell in love, and decided to settle. In 1924, a grandson was born named Alfred. Three years later, Alfred's mother died while giving birth to another boy. The Paulsen boys were sent to a German boarding school in Quito. Alfred's father soon suffered a massive heart attack, after a game of tennis, and passed away.

The boys, now orphans, moved in with their stepmother, but she had her own children to care for, so an aunt took them in. At sixteen, Alfred and his younger brother, Albert, fifteen, were ready to move on, traveling 3,500 miles northwest to Los Angeles. Alfred spent two years doing odd jobs before enlisting in the U.S. Army. Wounded while serving in Italy during World War II, he remained in Europe during the Allied occupation.

After the war, Alfred, by now using the surname of Paulson, returned to Los Angeles to attend UCLA. One day, in the school's cafeteria, he noticed an attractive young woman, Jacqueline Boklan, a psychology major, and introduced himself. He was immediately taken with her.

Boklan's grandparents had come to New York's Lower East Side at the turn of the century, part of a wave of Jewish immigrants fleeing Lithuania and Romania in search of opportunity. Jacqueline was born in 1926, and after her father, Arthur, was hired to manage fixed-income sales for a bank, the Boklan family moved to Manhattan's Upper West Side. They rented an apartment in the Turin, a stately building on 93rd Street and Central Park West, across from Central Park, and enjoyed a well-to-do lifestyle for several years, with servants and a nanny to care for Jacqueline.[7]

But Boklan lost his job during the Great Depression and spent the rest of his life unable to return the family to its former stature. In the early 1940s, searching for business opportunities, they moved to Los Angeles, where Jacqueline attended UCLA.

After Alfred Paulson wed Jacqueline, he was hired by the accounting firm Arthur Andersen to work in the firm's New York office, and the family moved to Whitestone, a residential neighborhood in the borough of Queens, near the East River. John was the third of four children born to the couple. He grew up in the Le Havre apartment complex, a thirty-two-building, 1,021-apartment, twenty-seven-acre development featuring two pools, a clubhouse, a gym, and three tennis courts, built by Alfred Levitt, the younger brother of William Levitt, the real estate developer who created Levittown. The family later bought a modest home in nearby Beechhurst, while Jacqueline's parents moved into a one-bedroom apartment in nearby Jackson Heights.

Visiting his grandson one day in 1961, Arthur Boklan brought him a pack of Charms candies. The next day, John decided to sell the candies to his kindergarten classmates, racing home to tell his grandfather about his first brush with capitalism. After they counted the proceeds,

Arthur took his grandson to a local supermarket to show the six-year-old where to buy a pack of Charms for eight cents, trying to instill an appreciation of math and numbers in him. John broke up the pack and sold the candies individually for five cents each, a tactic that investor Warren Buffett employed in his own youth with packs of chewing gum. Paulson continued to build his savings with a variety of after-school jobs.

"I got a piggy bank and the goal was to fill it up, and that appealed to me," John Paulson recalls. "I had an interest in working and having money in my pocket."

One of Alfred Paulson's clients, public-relations maven David Finn, who represented celebrities including Perry Como and Jack Lemmon, liked Alfred's work and asked him to become the chief financial officer of his firm, Ruder Finn, Inc. The two became fast friends, playing tennis and socializing with their families. Alfred was affable, upbeat, and exceedingly modest, content to enjoy his family rather than claim a spotlight at the growing firm, Finn recalls. On the court, Alfred had an impressive tennis game but seemed to lack a true competitive spirit, preferring to play for enjoyment.

"Al didn't care about winning," says Finn. "He never made a lot or cared about making a lot. He was brilliant, very sensitive and friendly, but he was happy where he was in life."

A natural peacemaker, he sometimes approached colleagues involved in a dispute and gave each an encouraging smile, instantly healing the office rift.

Jacqueline, now a practicing child psychologist, was more opinionated than her husband, weighing in on politics and business at social gatherings as Alfred looked on. She believed in giving her children a lot of love and even more leeway. Jacqueline brought the Paulson children up Jewish, and their eldest daughter later moved to Israel. Alfred was an atheist, but he attended synagogue with his family. Until he turned twelve, John had no idea that his father wasn't Jewish.

John attended a series of local public schools, where he entered a program for gifted students. By eighth grade, Paulson was studying calculus, Shakespeare, and other high-school-level subjects. Every summer, Alfred took his family on an extensive vacation, in the United States or abroad. By his sophomore year, John was going cross-country with friends, visiting Europe a year later.

John showed signs of unusual independence in other areas as well. Though the Paulsons were members of a local synagogue, the Whitestone Hebrew Centre, Paulson listed in his yearbook at Bayside High the "Jesus club" and the "divine light club" among his interests.

By the time Paulson entered New York University in the fall of 1973, the economy was floundering, the stock market was out of vogue, and Paulson's early interest in money had faded. As a freshman, he studied creative writing and worked in film production. He took philosophy courses, thrilling his mother, who loved the arts. But the young man soon lost his interest in his studies, slipping behind his classmates. Vietnam, President Nixon, and the antiwar and civil rights protests dominated the news.

"I felt directionless," says Paulson, who wore his hair to his shoulders, looking like a young Robert Downey Jr. "I wasn't very interested in college."

After John's freshman year, Alfred sensed he needed a change and proposed that his son take a summer trip, the Paulson family remedy. He bought him an airplane ticket to South America, and that summer John traveled throughout Panama and Colombia. Soon he made his way to Ecuador, where he stayed with an uncle, a dashing bachelor who developed condominium projects in the coastal city of Salinas. His uncle appointed Paulson his *hombre de confianza,* or trusted right-hand man. He kept an eye out for thieves trying to steal materials from his uncle, supervised deliveries at various construction sites, and kept track of his uncle's inventories.

For a young man from Queens, Salinas was a little piece of heaven. Paulson lived in the penthouse apartment of one of his uncle's buildings, the tallest in Ecuador, with a cook, a gardener, and a housekeeper. He found the women beautiful, the weather warm, and the beach close by. He grew to admire his uncle, a charismatic bon vivant who thoroughly enjoyed himself and his money. It was as if Paulson had been reborn into an affluent side of the family; he put off his return to NYU to extend his time in Ecuador.

"It brought me back to liking money again," Paulson remembers.

There was only one drawback: His family was conservative and proved too confining for a young man just beginning to enjoy his independence. Paulson wasn't allowed to date without a chaperone and could choose only young women from the right families, as designated and approved by his uncle.

One day, Paulson met a pretty sixteen-year-old at one of his job sites, a young woman who turned out to be the daughter of the chief of police of Salinas. He invited her back to his apartment for dinner, asking his cook to whip up something special. The cook quietly called Paulson's uncle to tip him off. Soon an associate of Paulson's uncle came to the door. "What's going on in there?! What's going on?!" he demanded. He pulled aside Paulson and said, "We can't have that type of person here."

The young woman fled the apartment, running into the night.

Eager to be on his own, Paulson moved to the capital city of Quito, before traveling elsewhere in Ecuador. When he soon ran out of money and needed to drum up some cash, he discovered a man who manufactured attractive and inexpensive children's clothing; Paulson commissioned some samples to send to his father back home in New York. Alfred took the samples to upscale stores such as Bloomingdale's, which ordered six dozen shirts, thrilling the Paulsons. The shirts continued to sell and Paulson hired a team in Ecuador to produce more of them, spending evenings packing and shipping boxes of the clothing, learning to operate a business on the fly.

Later, though, as orders piled up, Paulson missed a key delivery date with Bloomingdale's and the store canceled its order. He was stuck with one thousand unwanted children's shirts, which he had to store in his parents' basement. Years later, whenever Paulson needed a little extra spending money, he would return to Queens, grab some shirts out of a box, and sell them at various New York retailers.

Another time during his two years in Ecuador, Paulson noticed attractive wood parquet flooring in a store in Quito. He tracked down the local factory that produced it and asked the owner if he could act as his U.S. sales representative, in exchange for a commission of 10 percent of any sales. The man agreed, and Paulson sent his father a package of floor samples, which Alfred showed to people in the flooring business in New Jersey. They confirmed that the quality and pricing compared favorably with that available in the United States. By then, Alfred had left Ruder Finn, Inc. to start his own firm, but he made time to help his son. Working together, the Paulsons sold $250,000 of the flooring; his father gave John their entire $25,000 commission. The two spoke by phone or wrote daily while John was in Ecuador, bringing them closer together. It was John Paulson's first big trade, and it excited him to do more.

"I found it a lot of fun, and I loved having cash in my pocket," Paulson recalls.

Paulson realized that a college education was the best way to ensure ample cash flow, so he returned to NYU in 1976, newly focused and energized. By then, his friends were entering their senior year, two years ahead of Paulson, and he felt pressure to catch up. His competitive juices flowing, Paulson spent the next nineteen months accumulating the necessary credits to graduate, taking extra courses and attending summer school, receiving all As.

Among his classmates, Paulson developed a reputation for having a unique ability to boil down complex ideas into simple terms. After lectures on difficult subjects like statistics or upper-level finance, some approached Paulson asking for help.

"John was clearly the brightest guy in the class," recalls Bruce Goodman, a classmate.

Paulson was particularly inspired by an investment banking seminar taught by John Whitehead, then the chairman of investment banking firm Goldman Sachs. To give guest lectures, Whitehead brought in various Goldman stars, such as Robert Rubin, later secretary of the Treasury under Bill Clinton, and Stephen Friedman, Goldman's future chairman. Paulson was transfixed as Rubin discussed making bets on mergers, a style of investing known as risk-arbitrage, and Friedman dissected the world of mergers and acquisitions deal making.

An avid tennis player, like his father, Paulson sometimes invited friends to the Westside Tennis Club in Forest Hills, New York, where his father was a member, to play on the grass courts that served as home to the U.S. Open. But he rarely invited friends back home, and some never even knew he was a native of Queens. For years, Paulson would simply say that he was from New York City.

It was his classmate, Bruce Goodman, who began calling Paulson "J.P.," a reflection of Paulson's initials as well as a sly allusion to J.P. Morgan, the legendary turn-of-the-century banker. The nickname, which stuck for the rest of his life, spoke to Paulson's obvious abilities, his growing ambition, and his blue-blood aspirations. Paulson smiled when he heard the new nickname, appreciating the compliment and the double entendre.

Paulson graduated first in his class from NYU with a degree in finance. As the valedictorian of the College of Business and Public Administration, he delivered a speech about corporate responsibility. A dean suggested that he apply to Harvard Business School. Although Paulson was only twenty-two and didn't have much business experience, he cited the lessons of his business in Ecuador in his application; he not only gained acceptance but won the Sidney J. Weinberg/Goldman Sachs scholarship.

One day at Harvard Business School, a classmate, on the way to a meeting of Harvard's investment club, approached Paulson, telling him, "You've got to hear this guy Kohlberg speak." Paulson had never heard of Jerry Kohlberg, founder of investment powerhouse Kohlberg Kravis Roberts & Co., but he tagged along, one of only a dozen students to show up. Kohlberg, an early pioneer of so-called leveraged buyouts, brought two bankers with him, and they walked through the details of how to buy a company using little cash and a lot of borrowed money. Then Kohlberg detailed how KKR put up $500,000 and borrowed $36 million to buy an obscure company that they sold six months later, walking away with $17 million in profit.

For Paulson, it was a life-changing experience, like seeing the Beatles for the first time, one that opened his eyes to the huge paydays possible from big investments. Paulson calculated that partners at Goldman Sachs like Whitehead and Rubin made just $500,000 that year, a figure that seemed puny next to what could be made by Kohlberg Kravis Roberts & Co.

Jerry Kohlberg can make $17 million on just one deal, thought an astounded Paulson.

In his developing worldview, the acquisition of massive wealth deserved unabashed admiration. John Whitehead and Jerry Kohlberg played the game fairly, with intelligence and diligence. To Paulson, they seemed deserving of the rewards they commanded. During his second year in business school, Paulson undertook a research project to identify the key players in the leveraged-buyout industry. Upon graduation, Paulson assumed that he, too, would head to Wall Street.

Paulson graduated as a George F. Baker Scholar in 1980, in the top 5 percent of his class. But when firms came to recruit on campus, it was the consulting firms that offered the largest starting salaries, grabbing Paulson's attention. Wall Street was still battling a bear market. So Paulson accepted a job at Boston Consulting Group, a prestigious local firm that recruited only at upper-echelon schools.

Early on in his new job, Paulson was asked to help Jeffrey Libert, a senior consultant, advise the Washington Post Co. on whether to invest in real estate. Paulson initially was bullish on the idea—the Paulson home in Beechhurst had increased in value over the previous two decades and housing seemed like a good investment.

Libert, the same age as Paulson and also a native New Yorker who had graduated from Harvard Business School, showed Paulson a chart mapping the impressive growth of housing prices over the previous few decades. But when Libert factored in the rise of inflation over that period, the annual gains for housing turned out to be just 1.5 percent. Unless you can find an inexpensive home or building that can be purchased for less than its replacement cost, Libert argued, real estate isn't a very attractive investment.

"I was amazed to see that," Paulson says. "I wasn't an investor, so it didn't have meaning at the time, but the low rate of growth always stuck in my mind."

The work Paulson did at Boston Consulting Group was research intensive, and he excelled at it. An upbeat presence in the office, he flirted with the secretaries and other women in the office, most of whom liked Paulson much more than his less-approachable colleagues. But Paulson quickly realized he had made a mistake joining the firm. He wasn't investing money, he was just giving advice to companies, and at an hourly rate no less. To other executives at the firm, Paulson seemed out of place and uncomfortable.

"John would say, 'How can I make money off this' while others were giving advice," Libert remembers. "BCG was really about a bunch of geeks sitting around seeing who's smarter than the next guy, and that made him impatient. He seemed to have an instinctual sense of how to make money."

Paulson, for example, was taken with the story of Charlie Allen Jr., a high-school dropout who built an investment firm, Allen & Co., into a powerhouse in the first half of the twentieth century. "The shy Midas of Wall Street," Allen took taxis while members of his family enjoyed chauffeured Rolls-Royces. In 1973 Allen's firm took control of Columbia Pictures after an accounting scandal left it weakened, then sold it to Coca-Cola nine years later in exchange for Coke stock. Later Coke shares soared and Allen pocketed a billion-dollar profit. (Years later, Paulson would recall details of the transaction by memory, as if reciting the batting average of a favorite baseball player.)

Paulson wanted to move to Wall Street. But when he applied for various jobs, he found that his consulting experience accounted for very little. He didn't want to start at the bottom of the ladder with recent grads, placing him in a quandary. At a local tennis tournament, Paulson saw Kohlberg in the stands and approached him, telling the LBO doyen how much he had enjoyed his lecture at Harvard. Kohlberg invited the young man to drop by his New York office.

At their meeting a few days later, Paulson confided to Kohlberg, "I went into the wrong career." He asked for Kohlberg's help in finding a position on Wall Street.

Kohlberg didn't have any openings at KKR. When Paulson asked if Kohlberg might introduce him to other heavy hitters in the buyout world like Leon Levy at Oppenheimer & Co., Kohlberg picked up the phone and got him an appointment.

A few weeks later, Paulson went to Levy's Park Avenue apartment for an interview. He had never seen anything like it before—everywhere he looked he saw antiquities, collectibles, and objets d'art. Paulson couldn't help but gawk, unsure if the busts around the home were Roman, Greek, or of some other origin he knew even less about. Paulson worried that if he moved too quickly in any direction, he would knock over one of Levy's priceless pieces, a move unlikely to further his career. Sitting down, carefully, he began to talk with Levy, sipping coffee from delicate fine porcelain. It turned out that Levy was looking to expand his firm and needed a smart associate. By the end of the day, Paulson had landed a job.

Paulson was so eager to leave the world of consulting that he hadn't thought to ask many details about the firm he had joined. It turned out that Paulson had been hired by Oppenheimer, a partnership that owned a larger brokerage firm as well as an investment operation run by Levy and Jack Nash. When Paulson opened the door to his new office, he found another young executive, Peter Soros, sitting in his seat.

"What are you doing in my office?" Paulson snapped.

"What are you doing in *my* office?" Soros replied.

A stare-down ensued, as neither Paulson nor Soros would vacate the room.

"It wasn't the friendliest meeting," recalls Soros, a nephew of George Soros, who had been hired by another Oppenheimer executive, unbeknownst to Paulson.

Days later, Oppenheimer split up, with Levy and Nash leaving to start their own firm, Odyssey Partners. They convinced Paulson to join them. The move gave Paulson an enviable opportunity for hands-on experience working with Levy and Nash, who already were Wall Street legends with a string of successful investments. They later raised $40 million for John DeLorean, the auto executive famous for a sports car with gull-winged doors, among a string of high-profile transactions.

At Odyssey, Levy pushed Paulson to search for leveraged buyouts with the potential for huge, long-term upsides, Levy's specialty. He and his partners once paid less than $50 million to purchase the Big Bear Stores Co., a regional grocery chain, and immediately recouped their investment by claiming a fee that was almost as much as their entire investment. They gave management incentives to improve operations, and eventually walked away with a $160 million profit.

Paulson focused on underappreciated conglomerates selling at inexpensive prices. The firm bought a position in TransWorld Corp., a company weighed down by the struggling operations of its TWA Airlines. But TransWorld also owned Hilton Hotels, Century 21, and other profitable businesses. Levy and Paulson figured that if they broke up the company, investors would focus on the value of the other businesses and the stock would soar. So Odyssey bought a big position in the stock. But TransWorld resisted a breakup and fought back, resulting in a nasty public squabble. The Odyssey team eventually profited from the venture, but it taught Paulson a lesson in how difficult the buyout business could be.

After a couple of years, Levy and Paulson realized that Paulson didn't have the experience to excel at his job. Nash agreed a change needed to be made. Paulson was smart and presented his ideas well, but he hadn't learned the financial skills necessary to lead buyout transactions, nor did he have a thick Rolodex of contacts in the corporate world to pull them off on his own.

"As much as Leon and I liked each other, they needed someone more senior," Paulson says.

Looking for a new job, once again, Paulson now was more than four years behind his classmates from business school. Several investment banks offered him entry-level positions, where he would join the most recent business school graduates, but it was something he resisted. An opportunity at Bear Stearns suited him much better. The firm was just below the upper echelon of the investment banking business, and it didn't have extensive databases or other resources to help bankers compete. Banking wasn't even a focus at Bear; Dick Harriton's clearing operation was minting money loaning out customers' stock, Bobby Steinberg ran a top risk-arbitrage operation, and Alan "Ace" Greenberg was working magic on the trading floor.

What Bear did have in spades was a group of smart, hungry bankers who shared Paulson's lust for money. The firm was hoping to win business from the same financial entrepreneurs that Paulson was so enamored with and saw him as an obvious match.

Joining Bear Stearns in 1984, Paulson, now twenty-eight, quickly climbed the ranks, working as many as one hundred hours per week on merger-and-acquisition deals. Four years later he was rewarded with the title of managing director, catching up to and surpassing classmates from his graduating class. Other bankers boasted of their deal-making prowess and tried to impress clients with insights into high finance. But Paulson often took a more low-key approach, chatting about art or theater before discussing business. While he could snap at subordinates if they made mistakes, and often was curt and direct, Paulson impressed most colleagues with a cheerful, confident disposition.

"It was all about M&A in the eighties; bankers were Masters of the Universe. But John didn't take himself very seriously; he got the joke," recalls Robert Harteveldt, a junior banker at the firm who sometimes socialized with Paulson. "A lot of guys walked into a room, said they worked in M&A, and expected girls to melt, but John was debonair. He tried to charm women and was more interested in them than in saying who he was."

Paulson gravitated to Michael "Mickey" Tarnopol, a handsome senior banker and absolute force of nature. Upbeat and outgoing, Tarnopol was admired for the big deals he reeled in for the firm. He was held in equally high esteem for the lavish parties he hosted at his Park Avenue and Bridgehampton homes, his exploits on the polo field, and for a surprisingly sturdy marriage to his high-school sweetheart.

Paulson was impressed when Tarnopol succeeded in convincing a valued secretary to cancel her planned move to California, after Paulson and others failed to persuade her to stay at the firm. Amazed, Paulson asked him how he did it.

"A salesman's job starts when the customer says no," Tarnopol responded, a comment Paulson would take to heart and repeat years later.

Tarnopol opened doors for Paulson on Wall Street and introduced him to key investors. For his part, Paulson considered Tarnopol, who had no sons of his own, something of a "second father," according to one friend. Paulson was included in family occasions, played polo with Tarnopol in Palm Beach, Florida, and spent weekends at Tarnopol's Greenwich estate. Rather than emulate the veteran banker and settle down, however, Paulson became increasingly enamored with a newly discovered passion: New York's after-hours world.

JOHN PAULSON didn't seem like an obvious candidate to embrace the city's active social scene. Though friendly and witty, Paulson could be quite stiff and formal, usually donning a jacket, if not a tie, in the evening hours. If a conversation bored him, Paulson sometimes walked away midsentence, leaving companions befuddled.

But Paulson thoroughly enjoyed socializing and soon hosted parties for several hundred friends and acquaintances in a loft he rented in Manhattan's trendy SoHo neighborhood, where he mingled with wealthy bankers, models, and celebrities like John F. Kennedy Jr. Throngs attended Paulson's annual Christmas party, and he would place small presents for his guests under a tree.

Many evenings, Paulson and a group of friends enjoyed a late dinner before hitting popular dance clubs like Nello's, Xenon, or The Underground. Sometimes the group traveled from uptown clubs to downtown spots, all on the same night. Paulson joined Le Club, a members-only venue on Manhattan's East Side owned by fashion designer Oleg Cassini, where Paulson would chat with high-rollers such as billionaire arms dealer Adnan Kashoggi, record impresario Ahmet Ertegun, and Linn Ullmann, daughter of Ingmar Bergman and actress Liv Ullmann.

Despite his charm and flash, Paulson often chose to live in apartments that seemed grim to others, or were furnished in surprisingly pedestrian ways, with odd, plastic trees or ragged furniture. One of his apartments was located above a discount-shoe store.

At Bear Stearns, Paulson regaled younger colleagues with self-deprecating stories of dates that went awry, an appealing contrast to other bankers who took themselves far too seriously. Others at his level had cars waiting outside the office, but Paulson usually grabbed a bus or the subway, sometimes splitting a cab with Harteveldt, his junior colleague.

Before long, Paulson began to chafe at Bear Stearns. He was working long days and into most evenings, but too many bankers laid claim to the deals he had worked on, shrinking his slice of the profit pie. Paulson didn't play the political game very well, and was uncomfortable cozying up to the firm's partners, who determined annual bonuses.

In one deal, Paulson helped score a $36 million profit for Bear Stearns after the bank, along with an investment firm called Gruss & Co., made a $679 million buyout offer for Anderson Clayton Company, a food and insurance conglomerate. The $36 million score was a drop in the bucket at Bear Stearns, where it was divided among hundreds of partners. But Paulson noticed that Gruss, which hadn't previously undertaken a buy-out, divided the same $36 million among just the firm's five partners. To Paulson, there seemed to be a limit to how much money he could make at a large firm like Bear Stearns, especially since most of its profit came from charging customers fees rather than undertaking deals like Anderson with a huge upside. Yet those were the ones he pined for.

Few were surprised in 1988 when Paulson told Bear Stearns executives he was leaving to join Gruss. They long ago figured that Paulson at some point would want to launch a career making investments of his own.

Gruss & Co. specialized in merger-arbitrage, taking a position on whether or not a merger would take place and investing in shares of companies being acquired. The firm hadn't undertaken buyouts on its own, but the Anderson experience convinced the firm's founder, Marty Gruss, to test the waters more deeply. He asked Paulson to lead a new ef-fort to do similar buyout deals, hoping to potentially rival firms like

KKR. Gruss was so eager to hire Paulson that he agreed to make Paulson a general partner and give the young banker a cut of profits racked up by other groups at the firm.

Watching Gruss and his father, Joseph, up close, Paulson quickly picked up the merger-arbitrage business. By buying shares of companies being acquired, and selling short companies making acquisitions, Gruss was able to generate profits that largely were shielded from stock-market fluctuations. The ideal Gruss investment had limited risk but held the promise of a potential fortune. Marty Gruss drilled a maxim into Paulson: "Watch the downside; the upside will take care of itself."

Paulson's buyout business never really took off, however. The 1989 indictment of junk-bond king Michael Milken and a slowing economy made it hard to finance buyouts, and Martin Gruss seemed distracted, perhaps due to a recent second marriage. Soon he and Paulson parted company.

Despite Paulson's fierce ambition and his love of making money and landing big deals, other urges were pulling on the thirty-five-year-old.

"John was throwing great parties in his loft; he was enjoying his bachelorhood, shall we say," Gruss recalls. "John was very bright but he was a little bit unfocused; he had a tendency to burn the candle at both ends."

On his own, Paulson had more time to devote to his extracurricular interests. He certainly didn't feel undue pressure to make money. Several years earlier, Jim Koch, a colleague in a nearby cubicle at Boston Consulting Group, came to Paulson to ask for an investment in a brewery he was launching. Koch told Paulson that others at the consulting firm, along with several Harvard alumni from Paulson's graduating year, were investing in his company, and that Paulson would regret it if he passed on the opportunity.

Paulson gave him $25,000. Now the company, the parent of the Samuel Adams brand, was a raging success, and Paulson's investment was worth several million dollars. He also retained an interest in some of Gruss's businesses, receiving regular checks from the firm.

Paulson searched for new interests. He invested in a Manhattan night club, a disco, and various real estate deals. He bought an apartment building in Westchester with a friend, completed a triathlon, and traveled throughout the East Coast scouting various properties.

While many of his contemporaries had begun families, Paulson's circle of well-educated, highly cultured, and privileged friends tended to focus on enjoying life, too distracted to settle down. The group spent much of the summer in the Hamptons, the wealthy enclave on the south shore of Long Island. Weekends sometimes began with a lunch of grilled salmon and pasta for as many as one hundred people at a friend's home in Sagaponack, a town known for having the highest median income in the country. Lunch started around 1 p.m. and continued into the evening, with new arrivals joining as they came from work or nearby parties. The gatherings usually featured engaging conversation among friends in business, fashion, and the arts; good food; plentiful drink; and access to an assortment of recreational drugs for those who chose to partake.

Paulson often rode a beat-up ten-speed bicycle, usually with a baseball cap on backward, between friends' homes in the Hamptons, sweating as he arrived.

Few heads turned when Paulson walked into a room. But he often was surrounded by good-looking women. Of average height and build, with dark hair and brown, almost doleful eyes, Paulson was clever and intelligent, a good listener with an impish grin. Though the late 1980s were a time when brash, cocky traders and investment bankers ruled the New York social scene, Paulson chose not to flaunt his wealth or his education. There was something accessible, even vulnerable, about him, making it easy for friends to turn to Paulson for advice or a quick loan, or to borrow his Jaguar for a date.

"John was charming and fun; women always loved him," recalls Christophe von Hohenberg, a photographer and member of Paulson's pack. "He threw great parties and went to the best restaurants and clubs, and girls knew it."

Paulson was wary of those who seemed especially interested in his money, and appreciated it when one of the women, or a friend, volunteered to pick up the bill for dinner or drinks, although he usually grabbed it before anyone had a chance to open a wallet or purse.

Sometimes Paulson let the good times get a bit out of hand. Over Memorial Day weekend 1989, he was arrested for driving while intoxicated. He paid a $350 fine for the lesser infraction of driving while impaired.

But by 1994, the life of leisure was getting a bit tiresome to Paulson. He still dreamed of earning great wealth. It was time, he realized, to go back to work.

"Time was getting on; I realized I needed to focus," Paulson says.

The surest path to genuine wealth seemed to be investing for himself. So he started a hedge fund, Paulson & Co., to focus on merger-arbitrage, the specialty he had picked up from Gruss.

Paulson reached out to everyone he knew, mailing more than five hundred announcements about his firm's launch. But he didn't get a single response, even after waiving his initial $1 million minimum investment. Paulson never had managed money on his own, didn't have much of a track record as an investor, and wasn't known to most potential clients. He described some of his coups at Gruss and elsewhere, but it was hard for investors to tell how much responsibility he'd had for those deals.

Paulson called on bankers from Bear Stearns, some of whom had worked for him and now were well-heeled partners at the firm. They, too, all said no. A few wouldn't even return his calls. Others set up meetings, only to cancel them. Even Tarnopol, his old mentor, took a pass. Paulson had no more luck with his peers from business school who had become successful.

"I had lots of contacts and I thought money would pour in," Paulson recalls. "Some people said they would give me money, but only if they got a piece of my business. It was humbling."

David Paresky, owner of a big Boston travel agency and a potential client, asked Paulson to take a personality test, as he did with employees of his agency. He passed on Paulson's fund after telling a friend that Paulson's scores were underwhelming, the friend recalls.

So Paulson started his firm with $2 million of his own money. It was a full year before he found his first client, an old friend from Bear Stearns,

Howard Gurvitch, who gave him roughly $500,000. At this point, the firm consisted of just Paulson and an assistant; it was located in a tiny office in a Park Avenue building owned by Bear Stearns and shared by other small hedge-fund clients of the investment bank.

Paulson continued to woo investors, paying to speak at industry conferences and working with marketing professionals to hone his pitch and spread word of his new fund. He carried himself with a confidence that surprised some, given his limited track record.

Paulson even had a tough time finding people to work for him. At a 1995 dinner at a steak restaurant near Rockefeller Center in Manhattan, Paulson tried to convince Joseph Aaron to join his firm to help market the hedge fund to investors. After exchanging pleasantries, Paulson launched into a pitch detailing why he was sure he would succeed, emphasizing his rich pedigree.

"I finished number one in my class," Paulson said, Aaron recalls. A few minutes later, Paulson repeated how well he had done in school, boasting that he had graduated from Harvard University.

Aaron, a Southerner with deep connections in the hedge-fund world who courted investors with a charm and politeness that masked a keen understanding of the business, was amused by Paulson's obvious self-confidence.

"Really? Well, I graduated from the eleventh-best school in Georgia."

The tactics Paulson outlined sounded run-of-the mill to Aaron, who figured Paulson wasn't willing to share his insights—or just didn't have any.

"I'm not the guy for you," Aaron told Paulson at the end of the dinner.

At times, Paulson didn't seem completely put together. When Brad Balter, a young broker, came to visit, Paulson chain-smoked cigarettes and had spots of blood on his shirt collar from a shaving mishap. Paulson's head of marketing was stretched out in agony on a nearby couch, moaning about his back.

"I didn't know what to think; it was a little surreal," Balter recalls.

At times, Paulson became discouraged. His early investment performance was good but uneven, and he continued to have few clients.

He was sure of his abilities but questioned whether he could make the fund a success.

One especially glum day, Paulson asked his father, "Am I in the wrong business? Is there something wrong with me?" Alfred Paulson, who at that time was retired but helped with his son's accounting, tried to cheer him up, telling Paulson that if he stayed with the fund, it would succeed.

"It was hard to be rejected; it was a lonely period," Paulson recalls. "After a while I said, this is too much. He lifted my spirits."

Paulson clung to the message of a favorite quote from a commencement speech given by Winston Churchill: "Never give up. Never give up."

Paulson had more success in the then-struggling real estate market. In 1994, he heard about an attractive home available in Southampton. The couple who owned the house were in the middle of a divorce. Paulson contacted the wife, who sounded eager to sell the property, and together they agreed to a $425,000 price. At the closing, though, Paulson was shocked to learn that the home wasn't the woman's to sell—there already was a big mortgage on the property. For months Paulson kept an eye on the home, as it went through foreclosure and then was handed between banks before landing with GE Capital. He was told that the house would be auctioned the following Tuesday on the steps of the Southampton courthouse.

Paulson showed up early that August morning, just as rain began to fall. When he asked if the auction could be moved indoors, he was told that by law it had to be held outside the courthouse. Soon the rain picked up and some prospective bidders took off. The auction, with bids to increase in increments of $5,000, began with a bid by GE Capital at $230,000. Paulson quickly responded with an offer of $235,000. GE didn't respond, no one else emerged, and Paulson was able to walk away with his dream home at a bargain-basement price. Later that year, he purchased a huge loft in the SoHo neighborhood of Manhattan that also had been in foreclosure.

Paulson realized that if he could improve his investment performance, investors eventually would find their way to him. Because the firm was so small, he could focus on attractive merger deals that competitors wouldn't bother with or didn't have much faith in, such as those involving overlooked Canadian companies. Sometimes he would stray into investments unrelated to mergers, such as buying energy shares and shorting bonds of companies that seemed to have flimsy accounting.

By 1995, Paulson & Co. was big enough to hire two more employees; he pushed his young analysts to find investments with a big upside yet limited downside. "How much can we lose on this trade?" he would ask them, repeatedly.

The gains were solid but usually unspectacular, and sometimes Paulson appeared glum or cranky. When a trade went awry, he often closed the door to his office tightly and slumped in his chair. At times he would clash with his analysts. The yelling would get so loud that people down the hall sometimes popped their heads into the office to make sure that nothing was amiss. One time, Paulson turned beet red and got so close to analyst Paul Rosenberg's face that Rosenberg became scared. "Why are you acting like this? I'm on your side," Rosenberg said, according to someone in the room. Paulson just glared back.

Paulson once told an employee to go to a doctor's office on the Upper East Side to take a drug test, without giving him any explanation. The employee came back to the office and handed Paulson the cup of urine. He never heard about it again. Paulson castigated another employee for excessive use of the firm's printer, one more inscrutable action that left some on his team scratching their heads.

Paulson at times even became frustrated with his father's deliberate work. He also criticized his attractive new assistant, Jenny Zaharia, a recent immigrant from Romania who had landed a job at the firm after delivering lunch from the Bear Stearns cafeteria to Paulson and his employees. A college student in Romania, Zaharia left her family behind and was granted political asylum in the United States after her brother, George, a track star in Romania, defected during a European competition and later moved to Queens. Jenny, who had spent some time as a television reporter for a Romanian television station in New York, was tempted to quit, but she told others that she didn't have other options and needed the salary.

By late 1996, Paulson had just $16 million of assets. He was a small-fry in the hedge-fund world. Then he found Peter Novello, a marketing professional determined to help Paulson get to the big leagues.

"He had a reasonable track record but it wasn't phenomenal; it was a period when a lot of managers were making 20 percent a year," Novello recalls.

As Novello tried to lure new investors, they sometimes asked him about Paulson's activities outside the office. Rumor had it that Paulson partied hard.

"What difference does it make?"

"Well, we just want to see a level of stability," one investor replied.

"John didn't fit the profile of the average hedge-fund manger. He was living downtown in SoHo and in the Hamptons. He had a different lifestyle than [what the] institutional investors were used to seeing," Novello says.

Paulson's fund was hurt by 1998's Russian-debt default, the implosion of the giant hedge fund Long-Term Capital Management, and the resulting market tumult. His patience wore thin with one employee, Dennis Chu, who was left frazzled and unable to make clear recommendations to his boss.

"Just tell me what you think!" Paulson screamed at Chu, who eventually left the firm.

Sometimes Paulson hinted at what might have been aggravating him, noting that competitors and friends seemed to be pulling away. He told one analyst that an old roommate from Harvard, Manuel Asensio, was making a million dollars a year at his hedge fund shorting tiny stocks, "and we're killing ourselves here."

The fund lost 4 percent in 1998, enough to spur some clients to rush for the exits, leaving Paulson & Co. with about $50 million at the end of the year—down from more than $100 million at the end of 1997. Some deserted Paulson for larger merger specialists, some of whom managed to make a bit of money during the year.

"I was not a major player," Paulson acknowledges. "We were a little shell-shocked from the LTCM collapse so we were less aggressive getting back into the market later in the year like others."

On days the firm made money, Paulson was friendlier, even charming, a change in personality that both relieved and confused his employees. Some of them attributed his mercurial personality to his drive to be a major player. It was also, they realized, the nature of merger investing, which requires split-second decisions based on imperfect information. Others learned to appreciate Paulson's brutal honesty, such as when he dissected their investment recommendations, looking for holes.

While the market shakeout of 1998 cost Paulson clients, it also left him with ripe investment opportunities, enabling him to score impressive gains over the next few years. Just as important, he made a dramatic decision to alter his lifestyle. Paulson had continued to host blowout bashes at his SoHo loft in his early days of running the fund. But as he approached his mid-forties, almost everyone in his group of friends had married, and he, too, was beginning to tire of the social scene. Paulson took out a pad and pen and wrote down the characteristics he was looking for in a wife. The word "cheerful" topped the list. Paulson sensed he needed a partner who could help him deal with the ups and downs of his life.

"I figured I'd always make money, so that was unimportant to me," Paulson says.

He quickly realized there was a woman he was attracted to who fit the bill and was sitting nearby: his assistant, Jenny.

"Jenny didn't drink, smoke, or go out late at night; for me she was a breath of fresh air," Paulson says. "She was almost always smiling and cheerful."

Paulson quietly pursued Zaharia, asking her out almost every other week for more than a year, but she wouldn't agree to go on a date. Zaharia told Paulson that she'd only date him if he fired her and found her a new job. But Paulson couldn't bear to let Zaharia go and work for someone else. He offered her all kinds of enticements, including trips to Aspen, Miami, and Los Angeles. Zaharia had never been to those cities and was tempted to go with her boss, but ultimately refused, saying she didn't want to cross the lines of professional behavior.

Zaharia did agree to have lunch with Paulson, however, and the two began getting together at least once a week, though other employees were in the dark about the budding relationship. After more than two hundred meals together, and an occasional Rollerblading outing in Central Park, Paulson realized he was in love and proposed; six months later they wed. When Paulson finally told his employees, they were floored, having completely missed any signs that an office romance had been brewing.

Paulson went out of his way to embrace Jenny and her family. The couple agreed to wed in an Episcopal church in Southampton, and Paulson became friendly with the priest. Light streamed through the seaside church's Tiffany windows as the sun set and the ceremony began.

By 2001, Paulson was on more solid footing in his personal life. And his fund had grown as well. He managed over $200 million and had refined his investment approach.

Few outside the firm picked up on the change in Paulson, though. Erik Norrgård, who invested in hedge funds for New York firm NorthHouse Advisors, met Paulson around that time and decided his was "just another ham-and-cheese operation in a crowded space" of merger investors. Norrgård passed on him. Others heard rumblings about Paulson's wild past and steered clear, unaware that he had settled down into a quiet family life.

"If people knew him at all, it was as just another merger arb," says Paulson's friend and initial investor Howard Gurvitch. "He wasn't really on anyone's radar screen."

But something remarkable was about to happen to the nation, and to the financial markets, an upheaval that would change the course of financial history and transform John Paulson from a bit player into the biggest star in the game.

THE HOUSING MARKET DIDN'T SEEM LIKE AN OBVIOUS BENEFICIARY OF the age of easy money. As the World Trade Center toppled on September 11, 2001, and Osama bin Laden's lieutenants boasted of crippling the U.S. economy, the real estate market and the overall economy wobbled—especially around the key New York area. Home prices had enjoyed more than five years of gains, but the economy was already fragile in the aftermath of the bursting of the technology bubble, and most experts worried about a weakening real estate market, even before the tragic attacks.

But the Federal Reserve Board, which had been lowering interest rates to aid the economy, responded to the shocking September 11 attacks by slashing interest rates much further, making it cheaper to borrow all kinds of debt. The key federal-funds rate, a short-term interest rate that influences terms on everything from auto and student loans to credit-card and home-mortgage loans, would hit 1 percent by the middle of 2003, down from 6.5 percent at the start of 2001, as the Fed, led by Chairman Alan Greenspan, worked furiously to keep the economy afloat. Rates around the globe also fell, giving a green light to those hoping for a cheap loan.

For years, Americans had been pulled by two opposing impulses—an instinctive distaste of debt and a love affair with the notion of owning a home. In 1758, Benjamin Franklin wrote: "The second vice is lying; the first is running in debt."[1] The dangers of borrowing were brought home in the Great Depression when a rash of businesses went bankrupt under the burden of heavy debt, scarring a generation. In the 1950s, more than half of all U.S. households had no mortgage debt and almost half had no debt at all. Home owners sometimes celebrated paying off their loans with mortgage-burning parties, setting loan documents aflame before friends and family. The practice continued into the 1970s; Archie Bunker famously held such a get-together in an episode of *All in the Family*.

Until the second half of the twentieth century, borrowing for anything other than big-ticket items, such as a home or a car, was unusual. Even then, home buyers generally needed at least a 20 percent down payment, and thus required a degree of financial well-being before owning a home.

But the forces of financial innovation, Madison Avenue marketing, and growing prosperity changed prevailing attitudes about being in hock. Two decades of robust growth justified, and encouraged, the embrace of debt. Catchy television commercials convinced most people that debt was an ally, not an enemy.

"One of the tricks in the credit-card business is that people have an inherent guilt with spending," said Jonathan Cranin, an executive at the big advertising agency McCann-Erickson Worldwide Advertising, in 1997, explaining the rationale behind MasterCard's "Priceless" campaign. "What you want is to have people feel good about their purchases."[2]

By the summer of 2000, household borrowing stood at $6.5 trillion, up almost 60 percent in five years. The average U.S. household sported thirteen credit or charge cards and carried $7,500 in credit-card balances, up from $3,000 a decade earlier.[3]

Americans borrowed more in part because there was more money to borrow. Thanks to Wall Street's 1977 invention of "securitization," or the bundling of loans into debt securities, lenders could sell their loans to investors, take the proceeds, and use them to make even more loans to consumers and companies alike. Thousands of loans ended up in these debt securities. So if a few of them went sour, it might have only a minor effect on investors who bought the securities, so the thinking went.

The shift in attitude toward debt gave life to the real estate market.

More than most nations, the United States worked at getting as many people in their own homes as possible. Academic data demonstrated that private-home ownership brought all kinds of positive benefits to neighborhoods, such as reduced crime and rising academic achievements. The government made the interest on mortgage payments tax deductible, and pressure on Congress from vested interests in the real estate business kept it that way; other benefits doled out to home sellers and buyers became equally sacred cows.

Low-income consumers and those with poor credit histories who once had difficulty borrowing money found it easier, even before Alan Greenspan and the Federal Reserve started slashing interest rates. In 2000, more than $160 billion of mortgage loans were outstanding to "subprime" borrowers, a euphemistic phrase invented by lenders to describe those with credit below the top "prime" grade. That figure represented more than 11 percent of all mortgages, up from just 4 percent in 1993, according to the Mortgage Bankers Association.

Low borrower rates helped send home prices higher after the 2001 attacks. Until 2003, the climb in prices made a good deal of sense, given that the economy was resilient, immigration strong, unemployment low, and tracts of land for development increasingly limited.

Then things went overboard, as America's raging love affair with the home turned unhealthy. Those on the left and right of the political spectrum have their favorite targets of blame for the mess, as if it was a traditional Whodunit. But like a modern version of Agatha Christie's *Murder on the Orient Express,* guilt for the most painful economic collapse of modern times is shared by a long cast of sometimes unsavory characters. Ample amounts of chicanery, collusion, naiveté, downright stupidity, and old-fashioned greed compounded the damage.

A S HOME PRICES SURGED, banks and mortgage-finance companies, enjoying historic growth and eager for new profits, felt comfortable dropping their standards, lending more money on easier terms to higher-risk borrowers. If they ran into problems, a refinancing could always lower their mortgage rate, lenders figured.

After 2001, lenders competed to introduce an array of aggressive loans, as if they were rolling out an all-you-can-eat buffet to a casino full of hungry gamblers. There were interest-only loans for those who wanted to pay only the interest portion of a loan and push off principal payments. Ever-popular adjustable-rate mortgages featured superslim teaser rates that eventually rose. Piggyback loans provided financing to those who couldn't come up with a down payment.

Borrowers hungry for riskier fare could find mortgages requiring no down payments at all, or loans that were 25 percent larger than the cost of their home itself, providing extra cash for a deserved vacation at the end of the difficult home-bidding process. "Liar loans" were based on stated income, not stuffy pay stubs or bank statements, while "ninja" loans were for those with no income, no job, and no assets. Feel like skipping a monthly payment? Just use a "payment-option" mortgage.

By 2005, 24 percent of all mortgages were done without any down payments at all, up from 3 percent in 2001. More than 40 percent of loans had limited documentation, up from 27 percent. A full 12 percent of mortgages had no down payments *and* limited documentation, up from 1 percent in 2001.

For those already in homes, lenders urged them to borrow against their equity, as if their homes were automated-teller machines. Citigroup told its customers to "live richly," arguing that a home could be "the ticket" to whatever "your heart desires."

"Calling it a 'second mortgage,' that's like hocking your house," said Pei-Yuan Chia, a former vice chairman at Citicorp who oversaw the bank's consumer business in the 1980s and 1990s. "But call it 'equity access,' and it sounds more innocent."[4]

As lenders began exhausting the pool of blue-chip borrowers, they courted those with more scuffed credit. Ameriquest, which focused on loans to subprime borrowers, ran a suggestive ad in the 2004 Super Bowl showing a woman on a man's lap after an airplane hit sudden turbulence, saying "Don't Judge Too Quickly . . . We Won't."

Head-turning growth at Ameriquest, New Century Financial, and other firms focused on these subprime borrowers put pressure on traditional lenders to offer more flexible products of their own. Countrywide

Financial Corp.'s chairman, Angelo Mozilo, initially decried the lowered lending standards of other banks—until his company began to embrace the practices of the upstarts.

During the 1980s, Mozilo, a forceful executive and gifted salesman born to a butcher in the Bronx, taught employees how to sell mortgages quickly and efficiently, focusing on plain-vanilla, fixed-rate loans. The banking establishment didn't give Mozilo and his California operation much of a chance, but by the early 2000s, profits were soaring, and the company was the largest mortgage lender in the country.

Mozilo didn't so much run Countrywide Financial as rule over it. Rivals called him "The Sun God," both for how his employees seemed to worship him as well as for his deep, permanent tan. Mozilo drove several Rolls-Royces, often in shades of gold, and paid his executives hundreds of thousands of dollars. Mozilo's shiny white teeth, pinstriped suits, and bravado helped him both stand out and send a message: He was going to shake up the staid industry.

By 2004, competitors were biting at Mozilo's heels, and Countrywide began to adjust its conservative stance, pushing adjustable-rate, subprime mortgages, and other "affordability products." ARMs were 49 percent of its business that year, up from 18 percent in 2003, while subprime loans were 11 percent, up from less than 5 percent.[5] Mozilo said down payments should be eliminated so more people could buy homes, "the only way we can have a better society." He called down payments "nonsense" because "it's often not their money anyway."[6]

Mozilo was merely reacting to executives like Brad Morrice. In the early 1990s, Morrice worked at a mortgage lender in Southern California, watching housing prices in the region swing violently. In 1995, Morrice, along with two partners, pulled together $3 million to form New Century, a lender focused on borrowers with poor credit sometimes ignored by major lenders. They chose a name that seemed to foreshadow big changes on the way for the nation.

The New Century offer: People with bad credit could get loans to buy a home, albeit at much higher rates than those offered to borrowers with pristine credit. To limit their risks, New Century's executives had the good sense to sell their loans to investors attracted to the hefty interest rates. It was a blueprint followed by rival lenders. Orange County in Southern California quickly became the epicenter of subprime lending.

Morrice and his partners took New Century public in 1997, just as the housing market began to heat up. New Century, which billed itself as "a new shade of blue chip," reached out to independent mortgage-brokerage firms around the country, often tiny, local outfits that found customers, advised them on which types of loans were available, and collected fees for handling the initial processing of the mortgages. Brokers favored lenders like New Century that made loans quickly, and didn't always insist on the most accurate appraisals.

A revolution in home buying was under way: The same borrowers who once saw banks turn up their noses at them now found it easy to borrow money for a home. With immigrants rushing into Southern California, and those with heavy debt or limited or dented credit history trying to keep up with rising home prices, Morrice and his partners enjoyed a gold rush.

As profits rolled in, New Century's executives chose a black-glass tower in Irvine, California, as their headquarters, and treated their sales force of two thousand to chartered cruises in the Bahamas. Later, they held a bash in a train station in Barcelona and offered top mortgage producers trips to a Porsche driving school. A "culture of excess" was created, says a former computer specialist at the company.

Lenders like New Century relaxed their lending standards, a sharp break with past norms in the business. Regulators gave New Century and its rivals leeway, and New Century became the nation's second-largest subprime lender, competing head-to-head with older rivals like Countrywide and HSBC Holdings PLC. Wall Street was impressed; David Einhorn, a hedge-fund investor with a stellar record, became a big shareholder and joined the company's board of directors.

By 2005, almost 30 percent of New Century's loans were interest-only, requiring borrowers to initially pay only the interest part of the mortgage, rather than principal plus interest. But such loans exposed borrowers to drastic payment hikes when the principal came due. Moreover, more than 40 percent of New Century's mortgages were based on the borrowers' stated income, with no documentation required.

Some employees, like Karen Waheed, began having qualms about whether customers would be able to make their payments. She worried that some colleagues weren't following the company's rule that borrowers had to have at least $1,000 in income left over each month, after paying the mortgage and taxes.

"It got to a point where I literally got sick to my stomach," she recalls. "Every day I got home and would think to myself, I helped set someone up for failure."[7]

By 2005, "nonprime" mortgages made up nearly 25 percent of loans in the country, up from 1 percent a decade earlier. One-third of new mortgages and home-equity loans were interest-only, up from less than 1 percent in 2000, while 43 percent of first-time home buyers put no money down at all.

Rather than rein it all in, regulators gave the market encouragement, thrilled that a record 69 percent of Americans owned their own homes, up from 64 percent a decade earlier. In a 2004 speech, Federal Reserve chairman Alan Greenspan said that borrowers would benefit from using adjustable-rate mortgages, which had seemed risky to some, and were a type of loan the Bank of England was campaigning against. Greenspan clarified his comments eight days later, saying he wasn't disparaging more conservative, fixed-rate mortgages, but his comments were interpreted as a sign that he was unconcerned with the housing market. In the fall of 2004, Greenspan told an annual convention of community bankers that "a national severe price distortion seems most unlikely."

The Fed also chose not to crack down on the growing subprime-lending industry, even as some home loans were signed on the hoods of cars. In many states, electricians and beauticians were given more scrutiny and training than those hawking mortgages. Several years later, Greenspan said, "I did not forecast a significant decline because we had never had a significant decline in prices."

Lenders ramped up their activity only because a pipeline of cash was pumping hard, dumping money right in front of their headquarters. The pipeline usually went through Wall Street. After New Century issued a mortgage, it was bundled together with other mortgages and sold to firms like Merrill Lynch, Morgan Stanley, and Lehman Brothers for ready cash. New Century used the money to run its operations and make new loan commitments. The quasi-government companies Fannie Mae and Freddie Mac, pushing for growth, also became hungry for the high-interest mortgages from New Century and others, egged on by politicians pushing for wider home ownership.

"I believe there has been more alarm raised about potential unsafety and unsoundness than, in fact, exists. . . . I want to roll the dice a little bit more in this situation towards subsidized housing," Massachusetts Democrat Barney Frank, then the ranking minority member of the House Financial Services Committee, said about Fannie Mae and Freddie Mac in September 2003. Sen. Charles Schumer (D-New York) expressed worries that restricting the big companies might "curtail Fannie and Freddie's [affordable-housing] mission."

By selling its loans to Fannie and Freddie, as well as to the ravenous Wall Street investment firms, companies like New Century didn't need to worry much if they sometimes handed out mortgages that might not be repaid. Like playing hot potato, they quickly got them off their books. Checks and balances in the system were almost nonexistent. Home appraisers, for example, placed inflated values on homes, paving the way for the mortgage deals, knowing that if they didn't play along, their competitors would.

Banks like Lehman Brothers were eager to buy as many mortgages as they could get their hands on because the game of hot potato usually didn't stop with them. Wall Street used the mortgages as the raw material for a slew of "securitized" investments sold to investors. Indeed, one of the things the United States excelled at was slicing up mortgages and other loans into complex investments with esoteric names—such as mortgage-backed securities, collateralized-debt obligations, asset-backed commercial paper, and auction-rate securities—and selling them to Japanese pension plans, Swiss banks, British hedge funds, U.S. insurance companies, and others around the globe.

Though these instruments usually didn't trade on public exchanges, and this booming world was foreign to most investors and home owners, the securitization process was less mysterious than it seemed.

Here's how it worked: Wall Street firms set up investment structures to buy thousands of home mortgages or other kinds of debt; the regular payments on these loans provided revenue to these vehicles. The firms then sold interests in this pool of cash payments to investors, creating an investment for every taste. Though the loans in the pool might have an average annual interest rate of 7 percent, some investors might want a higher yield, say 9 percent. The Wall Street underwriter would sell that investor an interest in the cash pool with a 9 percent yield. In exchange for this higher rate, these investors would be at the most risk for losses if borrowers started missing their mortgage payments and the pool's revenue was lower than expected. Moody's or Standard & Poor's might give this slice, or "tranche," of the pool a BBB rating, or just a rung above the "junk" category.

Other investors, though, might be content with that 7 percent yield; they wouldn't see any losses until the BBB slice was hit. As such, these claims might command a higher, AA rating. Still other investors might want a safer investment yet and be comfortable getting only 5 percent a year; they would receive a slice of the pool with a much higher rating, say AAA.

Dozens of tranches, or claims on the packaged pools of assets, were created in a typical securitization, most rated AAA or close to it, and each paying investors interest based on expected payments of the pool. When Joe Sixpack sent his $1,500 monthly mortgage payment to New Century, the check, along with those of other home owners, would find its way to these "structured" vehicles, where they'd start paying off holders like a cascading waterfall. Part of Joe's payment first would go to satisfy holders of the AAA slice at the top of the pool, and then trickle down to holders of the tranches rated BBB, BBB− and BB−, each getting paid in full along the way. Losses would infiltrate up from the bottom. So the highest-rated pieces got the first chance at income but the lowest rate of return, while the lowest got the first losses and the highest potential return.

To try to ensure that losses wouldn't result, Wall Street firms made sure there was more revenue coming into the vehicle than it needed to pay out, just in case there were problems. Or they mixed in other kinds of revenue, such as claims on auto loans or even aircraft leases. To ensure proper diversification, loans were acquired from all over the country and from a variety of different lenders. The resulting investment product was called an asset-backed bond because it was a bond backed by a pool of mortgage loans or other assets.

Through these structures, Wall Street took piles of risky mortgages and created shiny AAA-rated investments—handsome new bonds made from much uglier bonds. The banks usually designed the securities to just barely achieve the credit agencies' requirements for their top ratings. They had created gold from dross.

Over three decades, as the market to "securitize" loans into investments grew, securities firms, investment banks, and commercial banks searched high and low for mortgages and other financial assets to package into new investments. After stocks tumbled in 2000, fees from the securitization market became even more important to the firms, making them more willing to buy up all kinds of mortgage loans, especially those with high interest rates, to serve as linchpins for these investments.

For investors, securitized investments were enticing. Stocks were on the ropes and it seemed a better option to plow money into anything housing related, since many other bond investments had skimpier yields. As comedian Jon Stewart later joked, just the aroma of a mortgage was enough to get investors salivating. An ingrained belief arose that the securitization process, by chopping up tens of thousands of loans of varying quality from all over the country into small investments, effectively spread risk from lenders to tens of thousands of investors around the globe. They might catch a cold but no one would likely be killed by a flu outbreak.

One key reason investors were so taken with mortgage-related investments was that companies like Moody's Investors Service and Standard & Poor's that were paid to place ratings on it all, blessed the pools of loans with top ratings. Analysts at these firms scrutinized all these debt investments, laboring for weeks before even warning that they *might* adjust a rating a smidgen. If these prestigious firms placed ratings as high as AAA on the mortgage-related investments, how bad could they really be? investors asked. (In truth, the rating firms tacked on disclaimers, in really fine print, that their ratings were just opinions.) Many investors didn't even realize they were making housing-related investments. They just focused on the top rating. Some had standing orders at various Wall Street trading desks to buy any U.S. debt rated AAA and sold with an attractive yield.

The real estate bubble would have burst early on were it not for overeager home buyers, of course. Surging housing prices created an illusion of wealth for home owners, encouraging them to save very little and spend more than they were making. Wages were stagnant, making it hard for first-time home owners determined to buy their own home. Undeterred, many borrowed heavily to afford their first home, or to move up to their dream home, complete with granite kitchen counters, stainless-steel appliances, flat-screen televisions, and surround-sound systems. Borrowers often asked for loans much larger than they could afford, sometimes exaggerating their salaries and other financial information to qualify.

The real estate market became the hobby that swept the nation, extended around the globe, and then back again. Reflecting the speculative frenzy, reality television shows debuted, including *Flip That House* and its competitor, *Flip This House*. Even the upper echelon got carried away. In the spring of 2004, Lakshmi Mittal, an Indian steel magnate, bought a twelve-bedroom house with a twenty-car garage in Kensington Palace Gardens, London, for an eye-popping $126 million.

Investors like Jeffrey Greene also drove prices higher. Greene, an old friend of John Paulson, had a voracious appetite for real estate in the early 2000s, purchasing hundreds of apartment buildings in Southern California, often at a rapid-fire clip. Greene never asked for a commission from real estate brokers bringing him deals, unlike some of his competitors. Instead, he hoped to be their first call when a new property came on the market. Because he had done so much buying, Greene became familiar with wide swaths of the San Fernando Valley and Hollywood. Within five minutes of getting a new offer for an apartment building or a home, Greene usually agreed to a deal at full price, forgoing time-consuming negotiations or inspections so he could be the first in the door.

"I could tell within five minutes, just from a phone call, if it was a good price," Greene recalls. "I knew the streets, I knew the rents, and I could picture the buildings. The brokers knew what I wanted."

By 2005, lenders had granted $625 billion of subprime loans, a fifth of all home mortgages that year, according to *Inside Mortgage Finance,* a trade publication. U.S. home prices had jumped 15 percent in the previous year and were on average almost 2.4 times annual incomes, compared with a seventeen-year average of about 1.7.[8]

Bulls were convinced that prices would continue to trend up, noting that homes hadn't fallen on a national basis in generations. A flattening of prices was as bad as it had gotten since the 1930s. Many experts at most conceded there might be bubbles in some local markets.

A December 2004 interview with Countrywide's Angelo Mozilo on the *Kudlow & Cramer* show on the cable-business network CNBC captured the tenor of the times:

LARRY KUDLOW, COHOST: *Mr. Mozilo, again, happy holidays to you.*
MR. MOZILO: *Thank you.*
KUDLOW: *You can't see it, sir, but underneath you, it says "bubble shmubble," which has sort of been our view . . . People buy homes, 'cause they like to and they can afford to. And . . .*
CRAMER: *Right.*
KUDLOW: *. . . homes are in short supply relative to demand.*
MR. MOZILO: *Right.*
KUDLOW: *Are you in the bubble shmubble camp?*
MR. MOZILO: *No, I'm probably in the bubblette camp to be honest with you. . . . There's a few areas of the country where we have some inventory, but on balance, as you said, Larry, the demographics are clear, there's tremendous demand for housing, and it's becoming more and more difficult to build housing and to get land and title than the capital that's needed to do it. . . . And so I think that we're going to have a very healthy housing market.*

CRAMER: *I have a quick question to ask Angelo. Angelo, fifty-one years. Did you get into the housing business when you were, like, eight?*

MR. MOZILO: *Fourteen, right—not far from you. I was in 25 West 43rd Street, fourteen years old, as a messenger boy.*

KUDLOW: *That's a great story. . . .*

MR. MOZILO: *It's a great country.*

CRAMER: *Yeah, it is.*

KUDLOW: *Number one.*

CRAMER: *It's a great American story.*

KUDLOW: *And earnings look great.*

MR. MOZILO: *It's a great country.*

KUDLOW: *Share looks great.*

CRAMER: *Yeah.*

KUDLOW: *No, really, it's a wonderful American story.*

CRAMER: *It's a great country, great country.*

KUDLOW: *And we wish you all the best in the holidays and the new year.*[9]

It became hard to miss the excesses, though. When Alberto and Rosa Ramirez began looking for a home in late 2005, they had realistic expectations. The couple, strawberry pickers who each made $300 a week in the fields around Watsonville, California, near Santa Cruz, pooled resources with another couple working as mushroom farmers and determined they could afford payments of $3,000 a month. When an agent showed them a four-bedroom, two-bath home in the city of Hollister for $720,000, they blanched. They had no assets, six children, and no money for a down payment.

But their agent assured them they could handle it, even though the initial monthly payment would be $4,800. The zero-down mortgage from New Century had a "teaser rate" that would put monthly payments at $5,378, but the agent said they could refinance and "get the payments down to $3,000 or less," Rosa Ramirez recalls.

The refinancing never happened, though, and cutting back on expenses didn't help much. About a year after buying the home, they could no longer make the payments.[10]

A Washington Mutual loan representative made a loan to a borrower claiming a six-figure income from an unusual profession: mariachi singer. The representative couldn't verify the income so he just had the singer photographed in front of his home dressed in his mariachi outfit. The loan was approved.[11]

E VERYONE seemed to be drinking the housing Kool-Aid, right? Well, not exactly.

A number of traders saw a real estate bubble forming, but precious few bet that it would burst. There was little incentive for even skeptics to make a radical wager against housing. Traders bucking the bullish consensus risked squandering big profits and ruining their careers if they were wrong. They might make money in a downturn, but who knew how long it would take for any slowdown to materialize? Any profits they might generate with a bearish stance likely would be offset by losses elsewhere at their firms, limiting their paycheck. Radical moves didn't lead to long careers on Wall Street. So even the bears sat on their hands, letting the bulls run wild.

For those utterly convinced a housing crash was in the offing, there was precious little they could do, anyway. Sure, you could sell a home and move into a rental, but that meant packing up the family and kids, and leaving behind neighbors and friends, never a fun task. A futures market on housing prices never took off. Shorting home builders and lenders was a possibility. Some bears favored a "derivative" investment called a credit-default swap, or CDS, that served as insurance protection for the debt of companies in the subprime-lending business. But these companies didn't always suffer when housing fell, because some of them benefited in a weak market by grabbing business from rivals or by selling out to larger companies. Besides, there weren't that many of these corporate bonds in the market; it was difficult to create CDS contracts to protect bonds that didn't exist.

Shorting risky mortgage loans seemed like the most obvious move for financial traders, but it was even more difficult to get one's hands on these "mortgage-backed bonds," or claims on pools of hundreds of different risky loans, to short them or create a CDS contract to protect this debt. Sometimes a bullish investor would buy an entire issue of mortgage-backed securities and resist lending it out, making it impossible for investors to short.

As a result, a shocking few pros in the mortgage-bond world bothered to predict where home prices were going. The direction of interest rates and inflation seemed more crucial to these bonds than the health of housing, which never seemed to hit big problems, anyway. Most analysts didn't even have basic data about things like the levels of foreclosures around the country, and how home-price appreciation differed, preferring to opine on whether one collection of mortgages looked more attractive than another. They were so involved with analyzing the limbs of each tree in the mortgage world that they didn't seem to know the forest even existed.

Bearish investors tend to act as a speed bump for a racing market, levying downward pressure by ganging up against a sector or company, and by sending a message of skepticism to those in the market. But until a group of bankers got together for a historic dinner in the winter of 2005, it was nearly impossible for investors to bet against housing or the growing pool of subprime-mortgage bonds. That was part of the reason housing was able to soar.

John Paulson, ever interested in a big score that could change his standing on Wall Street, would look to find a way to bet against the housing market. But how? Making his task even more challenging: While real estate was surging, Paulson had his hands full elsewhere.

3

JOHN PAULSON AT FIRST EYED THE HOUSING FRENZY WITH LITTLE MORE than passing interest; it was an express train bulleting by as he waited for his trusty local. He didn't play mortgages, derivatives, or real estate, missing out on much of the real estate mania. He had more than enough to deal with: When the stock market crumbled during the early part of the new millennium, mergers dried up, making it difficult for Paulson and others who invested in these deals.

But Paulson was becoming gutsier, playing the merger game differently than his peers. He began to short companies set to be acquired when he deduced that their merger agreements might collapse, a step most competitors were uncomfortable taking. And because Paulson had crafted mergers at Bear Stearns, he felt at ease taking big positions in stocks he was most certain *would* be acquired or receive competing acquisition offers, rather than simply spreading his investments evenly among a number of such companies.

The steps helped Paulson & Co. gain about 5 percent in 2001 and 2002, even as rivals suffered. Investors took a bit more notice of the firm, pushing it up to $300 million in assets by the end of 2002.

Paulson felt handcuffed, however, like a performer unable to show off his entire repertoire.

"I didn't like being narrowly tagged as merger-arb," Paulson says. "I had a broad skill set . . . high yield, bankruptcy, arbitrage . . . I always felt underutilized."

Paulson had done some debt investing at Gruss and he hungrily eyed beaten-down bonds amid the ongoing recession. But the rules of his funds limited his focus to mergers and other situations in which shares were exchanged. He found an opening, though, when some troubled companies sought bankruptcy protection and their debt was traded for new shares, something that Paulson told his investors was just another form of a merger.

So Paulson bought debt of troubled companies, like Enron, WorldCom, AT&T Canada, and European telecom provider Marconi Corp., all selling for pennies on the dollar. As the economy improved and the debt advanced in price or was exchanged for shares that climbed, Paulson & Co. scooped up profits, gaining 20 percent in 2003.

Paulson now managed $1.5 billion, a figure that sounded like a lot to friends outside the business. But the firm was dwarfed by its many rivals. With only nine employees, Paulson himself usually attended various meetings with companies, asking respectful questions from the back of the room as younger analysts from competing hedge funds blustered in front of the group. Paulson's hedge fund was such small potatoes that he worried it might not survive an ongoing consolidation of the business.

"In order to survive, I needed to be one of the larger players; midtier players would be squeezed out," he recalls. "I wanted to be a more significant participant in the industry."

Paulson was playing catch-up, much like he did during college and when he first was looking for a job on Wall Street. New investors weren't flocking to merger investing. And larger firms in his business had been in the game longer; some were operated by hallowed names on the Street, such as George Soros, Richard Perry, and Paul Tudor Jones, making it hard to compete.

"The leaders all came out of large, risk-arb trading desks from places like Goldman Sachs," Paulson remembers. "Once they had the lead, once they got an allocation [of money] from foundations or funds-of-funds and performed well, the doors to others were closed."

Paulson's outside marketing pro, Peter Novello, insisted to potential clients that Paulson wasn't like other investors. He might never match the huge scores that some rivals were scoring in adventurous areas, such as emerging markets. And Paulson's returns might be more unpredictable than those who carefully spread their money around. But Paulson's results would be impressive, Novello assured them. Just give him a chance.

"John piles into positions he believes in," Novello told a group of investors one day. "He has an investment-banking background, not a trading one like everyone else."

Finally, Novello succeeded in arranging meetings with some big investors. But Paulson sometimes seemed bored sitting through the barrage of simplistic questions, an impatience that worried Novello.

Once the conversation was steered to his complex trades, however, Paulson demonstrated a remarkable ability to explain his moves in surprisingly simple terms, as if he were a favorite professor teaching a challenging course. Numbers seemed like a favored language to Paulson, one that he could easily translate for even the uninitiated.

"In ten seconds their eyes lit up," Novello says. "It was so easy to understand."

One prospective client, Richard Leibovitch, visited Paulson for a one-hour meeting. He sat in an awkward reclining chair in Paulson's office and struggled to take notes on a coffee table, wondering why Paulson had original Calders on his walls but no formal conference room to host guests.

"It felt like a doctor's office," Leibovitch says.

Once they got going, though, the one hour turned into four, stretching into the evening. Paulson detailed the twists and turns of his trades with such relish that it captivated Leibovitch.

"He just didn't want to leave, so I didn't either," Leibovitch remembers.

Other investors were taken with Paulson's surprisingly self-deprecating manner, and the way he cited trades that went awry along with his successes. It helped that he was "one of the best-dressed managers we ever met," Novello says.

As Paulson's performance perked up, investors discovered his firm. Assets surged to $3 billion in 2004. Rather than live it up, however, Paulson turned more conservative, sometimes to the derision of friends who remembered his livelier bachelor days. He spoke in a more measured, serious tone and offered fewer glimpses of humor. Viewing the endless parade of dark suits and somber ties from his wardrobe, friends began to call him "the undertaker" behind his back. Paulson asked one old friend to clean up his language when he cussed in front of him. Paulson stopped speaking with Christophe von Hohenberg, a friend from his wilder days.

Some noticed Paulson becoming more deliberate and gaining more control over his emotions and temper. Paulson also adopted a healthier lifestyle, eating smaller portions of healthier food throughout the day— a piece of fruit for breakfast, salad or fish for lunch. For a snack, he stopped at a produce stand for a bag of grapes or cherries. He encouraged those working for him to follow in his footsteps, handing out copies of books advocating vegan or wholesome diets, such as T. Colin Campbell's *The China Study* and Roy L. and Lisa Walford's *The Anti-Aging Plan*.

One day, Paulson saw Keith Hannan, his stock trader, eating pizza at his desk and became incensed, an employee recalls.

"That stuff's going to kill you!"

Some employees started eating less-healthful food on the sly, sometimes out of drawers, though Hannan and others began to embrace Paulson's healthier diet.

Some of the Paulson team speculated that the early death of Paulson's father had sparked his interest in healthful food. But Paulson gave Jim Wong, his head of investor relations, another explanation.

"He told me, 'If I can stay alive longer, I can compound my wealth longer,'" Wong recalls. "He was joking, and yet he wasn't." It was a hint at what was driving Paulson.

Paulson's domestic life became his new passion. He hurried straight home after work most evenings to be with Jenny and their two young daughters. Paulson was one of the only investors to take his wife on a ski trip to Utah sponsored by a brokerage firm. And he began a tradition of taking his family on annual summer trips abroad.

Though the firm raked in tens of millions of dollars per year, Paulson's offices were understated, even Spartan. He clung to a few pieces of worn furniture, including a black leather couch that he bought in 1994 from a Bloomingdale's warehouse. That wasn't out of character. Paulson tended to hold on to things close to him. For years, he was smitten by a black 1986 Jaguar with a doe-skinned interior. It was the first car he ever owned and he refused to give it up, even after the car began having electrical problems. One day on a drive back to New York from Southampton, the Jaguar's engine caught fire and Paulson had to quickly ditch it on the side of the road before it was engulfed in flames.

"I get attached to things and I look for good value," Paulson explains.

He frequently walked to work or a meeting, sometimes bumping into clients along the way. Some of them were surprised Paulson didn't take a car service like most other hedge-fund managers.

On a business trip to England in 2003, Paulson stayed at Peter Soros's country home in the English countryside. After dinner, Paulson excused himself and walked into a nearby room to arrange a flight back home. Rather than book a private plane, Paulson spent forty-five minutes on the phone with a representative of American Airlines, haggling for a better business-class fare back to the United States.

"Can you do better than that?" Paulson asked of the representative.

Listening from another room, his incredulous host shook his head, smiling.

"It wasn't even a first-class seat" he was negotiating for, Soros recalls, by then a close friend.

Paulson liked to track real estate, and he noticed prices heating up in 2004. He sold his SoHo loft, pocketing more than $1 million in profit. Paulson wasn't yet wary of the market, however; he just needed more space for his growing family. On the lookout for a new place to live, Paulson heard about a home languishing on the market—a 28,500-square-foot building on the Upper East Side, just off Fifth Avenue, a magnificent six-story limestone mansion with an indoor pool and a tragic past.

Built in 1916 by legendary architects Delano and Aldrich for the patrician banker and horse breeder William Woodward Sr., the home, one of New York's largest residences, was the backdrop of lavish parties thrown by William Woodward Jr. and his wife, Ann, a former actress and model.

Their giddy days ended when she shot her husband to death at point-blank range in the middle of the night at their Long Island estate after she said she mistook him for a prowler. *Life* magazine dubbed it "The Shooting of the Century." Ann was cleared by a grand jury, but the case was full of intrigue. She later committed suicide, shortly after Truman Capote published a thinly veiled account of the case in 1975.[1]

After the shooting, the New York home was transformed into the Town Club, where a group of members enjoyed high-stakes games of gin and bridge. The residence became rundown, however, allowing Paulson to purchase it for $15 million, well under the original $27 million asking price.

D ESPITE THE BARGAIN he had found in his own home, Paulson began to sense that real estate was getting out of hand. He heard about homes similar to his own being sold in Southampton for five, seven, and even ten times what he had paid a decade earlier. Developers and buyers seemed on a building-and-buying spree.

"It was out of control," Paulson remembers. "The amount of appreciation relative to what people were earning was startling."

Paulson sold his Southampton home, figuring that he would find another bargain. When he heard about an attractive home nearby, though, he was astonished at its $13 million asking price. In the end, he decided to rent.

Others were getting caught up in the frenzy, however. A friend purchased forty-five acres of land from a farmer for $3 million and then flipped it for $9 million. He watched it quickly sell for $25 million. The rapid appreciation stunned Paulson. He warned friends about their real estate investments, but they ignored him, insisting that there were very few lots available; prices were bound to rise further.

"I kept saying, 'This isn't sustainable,' but no one seemed to listen," Paulson recalls.

He hadn't yet translated his concern about his high-end world to the national market, nor did he have much reason to, given that he still focused on merger investing. That all changed, however, when Paulson received an unexpected phone call from an old friend.

A S PAOLO PELLEGRINI picked up the phone in the spring of 2004, he debated how to ask John Paulson for a job. A career Web site operated by the Harvard University Business School listed an opening for a chief financial officer at Paulson's hedge fund.

Pellegrini didn't have high hopes. He hadn't worked with Paulson in years and they hadn't stayed in close contact. Pellegrini already had sent out hundreds of fruitless letters to prospective employers. Moreover, Pellegrini was sure that he wasn't nearly qualified enough for the job.

But Pellegrini had drained his bank account and didn't have many other options, so he took the chance. He half-expected Paulson to laugh at his boldness. Instead, Paulson sounded happy to hear from him. Then Paulson delivered the bad news: The job already was filled.

"What about a job as an analyst?" Pellegrini quickly countered.

Paulson sounded uncomfortable.

"Well, Paolo, usually those jobs are for young people out of school. There's a lot of grunt work involved, and you don't make many decisions."

"I'm fine with grunt work," Pellegrini responded, with as much enthusiasm as he could muster. So Paulson suggested they get together.

When they met in Paulson's office, the hedge-fund manager was friendly but exceedingly blunt.

"It looks like your career is going nowhere," Paulson said, looking over Pellegrini's résumé. "You've been doing nothing, really, since Bear."

He's more or less accurate, Pellegrini thought.

"But you're a smart guy and a hard worker," Paulson continued. A young associate recently had left the fund to attend business school, creating an opening.

Paulson set up an interview for Pellegrini with two of his associates. It was a last chance for Pellegrini to make something of a career that began with much promise but had stalled out, quite badly.

Born in Rome in 1957, Pellegrini moved to Milan at the age of five when his father, Umberto, a physicist, was hired to teach electronics at Politecnico, Milan's prestigious engineering school. On the side, Umberto ran a company that manufactured electronics for Italy's military and later built the country's first minicomputer. The family led a comfortable life in a neighborhood near the university and enjoyed skiing vacations in the Dolomites section of the Alps. But Umberto was a reluctant capitalist, more focused on the technical and intellectual challenges of his work than on his pay. Pellegrini's mother, Anna, taught high-school biology and pursued her own research, sharing her husband's distaste of money.

In many ways, the Pellegrinis' attitudes reflected a period of economic upheaval and frustration in Italy, as a series of governments clamped down on foreign-currency holdings and took other restrictive measures to try to stem runaway inflation.

Early signs suggested that Paolo didn't quite share his parents' perspective. At the age of six, he used toy Lego pieces to build a huge replica of a bank, startling his parents. From the age of twelve, he worked at his father's company, writing computer code and showing unusual interest in the business world.

"I always liked money," Pellegrini recalls. "My parents were puritanical about it; I think it was a reaction to them."

Paolo excelled in school, especially in math and physics, but his grades dropped in high school as he showed little interest in a curriculum featuring Italian literature, philosophy, Latin, and Greek.

Most summers Pellegrini worked at various international companies operating in Italy, or could be found in front of a computer at his father's company.

"Programming computers taught me to break down problems and set up intellectual experiments to verify and demonstrate theories, and to run simulated experiments," Pellegrini recalls. "My dad indirectly provided certainty that I could handle it all because he had."

At the University of Milan, Pellegrini finally could focus on the computer sciences and electrical engineering courses that intrigued him, and he received top grades. He spent one summer working for Hewlett-Packard in France and another in Boston working for Honeywell.

Most graduates served in the Italian army after school, but after five years of university Pellegrini already was a year behind contemporaries in the United States, and he was in a rush to catch up. So he found an entry-level job at a computer-equipment company in Holland. Pellegrini quickly became bored, though, quitting after just two years to attend Harvard Business School.

Class work came easily to Pellegrini, even though English was his second language. He received honors in his first year at Harvard and was described by one professor as having one of the "most creative mathematical minds" he had ever seen in a student.

"I remember him very well, he was really special," says Elon Kohlberg, a professor at the school. Pellegrini was "sort of like those annoying kids who are just too smart for their own good. Whatever comes up they can just poke holes in it."

Pellegrini aced a class on regression analysis, a course that Harvard later abolished because students complained it was just too hard, Kohlberg says.

During his first summer in business school, Pellegrini worked at the investment-banking department at Bear Stearns, sharing an office with John Paulson, impressing him by developing a detailed, proprietary database of merger deals.

At Harvard, Pellegrini felt uncomfortable socializing with his classmates; he was a bit older than most of them, and was concerned that his English wasn't up to par. The six-foot-two Pellegrini was more relaxed in one-on-one settings. He soon discovered that his accented English held a special charm for certain women. Pellegrini dated a series of classmates but found himself looking forward to seeing fellow student Claire Goodman, the daughter of legendary New York State Senator Roy Goodman, to whom he gave regular tutoring sessions.

Their relationship blossomed, as Goodman's outgoing personality seemed to complement Pellegrini's more introverted nature. A year later they married; John Paulson was among the attendees. After Pellegrini graduated from Harvard with distinction in 1985, the young couple moved to New York. He landed a job at investment-banking firm Dillon, Read & Co., and Goodman took a job at First Boston.

Pellegrini seemed on the fast track to success. He quickly received a promotion, joining Dillon Read's mergers-and-acquisitions department, and then was hired away by the prestigious banking firm Lazard Freres & Co. for its international mergers and acquisitions group. The firm didn't have an insurance-industry expert and turned to Pellegrini, who enjoyed the challenge of figuring out a new industry.

Clients and colleagues seemed taken with his unique style. Well dressed and possessing boundless enthusiasm, Pellegrini was passionate about his deals, pushing hard to get buyers and sellers on the same page. Working on a floundering deal with David Nelson, a senior banker at Chase Manhattan Bank, Pellegrini pushed the various parties toward a compromise, impressing others at the negotiating table.

"Paolo wasn't your typical investment banker, he was full of life, almost flamboyant, with a tremendous amount of positive energy," recalls Nelson, who helped arrange financing for some of Pellegrini's insurance acquisitions. "Most guys were Anglo-Saxon, white-shoe bankers, but [Paolo] was this bigger-than-life, good-looking guy with Romanesque features and a distinctive accent driving the conversation."

But Pellegrini found it difficult to woo clients, blaming his unfamiliarity with American social norms. He once watched a playoff basketball game with the two top executives of a large insurance company and struggled the entire night to come up with topics of conversation or a single player he was familiar with.

The best Pellegrini could muster to fill the awkward silence: "So you like basketball in Chicago?"

Other times, the cutting, sarcastic humor he displayed that went over so well in his native land seemed to offend clients in the United States.

Pellegrini failed to gain a promotion at Lazard, even as contemporaries vaulted past him. He became seen as a laggard and his work suffered. Pellegrini turned brusque with colleagues, convinced that his accent raised doubts among clients about whether he fully understood the nuances of the complicated transactions.

"I was an outsider, it wasn't my home turf, and my accent made clients worry that I'd miss the fine print. It tilted the balance away from me," he recalls. "I was never the first call for companies; we had difficulty relating personal experiences."

Pellegrini was bursting with new ideas about how companies could raise money or undertake innovative merger structures, but the nitty-gritty of the banking job overwhelmed him. Pellegrini tried to focus on big-picture issues, ignoring details such as his appointment schedule. That led some to question his competence. Traveling to Rome with a group of senior Lazard bankers for a big meeting, Pellegrini had trouble guiding them to the meeting's location and they arrived a half hour late, frustrating the group.

"Everyone assumed I knew my way around because it was Rome but I didn't; it was embarrassing," he says.

Pellegrini paid a coach to help him become an "active listener," to better understand his clients and their needs, and he hired another coach to help eliminate his accent. He couldn't shake it entirely, though. When Pellegrini became uncomfortable in public, he found it difficult to express himself, seeming stiff and awkward.

A flurry of successful insurance deals improved Pellegrini's stature at the firm, however, and by 1993 he was on his way to becoming a partner. Riches and prestige were sure to follow. That year, Lazard's senior banker, Felix Rohatyn, set up a meeting for Pellegrini with the chief financial officer of Xerox Corp. to discuss a possible sale of the company's flagging life-insurance subsidiary. Pellegrini was competing for the business with a fierce rival, Morgan Stanley's star banker Gary Parr, even as rumors swirled that Lazard was quietly wooing Parr to join the firm, perhaps to lead Pellegrini's insurance group. Pellegrini tried to get out of the assignment, but he couldn't extract himself.

As Pellegrini researched Xerox Life to prepare for the meeting, he concluded that it had deep problems. But he tried to strike an upbeat tone with the Xerox executives, encouraging them to pursue a sale because merger activity was so buoyant.

"You can turn chicken shit into chicken salad in this market," Pellegrini told them with enthusiasm, trying to drive home his point.

Suddenly, the room went silent. The jaws of the Xerox team seemed to drop. They were shocked and insulted by Pellegrini's coarse description of a unit that they didn't consider to be operating so poorly. Pellegrini tried to backtrack, but it was too late; the damage had been done.

Days later, his boss, Luis Rinaldini, a hard-driving Argentinean, called Pellegrini into his office—Xerox wanted him off the account. At that moment, Pellegrini was certain that his once-bright future was in jeopardy.

"It was a lesson to me that people are always waiting at the pass to shoot at you," Pellegrini recalls. "I knew my career was in trouble."

As his anxieties built, Pellegrini's marriage to Goodman began to crumble. Word of their troubles, which soon led to a divorce, spread within Lazard. Pellegrini took comfort in a special bond he had developed with his two young sons. He frequently brought them to the office and boasted of their exploits to colleagues, showing a tender side that softened their view of him.

But when Kendrick Wilson took over Lazard's investment-banking group, the pressure grew. Wilson, a no-nonsense former Marine who had served as an officer in the Army Special Forces in Vietnam, had little patience for Pellegrini and his grand schemes. One day, Pellegrini brought Wilson an idea for an improved version of an employee stock-option plan that could be pitched to Lazard's clients. Wilson was dismissive and sarcastic, telling Pellegrini to stick with mergers.

"Just get it done, Paolo," Wilson implored him, repeatedly.

Pellegrini turned stubborn, unwilling to back down from his boss, colleagues, or rivals, even over minor points of disagreement. Some at Lazard buzzed about a screaming match between Pellegrini and another top banker, Chris Flowers. When Wilson heard a client complain about how rudely Pellegrini interacted with others at the firm, Wilson had had enough. He fired Pellegrini in 1995, after nine years at the firm, telling him that "a knife-and-fork role isn't suited for you."

"He's very, very smart, and his analytical skills are extraordinary," Wilson recalls, "but he's a classic hot-blooded Italian; he got into situations where everything was a zero-sum game."

Pellegrini says more bluntly, "He thought I was full of shit."

Pellegrini was thirty-eight years old, unemployed, and newly single.

He threw a party at his apartment, trying to meet some new friends, but he was too uncomfortable to enjoy it very much, retreating to a corner of the room. His job prospects weren't much better. Lazard was a top-flight Wall Street firm, but nine years as a vice president without a promotion raised all kinds of questions in others' minds.

Pellegrini still had big ideas, however. He started an insurance company in Bermuda with Bill Michaelcheck, a former Bear Stearns colleague, to invest insurance premiums in hedge funds. He threw himself into developing complicated models. The idea was a success for Michaelcheck, who turned it into a separate business to invest in hedge funds, but it didn't do much for Pellegrini, who left after a couple of years.

He found more luck in love, marrying Beth Rudin DeWoody, the daughter of the late New York real estate mogul Lewis Rudin, in a 1996 wedding in Bermuda officiated by former New York Mayor David Dinkins. Pellegrini now was part of a wealthy, well-established family.

Instead of relaxing, however, he began to worry about what would happen if DeWoody ever left him. Pellegrini was tapping into his 401(k) retirement savings to make hefty child-support payments for his two sons, who attended expensive New York private schools. The payments had been set when Pellegrini was working at Lazard and making much more money than he now was making from irregular consulting gigs in the insurance industry.

Pellegrini and DeWoody lived an expensive lifestyle, and bills for art, evenings of entertainment, and a deluxe apartment added up quickly; Pellegrini favored expensive clothing, trying to keep up appearances and to fit into a privileged social scene. But he chafed at how little money was coming in and at the fact that the couple depended on DeWoody's family to pay for their lavish lifestyle. His growing insecurities began to weigh on their marriage. Pellegrini tried to get his wife's family to stake him some money to trade in the stock market, but they refused, asking to first see evidence that he could trade profitably. As Pellegrini watched other men his age lose jobs and have difficulty making much of their lives, he worried that he would, too. He pushed DeWoody to adjust their prenuptial agreement to increase any payout to him, telling her that the terms gave her encouragement to leave him. But lawyers within the Rudin organization wouldn't budge on the agreement.

DeWoody tried to boost her husband's confidence. "You just need the right situation, where someone believes in you and you don't have to deal with clients," she told him.

Pellegrini never felt reassured, though. "A number of Beth's friends had disposed of their husbands, and I felt that pressure," he recalls. "I felt vulnerable and expendable."

In 2000, Pellegrini finally snapped, waking DeWoody in the middle of the night to demand sweetened terms from the prenup agreement and threatening to leave her. That's it, DeWoody decided. She ignored his demands and Pellegrini walked out. A few days later, he tried to get his wife to take him back, but by then she was set on a divorce, no longer willing to deal with his insecurities.

"I could have handled it better," Pellegrini acknowledges.

Pellegrini moved out of their Gracie Square home to an apartment in Westchester, receiving $300,000 from DeWoody in a divorce settlement, a pretax payout that he figured might have to last him through retirement. Being financially successful was at the top of Pellegrini's life goals, right up there with having a happy family life. He had failed miserably at both.

"I was forty-five and had zero net worth," Pellegrini recalls. "And from my perspective, I had no prospects."

Pellegrini's bright ideas kept coming, though. He developed a new method to use "statistical arbitrage" to trade stocks, though he couldn't make much money with it. A stint at Tricadia Capital, a hedge fund founded by Michaelcheck's Mariner Investment Group, Inc., gave Pellegrini an education in the world of securitized debt and credit-default swaps (CDS), which the firm was heavily involved in.

But Pellegrini didn't make many friends at Tricadia when he suggested that the firm find ways to short collateralized-debt obligations, even as others at the firm were buying and creating versions of these debts. After a derivative-focused company that Pellegrini hoped to set up for Tricadia failed to get off the ground, he began searching for a job once again. It was that development that led him to the interview that Paulson set up for him with two of Paulson's executives, Andrew Hoine and Michael Waldorf.

The meeting started with Hoine and Waldorf asking Pellegrini for his views on various European industries. Pellegrini had no clue—his most recent experience was with CDS trading. He hadn't taken the time to brush up on other areas. Pellegrini tried to compensate by acting more cocky than he actually felt, but he could see Hoine and Waldorf becoming annoyed with him as the meeting progressed.

Afterward, Pellegrini waited at home for days, hoping to hear back from Paulson. Pellegrini almost gave up. Ten days after the interview, he finally received a call. "Well, you managed to piss off my partners," Paulson said. "If you hadn't been such a jerk, you would have gotten a job earlier."

"If I came off as a jerk, I didn't mean to," Pellegrini responded, quietly.

Paulson agreed to give Pellegrini a chance. His employees didn't like him very much, but Paulson viewed Pellegrini as a smart gamble, a bright, well-educated analyst who might yet become an asset. He told Pellegrini it would take him a year or so to learn the merger-arbitrage business, and welcomed him aboard. Pellegrini was forty-seven, a year younger than his new boss and thrilled at the opportunity to show he wasn't washed up.

THE EARLY MONTHS at Paulson & Co. were tough on Pellegrini. Worried about being overwhelmed by the details of his job, as he had been at Lazard, Pellegrini arrived at the office before 6:30 a.m. each morning, among the first to arrive. He wanted to try to have a few recommendations ready when Paulson walked in. He had another motive: Pellegrini found early-bird $18 parking a fifteen-minute walk from their office at the corner of 57th Street and Madison Avenue. The price doubled if he arrived after 7 a.m. Pellegrini wasn't sure how long he would have the job, so he needed to save his cash.

Pellegrini took advantage of a full, catered lunch from a local upscale eatery that Paulson offered his employees. When Pellegrini returned home to his apartment in the Westchester suburb of Mamaro-neck around 8 p.m., he usually made something light, like tomato salad, cheese, and bread.

He had no television in his small one-bedroom rental. He chose to live close to a train station and his favorite golf course. For entertain-ment, Pellegrini began to catch up on classic American writers, such as Edith Wharton and Henry James, authors he never had a chance to enjoy in school. Pellegrini found a connection with their stories of out-siders struggling to break into high society, including New York's upper-crust scene, something he had failed to do at Lazard Freres and through his marriage to DeWoody.

"I could see the divide between people who are successful and opti-mistic and those at the other end, having trouble keeping up," Pellegrini says. "There's sadness about not realizing one's hopes and expectations."

Pellegrini didn't have many friends in the area, but his sons stayed over on weekends, sleeping on a pullout couch in the living room. Pellegrini felt the likelihood of turning his life around was dropping with each day, but he wasn't ready to give up.

"Somehow I needed to manage to stay in the United States and sup-port myself; I didn't want to be in another country and not be able to see my kids," he says. "That kept me going."

Pellegrini put in long hours analyzing international mergers but couldn't come up with many good ideas for the fund. It took him longer to get up to speed than he expected, and he was as disappointed in his work as Paulson was. When Paulson met his investors, he often brought along a few associates to introduce them and show off their education and backgrounds. Pellegrini usually was left back at the office, even though he was two decades older than most of the other analysts. He didn't complain.

"I didn't have a great story to tell about myself and my experience," Pellegrini says. "I produced usable work, but it was difficult for me to carry on conversations with clients. It was nice of John to give me the job and stick by me."

Pellegrini was so relieved to land the position that he missed fleeting signs that Paulson himself might be losing his touch.

Some ridiculed Paulson's focus on mergers, which seemed out of step with the instant wealth being created in housing. At a cocktail party in Southampton in late 2004, Paulson and a friend, Jeffrey Tarrant, stood in the corner of the room discussing how overheated the real estate market had become, when Stephan Keszler wandered over, a drink in his hand. Keszler, a dashing, six-foot-three, fair-skinned native of Munich, wearing tattered jeans and a blue blazer, was well-known in the Southampton scene as a real estate success story. He had spent twelve years purchasing and renovating upscale homes in the area.

Inserting himself into the conversation, Keszler was dismissive of his friends' caution.

"What are you guys trying to do, a 10 percent to 12 percent return? How does that help anyone—you can't do better than that?" he asked. "I'm doing more than 25 percent a year; I can double my money in a few years."

Paulson and Tarrant turned uncomfortable. In high school, mother jokes were the meanest put-down, but among the Southampton set, it didn't get much lower than knocking someone's investment prowess.

"Good for you," Paulson responded, "but I hope you know when to get off. Real estate has gone down in the past; why won't it end badly this time, too?"

Keszler chuckled and shook his head, before walking away.

Part of the reason Paulson had grown concerned about real estate was that the Federal Reserve finally had begun to raise interest rates, which eventually would push borrowing rates higher, taking away the economy's punch bowl.

"Who's the most vulnerable to higher rates?" Paulson asked a group of staffers back at the office.

Paulson became intrigued about whether consumers, many of whom already were struggling with debt, might have difficulties handling a rise in rates. Investment banks and financial firms also were heavy borrowers, Paulson told one of his traders. Some had more than $25 of assets for each $1 of equity they held. They might also be vulnerable as rates rose, Paulson said.

He started to look into buying protection for his firm, in case all the borrowing in the economy led to deep troubles. He wasn't the only one getting worried, however. Enough investors had purchased "put" contracts on the Standard & Poor's 500—futures contracts that rise in value when stocks plunge—that the contracts had become too expensive to Paulson.

Paulson had examined shorting shares of some financial-service companies, but some companies in that business recently had received takeover offers, sending the stocks racing higher, burning those who shorted them with deep losses. Was there any better insurance?

One day in October 2004, Pellegrini, still nervous about his standing at the firm, got up the nerve to approach Paulson in the hallway to tell his boss that there might be a better way to protect the firm's portfolio. Why not buy credit-default swaps?

Paulson and his team weren't very familiar with the world of credit-default swaps, beyond a vague understanding that these instruments provided insurance against losses from debt investments. Though trading of CDS contracts had soared in volume in recent years, it was a complicated, esoteric world. Paulson was one of many investors who shied away from using these "derivative" investments, described as such because their value derives from the change in some underlying asset.

Pellegrini knew something about CDS trading from his previous job, he told his boss, and was glad to help. The beauty of CDS, Pellegrini explained, was that they are like insurance contracts—the annual premium you pay for the protection is the only downside, unlike a bet against a stock that can result in deep losses if the shares soar.

Pellegrini tried to judge his boss's reaction, and whether he was out of line. But Paulson liked to encourage his staff to develop novel approaches to problems, and he seemed intrigued, a small smile forming on his face. He asked Pellegrini to research how the firm could buy CDS contracts on financial companies, which Paulson was especially worried about due to all their borrowed money.

In truth, Pellegrini didn't know that much about how credit-default swaps were traded, other than watching others do it at Tricadia. So he arranged for tutorials by various brokerage firms on the ins and outs of credit-default swaps. The fund made its first purchase of CDS protection on a company called MBIA, Inc., which insured all those mortgage bonds backed by aggressive loans. The annual cost of insuring $100 million of MBIA's debt was a puny $500,000. In other words, if MBIA ran into problems and its debt became worthless, Paulson would get paid $100 million thanks to CDS protection that cost just $500,000 annually. It seemed a no-brainer to Paulson.

Over the next two months, MBIA's profits climbed, and the price of its debt remained strong, making it clear to Paulson and Pellegrini how difficult it could be to take a stance against a single company. Soon, their position faced some small losses. They discovered that the value of CDS protection falls as the underlying debt gets closer to maturity. Paulson and Pellegrini were dipping their toes into the water, still figuring out how to bet against the housing market.

But in Northern California, far from Wall Street's frenzied trading desks, an obscure investor already was zeroing in on real estate, well ahead of Paulson & Co., certain that he had discovered the trade of a lifetime.

4

WHEN MICHAEL BURRY WAS BORN, IN 1971, HIS STEEL BLUE eyes seemed crossed in an unusual way, drawing immediate concern from his parents. A local pediatrician in Johnson City, New York, a suburb of Binghamton, dismissed the Burrys' worries, assuring them that the boy had a lazy left eye that would improve with time. But James Burry couldn't shake a feeling that something was wrong with his son.

Over the next year, he and his wife, Marion, brought Michael from doctor to doctor, searching for a better explanation. Finally, an ophthalmologist diagnosed retinoblastoma, a dangerous cancer that strikes one in twenty thousand children. They drove three hours to Columbia Presbyterian Medical Center in New York City, where doctors removed the boy's left eye, to prevent the tumor from spreading.

Before he turned two, Michael was fitted with a glass prosthesis. It was an approximation of his natural eye, the best they could produce at the time, but it had no movement, making it quite obvious.

Later, Michael had difficulty adjusting to the artificial eye. His depth perception was poor. Intense pain in the socket often forced him to leave class to visit the school nurse. One day in second grade, older children gathered around, cheering Burry to "take it out, take it out." Reluctantly, he complied, drawing even more unwanted attention.

In 1977, when Burry was almost seven, his father landed a transfer to an IBM plant in Northern California. The family, which by then included three more sons, moved to South San Jose, a middle-class city in Silicon Valley. An IQ test at his public school showed that Michael was highly intelligent, and he was placed in advanced science and math classes. Reading came slowly to him, but he persisted and soon was devouring books, especially escapist fantasies and biographies of sports heroes.

Burry was forced to wear safety glasses to protect his eye. Frustrated and embarrassed, he sometimes would smash the glasses, which slid down on his nose and sometimes obstructed his field of vision, telling his parents they had broken during a game, hoping the glasses wouldn't be replaced.

Marion, who had been raised in a poor, Catholic family in Wilkes-Barre, Pennsylvania, sometimes dressed her sons in discount clothing from a local Kmart. They became a focus of derision for his middle-school classmates, who were children of engineers and other employees of local technology companies. Michael turned shy around some of them.

"I never had more than one or two friends, if that," Burry recalls. "I always was a bit of an outsider."

His father often worked late, and his mother, a biology major in college who had returned to school to pursue a master's degree, holed up in the library most afternoons. So after school, Burry was left to pick up his three brothers at the homes of various friends, warm a tray of TV dinners, and help with their homework.

Michael's parents frequently argued loudly as he huddled in a bedroom listening. They divorced during the summer after he finished fifth grade, and Michael and his brothers moved with their father to a nearby town. His father, the first in his family to graduate from college, was a stern disciplinarian who hated to see his sons idling, especially in front of a television. Some afternoons, he made the boys carry piles of bricks from the backyard of the house to the side. The next day, they'd haul the bricks right back to the backyard, just so James could keep them occupied. Most weekends, he would lock the boys out of the house, forcing them to play outdoors.

Each summer, James brought his sons camping in the Sierra Nevada Mountains, where they lived in an army-surplus tent for weeks at a time, sharing it with their black Labrador retriever. The former Marine taught his boys to shoot deer with a bow and arrow and to ride a Yamaha 80cc motorcycle on mountain trails and dirt access roads. One night during each trip, they emerged from the woods to dine at a nearby restaurant, drawing stares for their scruffy appearance. Burry lugged a stack of books to the campsite and read for hours by the fire, avoiding gathering wood or cleaning the tent, a deriliction of duty that infuriated his father. James Burry respected education but was suspicious of any act that required a lot of sitting around.

One day, Michael noticed the stock quotations in the business section of the local newspaper and asked his father to explain them. James was skeptical of the stock market but pointed to the symbol for American Motors, the maker of army jeeps, then trading at $4 5/8 a share. He piqued the interest of his son, and Michael tracked American Motors shares every day for more than a year, fascinated by each little move, and the fortunes that his father explained were made and lost along with them.

Michael quickly became enamored with making money. Sometimes he'd wash dollar bills, drying them off with a towel and placing them between the pages of thick books on his shelf to make them look crisp and new. Working odd jobs on Sundays and holidays, including an $11-an-hour stint at a local IBM research lab, he built a small savings account that he began to invest in mutual funds. Once, when the funds dropped sharply and he struggled to figure out why, his father wagged a finger.

"I told you, I told you," James Burry said. "They're going to take all your money."

His parents had remarried each other by the time Michael began Santa Teresa High, though the squabbling continued. As an outlet, he turned to sports, joining South Valley Aquatics, a prestigious local swimming club. He embraced the team's daily regimen, waking at 4:30 a.m. for practice and doing five hours of laps each day. He discovered a fierce competitive streak and relished his coach's positive feedback.

At school, Burry became more comfortable airing his opinions. The better his grades became, the later his father let him stay out at night. Michael soon began to equate academic achievement with freedom. He reckoned that if his grades were good enough, he'd be allowed to choose a college far away. That was all the incentive he needed; he scored As in almost every subject and aced the SATs, the college aptitude test. As he grew, his body adjusted to the artificial eye and he became more adept at taking care of it, another boon to the young man's self-assurance.

At a local swim meet, Burry's coach talked him up to Harvard University's swim coach, who suggested that Burry had a great shot to gain acceptance to Harvard. With help from a supportive English teacher, Burry sent in an application. But his guidance counselor submitted an incomplete form and Harvard rejected him. Burry was dejected for weeks, despite gaining admission to UCLA.

Partly to please his father, Michael enrolled in premed courses at UCLA, like many of his classmates. But he couldn't seem to blend in with the other students, feeling out of place in sunny Southern California. On most nights, classmates headed out to party while Burry waved good-bye from the dorm's study area.

Burry seemed cocky and tactless to some, and he couldn't figure out how to change the perception. It was as if he were missing some sensitivity chip. During his freshman year, he remarked that the school's premed classes seemed too easy. Other times he suggested that most of the undergraduate body was lazy, and he ridiculed the lengths that classmates took to be accepted by various fraternities and sororities.

He forced himself to listen rather than dominate conversations but continued to feel strangely disconnected from his classmates. Years later, Burry would be diagnosed with Asperger's syndrome, a variant of autism characterized by difficulties in social interactions.

His relationships with UCLA's faculty sometimes were just as strained. As a junior majoring in English, he was accused by a teaching assistant of plagiarizing a term paper. The instructor didn't have any proof; he simply said, "All I know is an undergraduate didn't write this."

Around this time, Burry rediscovered a passion for the stock market, drawn by what he considered to be the meritocracy of investing. It didn't matter if a mutual-fund manager was perceived as arrogant or was socially awkward, Burry figured, just as long as he produced good returns. Making a lot of money seemed among the most concrete and objective signs of success.

He opened a brokerage account with his summer earnings and

skipped lectures to focus on his portfolio, purchasing class notes near the end of each quarter to help cram before final exams.

Burry soon switched his major to economics, while still juggling premed courses. In 1991, Burry was accepted to Vanderbilt University's medical school, where he thrived. A local ocular plastic surgeon succeeded in attaching his long-dormant extraocular muscles to a hydroxyapatite ball implanted in his left socket, and a more natural-looking artificial eye was made to fit over the ball. The result was realistic movement in the eye for the first time.

During Burry's third year of medical school, his father died after a short battle with lung cancer. The death was so sudden that Burry never had a chance to say good-bye; he was unable to hold back tears long enough to speak at the funeral.

In the wake of his father's death, Burry adopted a detached aloofness. Classmates saw him as unapproachable, and he did little to try to change the perception.

"Everyone there was incredibly good-looking and superintelligent; I felt like a lower quintile as a person," he recalls.

Instead of using inheritance money to pay off mounting student loans, Burry poured it into the market, finding comfort and profit in his investments. Eager to share his budding investing views, Burry started an early Web site to discuss stocks, posting lengthy pieces several times a week. Several months later, an executive of the MSN online network came across Burry's site and offered him $1 a word if he'd become an MSN columnist.

"A dollar a word? I can write a lot of words," Burry joked, hungry for extra cash. He became known as "The Value Doc," weighing in on various stocks.

Burry's writing was raw, and his knowledge of the market had gaping holes. But he conducted valuable research on overlooked stocks and his insights seemed to resonate with readers.

Many evenings, Burry wandered into a local Office Depot, rummaging through the new items. He was imagining what it might be like to run his own business. His behavior drew stares from the stores' employees, though they soon learned Burry was harmless and better left alone. Burry's life became a grueling mix of stock research, online postings, and a demanding medical internship. He avoided spending much time with fellow students.

Burry finished medical school in 1997, facing $150,000 of tuition-related debt. He accepted a residency in pathology at Stanford University Hospital and moved back to his childhood home in San Jose, claiming a bedroom down the hall from his brother.

That fall, on a dare from a friend, Burry placed a personal ad on Match.com. He chose a blunt approach: "I'm single and have one eye and a lot of debt." Just minutes after posting the ad, Burry received an e-mail from Anh-Thi Le, a woman who worked in corporate finance in nearby Palo Alto and was thrilled to find someone downplaying his qualities rather than exaggerating them. A whirlwind, three-week courtship and an engagement with Anh-Thi Le ensued.

Burry soon suspected that he didn't measure up against his more-focused medical colleagues. But he was making thousands of dollars a month through his trading and the online column, enough to buy a black Dodge Dakota truck and enjoy some extra spending money.

On his way to the hospital each morning, Burry drove through the heart of Silicon Valley, passing the world's most prestigious venture-capital firms. The local technology industry was humming, but Burry felt strangely out of place. One afternoon in 1999, a dozen doctors crowded around a small computer terminal in the clinic, almost cheering as shares of the latest technology wonder, Atmel Corp., soared. They debated which high-tech stock was more attractive, Applied Materials, Cisco Systems, or Polycom. Burry, who by then had switched to become a neurology resident, and at night was posting online columns arguing that all those stocks were wildly overpriced, bit his lip, wary of letting them know about his side job.

This isn't going to end well. Sell! Sell! Sell!

The bursting of the dot-com bubble in the spring of 2000, and the sudden losses suffered by his fellow doctors, confirmed to Burry the tendency of markets to go to extremes. By then he was posting late-night articles on a Web site of his own, valuestocks.net, after a long day tending to patients.

By the time his residency ended in June 2000, Burry, twenty-nine, had had enough of medicine. He had married Anh-Thi, and she, too, had moved into his parents' house, where the couple lived with Burry's brother.

Although Burry didn't know what a hedge fund was, he had read how Warren Buffett began his career with a partnership, to invest for himself and others. Burry figured he'd do the same. He obtained a one-year for-bearance on his loans, and his family agreed to buy small stakes in his firm, giving Burry time to make a go of it. Anh-Thi emptied her retirement account to give her new husband more cash to invest. His broker at Bank of America, Alison Sanger, set him up with an account, and Burry's hedge-fund career was under way.

Two weeks later, a New York investor named Joel Greenblatt called Burry, disturbing the quiet of his living-room office, next to the drum set.

"Michael, I've been reading your work for a while, and I read that you're leaving medicine," Greenblatt said. It turned out that Greenblatt had been monitoring Burry's Web site. "You're a really talented analyst. My firm would like to make money from your ideas."

Greenblatt, who managed his own hedge fund and had published an investing book with a cult following, flew Burry and his wife to New York for a meeting, putting them up in the penthouse suite of the Intercontinental Hotel. A friend urged Burry to dress up for the meeting, so he stopped at a Tie Rack store and struggled to put on a blue tie as he rode the elevator. Greenblatt greeted him wearing an open-collar shirt; his partner, Rob Goldstein, was dressed in a sweater and jeans, putting Burry immediately at ease.

Greenblatt skipped the chitchat. He told Burry that he wanted a stake in his new business.

"I want to give you a million dollars," Greenblatt told him, pausing for effect.

Without missing a beat, Burry replied: "After tax."

Burry sold Greenblatt a 22.5 percent piece of the business, using the proceeds to pay off his school loans. He named his firm Scion Capital, inspired by *The Scions of Shannara*, a Terry Brooks fantasy novel. Burry would be a scion of investing greats such as Buffett and Benjamin Graham, although he would chart his own path. Back in California, he eventually rented a small office in a suburban office park, blocks from the headquarters of Apple Computer. The office once had been Apple cofounder Steve Wozniak's, which Burry took as an auspicious sign.

Burry wasn't very good at courting clients, but he figured if his results were strong enough investors would line up. Early on in his fund, after top executives of Avanti Software were charged with stealing secrets from a rival and the stock plunged to $2 per share, Burry determined that customers still were relying on Avanti's products. So he bought all the shares he could afford. Just months later, he watched the stock shoot up to $22, his first coup.

As WorldCom weakened, Burry's clients urged him to buy the discounted shares. But he resisted, unable to figure out why the telecom giant's profits were so much fatter than those of its competitors. The company must be fudging its accounting, he concluded. In the summer of 2002, WorldCom admitted to accounting fraud and filed for bankruptcy, vindicating Burry. He beat himself up, though, for not profiting from the shares' collapse. He kept asking himself, what could I have done differently?

Leafing through the finance section of a local bookstore, Burry found a particularly dense tome, *Credit Derivatives & Synthetic Structures: A Guide to Instruments and Applications,* that explained the knotty world of credit-default swaps, or CDS. The terminology sounded complex, and it was a slow slog getting through the jargon. But for Burry, it was like stumbling into an alternative world he never knew existed, one rife with possibility. While CDS contracts rarely garnered any mention in newspapers or on financial television, and most stock-focused investors hardly knew of them, Burry discovered that the CDS market had soared to $2 trillion from about $100 billion the previous decade, becoming among the world's largest financial markets.

Burry quickly realized CDS contracts were not very different from everyday insurance contracts. A buyer of a CDS contract agreed to pay a premium, in regular installments, as with any insurance contract, in exchange for protection sold by the seller of the CDS. But instead of guarding against damage to a house or car, CDS contracts offered a relatively easy way to prevent damage to an investment portfolio resulting from a company running into problems paying its debts.

If Burry was holding $1 million of IBM bonds, and was worried that the company might miss a debt payment, he could just buy a CDS contact costing as little as $10,000 annually, and receive a guarantee from the seller of the CDS to make him whole in the event IBM defaulted. If IBM ran into problems, or even looked like it might do so, the value of the CDS insurance contracts could be expected to rise in value. But if IBM proved a solid creditor, the CDS insurance contract would expire, and the buyer of the insurance would have lost only the annual cost of the insurance, just like any holder of insurance if a catastrophe never materializes.

Shorting shares of IBM could lead to big losses if the stock somehow soared, but losses from CDS contracts were capped. To Burry, CDS insurance seemed like the perfect kind of investment to own the next time he spotted trouble.

By 2003, Burry was managing $250 million of client money, making $5 million a year. He and his wife, with two children in tow, found a six-bedroom home in the nearby upscale community of Saratoga. It had sat on the market for more than two years, as the dot-com collapse weighed on local housing. The owners had asked $5.4 million for the home. Burry offered $3.8 million, and his bid was accepted.

Burry had a growing sense that other parts of the country might have their own housing problems. A number of investors were warming to shares of home builders and other real estate businesses, which seemed inexpensive given their growing earnings. But Burry's doubts grew as he studied the market.

He began to dig into the history of housing and why certain neighborhoods decay, and discovered that the value of land went nowhere in the sixty years preceding the 1940s, when the government began subsidizing the home purchases of returning GIs.

"It struck me that three generations had passed" since the last ugly period of real estate, says Burry, who wrote a long letter to his investors in the middle of 2003, warning about looming housing dangers. "There were no senior family members left who could, from experience, warn their children and grandchildren about the dangers of falling home prices; everyone felt that home appreciation was a right."

He read that PMI Group, one of the largest insurers of home mortgages and a stock that had become quite popular, had moved beyond its traditional business of writing insurance for individual mortgages to now insure mortgage-backed securities, or MBS. The world of MBS and other complex-bond investments seemed to exist in another galaxy from Burry's easy-to-follow stocks, but he decided to try to understand them.

Banks and other lenders who made home loans didn't usually hold on to them anymore, Burry realized. Instead, 80 pecent of home mortgages were sold to Wall Street firms and large companies, like Fannie Mae and Freddie Mac, soon after the closing on a home. These players pooled a hundred or so home mortgages, and used the stream of cash from the monthly principal and interest payments of the loans to back bond investments called mortgage-backed securities that were sold to investors around the globe. Burry also learned about the various slices, or tranches, of mortgage-backed securities, and how each carried a different yield and risk profile.

To PMI's executives, insuring against missed payments from these MBS slices seemed like a natural extension of their traditional business. But Burry couldn't help wonder whether PMI might be hurt if real estate slowed and borrowers ran into problems, something that could send the value of all those mortgage bonds falling. Remembering his experience with WorldCom, he picked up the phone to dial Veronica Grinstein, his broker at Deutsche Bank, at her office in New York.

"You guys trade credit derivatives, don't you?" Burry asked her. "How do I get started trading?"

Over the next few months, Burry purchased credit-default swaps protecting $800 million of bonds issued by a range of financial companies, including PMI and other mortgage insurers, as well as housing-related institutions like Fannie Mae. If the debt went bad, the value of his protection would soar in value, Burry figured; if it didn't, he was out just the $6 million or so annual cost of the insurance. By the end of 2003, 20 percent of Scion's portfolio was made up of these CDS contracts. He kept buying more throughout 2004. Scion's positions fell in value as housing strengthened throughout the year, but Burry offset the losses with gains from stocks in the rest of his portfolio, like McDonald's.

By the spring of 2005, Burry was managing about $600 million of investor money. He had also agreed to payouts totaling about $100 million over the course of five years for CDS protection against $6.5 billion of debt issued by various financial companies. But his positions dropped further in value as housing climbed. Burry grumbled to his wife that the Fed chairman Greenspan had replaced the tech bubble with a housing bubble. The country, he complained, eventually would suffer.

"It's just not right; it's manipulation," he insisted. His wife nodded patiently, already accustomed to her husband's periodic rants.

Years earlier, during an e-mail discussion on his Web site about the origins of past real estate bubbles, an older reader warned Burry: "Watch the lenders, not the borrowers—borrowers will always be willing to take a great deal for themselves. It's up to the lenders to show restraint. When they lose it, watch out."

So that's where Burry looked next. Traditional lenders, such as Bank of America, J.P. Morgan Chase, and Countrywide, were being elbowed out of the mortgage business by upstart lenders with vaguely New Age names, including Ameriquest, Novastar, and New Century Financial.

Burry trolled the Internet for mortgage-lending Web sites; the terms were foreign but they seemed slightly ominous. "Interest-only loans" reminded Burry of a type of loan flogged in the 1920s by door-to-door mortgage salesmen and later sworn off by bankers because borrowers had problems making the payments. Burry did a Google search for terms such as *quick approval* and *no down payment* and was stunned by the number of hits he got. Burry found some borrowers were taking out loans that were bigger than the purchase price of homes they were buying. A fifth-grader with an allowance could qualify for some of the loans offered, it seemed.

Burry holed up in his office, hour after hour, wearing a T-shirt, surfer shorts and Birkenstocks, reading abstruse mortgage documents. Then he'd turn off the lights, close his eyes, and think.

Lenders have finally lost it, he realized. *I have to take advantage of this.*

Burry's wagers against various financial companies hadn't worked so far. But maybe there was a way to bet against mortgages themselves. He called a trader, asking if he could buy CDS protection for pools of risky mortgages, rather than on companies in the mortgage business, as he had done so far. The bank might be able to write a CDS contract for him, the trader responded, but it would take time to work out the complicated language of the agreement. And it wasn't the kind of thing Burry could sell to another investor.

No dice, Burry said. He was worried that if he entered into such a deal, he'd be stuck. If financial markets quaked and the bank suffered, it might not make good on its end of any contract with him.

Burry had another idea, though. He called Angela Chang, who had replaced Grinstein as his broker at Deutsche Bank. I want to be your first call when they standardize these things, he told her, making them easy to buy and sell. Wall Street loved to roll out new products—protection on toxic mortgages had to be their next trick, Burry concluded.

"It's going to happen; you'll be selling it eventually," Burry said. "When this starts, call me right away. It's going to be huge."

Hanging up, Burry thought, *This will be my Soros trade.*

BACK IN NEW YORK, Greg Lippmann, a trader at Deutsche Bank who had never quite fit in on Wall Street, was meeting with a few rivals to plot a change in the way debt was traded. He would set the groundwork for Burry and others to bet against housing, just as Burry had anticipated.

From the time he first arrived at Credit Suisse First Boston a decade earlier, Lippmann seemed out of place. He wore his hair a bit long and slicked back, as if he was an extra in the movie *Wall Street.* A strong chin further distinguished him. Lippmann favored European suits, and his shirts often were untucked and loose. Lippmann didn't have even a fleeting interest in sports and couldn't keep up with much of the banter on the trading desk. But he knew where to find the best sushi in the city and eventually published an online guide to the best restaurants in New York, earning him the moniker of the "Robert Parker of raw fish."[1]

On the trading desk, Lippmann had the confidence of a veteran, and he seemed not to care what his colleagues thought of him. He was so over the top and had so many affectations—such as pronouncing the word "tranche" with a soft *ch*, as if to remind colleagues that it was the French word for slice—that they grew to enjoy his company.

"He always struck me as a little odd," recalls Craig Knutson, a colleague at First Boston. "But he was an easy guy to like. He wasn't looking for others to accept his viewpoint or who he was—it was like he didn't care."

Lippmann traded the riskiest slices of securitized bond deals. These slices, at the bottom rung of deals, paid off big-time if the loans backing the debt paid off, but saw the first losses if they didn't. This section of the market had such little activity that Lippmann was forced to get on the phone with a potential investor and wax poetic about the beauty of these obscure debt slices. Nearby, traders listened with appreciation, or sometimes rolled their eyes. Lippmann told them that he considered himself "more of an art dealer than a broker."

In 2000, after Lippmann was hired by Deutsche Bank, he warned colleagues about the risks of mobile-home companies. He soon learned the dangers of challenging the market's bullish consensus. When Lippmann offered lowball bids to purchase debt of these companies, making it clear how little he valued it, a senior salesman turned to him with a scowl, saying, "You're making us look stupid." Six months later, mobile-home debt collapsed in price.

Lippmann eventually rose to become a senior trader, running a group that dealt with mortgage-related bonds and other complicated debt investments. But he still couldn't bring himself to conform. Lippmann sometimes wore his sideburns unusually long and thick, ending in a point below the ear, Elvis Presley–like. At times, he wore bulky, pointed, brown dress shoes and a brown pinstriped suit, amid a sea of blue and beige at the trading desk.

By early 2005, Lippmann was thirty-six years old and impatient to grow his firm's lagging mortgage-bond business. But he ran into an issue frustrating others in the market: There just weren't enough mortgages to go around. Thousands of investors all over the globe were eager to buy slices of mortgage bonds backed by risky loans because they carried such high interest rates. For all its growth, though, the subprime-mortgage market couldn't keep up with the investor demand.

Lippmann's radical thought was, *What if an investment could be created to mimic the existing mortgages? That way, new mortgages wouldn't have to be created to satisfy hungry investors; rather, a "synthetic" mortgage could be sold to them.*

In February, Lippmann called traders from Bear Stearns, Goldman Sachs, and a few other firms struggling with the same issues, inviting them, along with a battalion of lawyers, to a conference room at Deutsche. Sitting around a blond-wood conference table, they debated ideas into the night, while picking at take-out Chinese food. Their light-bulb idea: Create a standardized, easily traded CDS contract to insure mortgage-backed securities made up of subprime loans. Yes, they'd be signed contracts between two parties, rather than a loan. But since they were contracts that insured all those aggressive mortgages, they would smell, touch, and feel like the mortgages themselves, rising when they looked safer and falling as borrowers ran into problems.

"We called up the guys we felt like we knew and could work with," Lippmann told a reporter. "It's not very glamorous. . . . Just a bunch of guys eating Chinese discussing legal arcana."

The discussions went back and forth for months; other banks soon demanded to be part of the conversations. By June, the group had introduced a new, standardized credit-default contract that would adjust in price as the underlying mortgages became more or less valuable. A buyer of a CDS contract protecting $1 million of risky debt would pay annual premiums to the seller of the contract. If the debt became worthless, the seller of the protection would hand over $1 million to the buyer. Buyers of the CDS protection would be paid in cash by those selling the insurance when something happened to affect the cash flows of the bonds underlying the CDS, something they called pay-as-you-go. Those bullish on subprime mortgages would sell the insurance and pocket cash, while bears might buy it. And because the language of the contracts was standardized, they could easily be traded, like any other bond.

Just as bettors on the Super Bowl enter an array of wagers on a single game, such as which team will score first and how many points will be racked up at the end of each quarter, to multiply the bets on the game, Lippmann and his colleagues had invented derivative instruments to multiply the wagers on a single, finite pool of home mortgages. The credit-default swaps were tied to actual mortgages—but the number of insurance bets on subprime loans now was essentially unlimited. Finally, Burry and other housing skeptics had a way to short the market, while those who were bullish, such as insurance giant AIG, could make extra money by selling the insurance, confident they would never have to pay out any claims. Their actuaries produced sophisticated models that showed the chances of a housing meltdown were minimal.

With a feat of financial and legal engineering, the subprime mortgage market had effectively grown by leaps and bounds, a fact that would come back to haunt both Wall Street and global economies. In the months ahead, the bankers created similar insurance contracts for securities backed by loans for commercial buildings and collateralized debt obligations. They'd even create a CDS insurance contract for an index that tracked a group of subprime mortgages, called the ABX, a sort of a Dow Jones Industrial Average for risky home mortgages.

Lippmann and the other bankers had no idea of the impact their change would have on Wall Street, banks, and the entire global economy. They just wanted another product to sell to their clients.

In fact, when the trading of CDS on subprime mortgage–backed securities began, Lippmann's first move was to *sell* protection on about $400 million of subprime mortgages to a hedge fund. He was oblivious to any looming problems for housing.

MICHAEL BURRY was taking his four-year-old son to an ophthalmologist in nearby Sunnyvale for a checkup when he received a call on his cell phone from his broker, Angela Chang. He stepped outside the waiting room to the nearby parking lot to take it.

"Okay, Mike, we're ready to sell that protection you asked about," she told him. Lippmann and the other bankers had just finished the paperwork on the "synthetic" CDS and were offering them to clients.

Burry could hardly contain his excitement. Pacing the length of the parking lot, Burry listened as Chang described details of the investment. Deutsche would sell him CDS protection for six slices of mortgage-backed securities backed by the iffiest subprime mortgages, each with a $10 million face value. The bank had lined up a European pension fund that was bullish on housing and willing to sell the protection and pocket some cash to juice its returns. Deutsche would act as the middleman. The slices of the mortgage securities were rated BBB, or one notch above the "junk bond" category, the lowest level of so-called investment-grade bonds. That seemed safe enough to the pension plan.

Burry's cost to buy CDS protection for each of the six slices would be about 155 basis points above the London Interbank Lending Rate, or about $155,000 annually—just under $1 million for all six, Chang said. Do you want it?

"Yes, yes," Burry quickly responded.

Over the next few months, Burry stepped up his research, poring over prospectus documents for hundreds of pools of bonds, trying to locate those pools holding the riskiest mortgages. He felt he didn't have much time to act—thousands of hedge funds and other kinds of investors were searching for attractive trades and were bound to find these investments.

Burry focused on pools stuffed with mortgages of borrowers from California, Nevada, Florida, and other frothy real estate markets. He became especially enthused when he found securities with names from Southern California, the epicenter of the subprime lending market, like SAIL (Structured Asset Investment Loan Trust), SURF (Specialty Underwriting and Residential Finance Trust), and HEAT (Home Equity Asset Trust). He told his brokers to buy protection on all of the mortgage pools.

He asked Chang who was selling him the CDS insurance. Institutions and wealthy European families, she told him, along with some other hedge funds. They were comforted by the top-grade investment ratings being placed on the mortgage bonds granted by credit-ratings companies like Moody's and Standard & Poor's.

"Well, they're totally wrong," Burry told her with insistence.

One night, late in the office, shades drawn tight, Burry tried to imagine what would happen if his analysis proved accurate. Sure, he'd make a ton of money holding mortgage protection, which likely would jump in value. But if real estate collapsed, some of the brokerage firms he traded with might be crippled. Perhaps they wouldn't be able to pay Burry his money. As a result, Burry began to avoid doing business with investment firms with big mortgage holdings, like Lehman Brothers and Bear Stearns. He focused his trades on other brokerage firms.

By the late summer of 2005, however, Burry realized that the first batch of insurance that Chang had sold him protected mortgages that weren't quite as risky as others he was discovering. He began to isolate mortgage pools with a high percentage of loans in which buyers took out two loans—one for the mortgage and one for the down payment, a "simultaneous second lien." Essentially, these houses had no equity whatsoever, making the loans risky if housing prices fell or even flattened. The protection was still dirt cheap, so he kept buying more. Burry felt like a kid in a half-priced candy store, trying to gobble up as much of the merchandise as possible before the other children found out about the markdown. Could it be that no other investors had caught on?

After doing one trade, Burry received a call from his broker at Goldman Sachs.

"What are you *doing*?? You're just buying, buying, buying. No one else is just going one way."

"I'm just buying, yeah. I think the whole system is going to hell."

Burry felt an urgency to boost the size of the trade—he was convinced that it was going to be huge, maybe even historic. Burry began calling and meeting with clients in an effort to try to start a new fund to just focus on buying up mortgage protection. He called it Milton's Opus LLC, an ode to John Milton's *Paradise Lost*, the seventeenth-century narrative poem. He argued that a new paradise was about to be squandered as housing crumbled.

In late 2005, Burry wrote an impassioned letter to his investors, trying to drum up interest in his new fund:

> Markets erred when they gave America Online the currency to buy Time Warner. They erred when they bet against George Soros and for the British pound. And they are erring right now by continuing to float along as if the most significant credit bubble history has ever seen does not exist. Opportunities are rare, and large opportunities on which one can put nearly unlimited capital to work at tremendous potential returns are even more rare. Selectively shorting the most problematic mortgage-backed securities in history today amounts to just such an opportunity.

As they learned what Burry was up to, however, some of his investors grew unhappy. Burry was supposed to be a stock investor, not someone buying up all these derivatives. To many of his clients, Burry remained a former doctor who had taught himself about the world of investing. He had a lot of potential but still was learning. Now he was making what seemed like a simplistic argument about problems in the subprime part of the housing market. Investors with degrees from some of the nation's leading business schools were comfortable relying on the complicated risk models developed by Wall Street's sharpest minds, models that predicted minimal housing-related losses. And here was Burry saying the emperor wore no clothes. Many of the clients didn't even bother to read his lengthy letter.

Longtime backers also raised questions.

"Why are you so sure this is a top" for housing? asked Rob Goldstein, one of his original investors.

Another client cited sophisticated models developed by Wall Street firms showing that any housing-related losses would be contained, even in the event of a slowdown in housing prices.

"What model are *you* using?" the investor demanded of Burry.

Burry responded that the models Wall Street relied on were based on the performance of mortgage loans made over the past two decades.

They didn't reflect the recent surge of aggressive home loans. As such, they were as good as useless.

"It's just a series of logical, commonsense conclusions," Burry told the investor. "Three to five years, just give me three to five years" to make the trade happen.

After spending so many long hours knee-deep in the intricacies of mortgages, Burry found he often was unable to clearly summarize his views. He became impatient that he couldn't convince investors of his thesis and began to leave the fund-raising to his team.

Every day, Burry rushed into the office of his chief financial officer, brimming with hope.

"Have we heard back yet?" he would ask, referring to potential clients in his new fund.

The answer usually was disappointing. Burry bought some positions, holding CDS protection on $1.1 billion of subprime mortgage pools by early 2006. But it wasn't nearly enough for him.

This should be my big trade! he fretted.

Burry turned sullen and reclusive, figuring someone else would catch on and buy the mortgage protection, driving up the price and profiting when housing turned sour. Most days, he sat alone in his office for hours at a time, shutting his door and playing heavy-metal music on a stereo system so loudly that it worried his employees. Soon, they became afraid to approach him.

The cost of some of the mortgage insurance soon rose a bit, making Burry furious. His trade seemed to be slipping away. Heavy-metal bands like Megadeth and Disturbed blasted out of his office, the bass shaking the entire floor. Metallica's "Kill 'Em All" and Pantera's "Cowboys from Hell" topped Burry's playlist.

Eventually, Burry could no longer take the stress and frustration. He threw in the towel and ended his efforts to launch the fund, unable to find enough investors who believed in him and his bearish views.

5

A

S 2005 BEGAN, GROWING CONCERNS ABOUT THE HOUSING AND debt markets gnawed at John Paulson. He wasn't convinced that a housing storm was over the horizon, and didn't think that risky mortgages were much of a danger. But he noticed some threatening clouds and felt compelled to find protection, an umbrella just in case the rain started to pour. He just didn't know where to find it.

"You can't short a house," Paulson told a colleague, regretfully, as he surveyed the booming real estate market.

The CDS insurance that Pellegrini championed wasn't doing much for the firm, but it couldn't hurt to buy some protection on a few other financial companies, Paulson figured, particularly those dependent on consumers, who seemed up to their eyeballs in debt. So Paulson directed his trader, Brad Rosenberg, to buy CDS contracts to insure the debt of two big lenders, Countrywide Financial and Washington Financial, companies that Pellegrini had been studying.

But rumors soon circulated that the companies might receive big takeover offers, sending their stock and bond prices soaring. That weighed on the value of CDS protection on the companies' debt, rattling Paulson and his team. The losses were small but the fund already lagged its competitors during the early part of the year, leaving little room for error if Paulson wanted to keep the firm growing.

One afternoon, Pellegrini walked into Paulson's office clutching a spreadsheet. He was there to discuss the latest chatter about who might buy Countrywide, rumors that were sending shares higher and sparking still more losses for Paulson & Co.

As he turned to leave, Pellegrini threw out an idea.

"By the way, if you're concerned that someone might bid for Countrywide, why don't we figure out how to short mortgage securitizations," Pellegrini suggested. "If they go bad, they stay bad—it's a one-way street."

It was a phrase he had overheard from his ex-boss, Arif Inayatullah, at his last job, at Tricadia Capital. Insurance for bonds backed by risky mortgages couldn't be affected by any individual corporate takeover, so it might be a perfect way to get protection for any problems that might arise in the mortgage market.

Paulson was immediately intrigued; a smile grew on his face. As interest rates rose, all those adjustable mortgages would reset at higher levels, and consumers would have difficulty meeting their monthly payments, Paulson quickly realized. That would put pressure on the mortgage-backed bonds.

Later, Paulson came to Pellegrini still more animated, telling him that the Fed wouldn't want to trim rates to help borrowers because it might cripple the already-weakening dollar and stoke inflation. So when interest rates climbed, a rash of home owners would be unable to pay their monthly mortgages, and the value of the mortgage bonds based on those loans would tumble in value.

Pellegrini agreed. But when he asked his boss which slice of mortgage bonds the firm should bet against, Paulson seemed confused. He didn't seem to understand what Pellegrini meant.

"Yeah, there's billions of dollars of this stuff out there."

Paulson's eyes widened. "That can't be!" he replied, with apparent shock.

Pellegrini only recently had learned of the complexities of the mortgage market, thanks to a series of tutorials from the firm's brokers at Bear Stearns and contacts at other firms, and after attending an industry conference. The lessons were brief, and he still wasn't sure of all the details of that market, but they made Pellegrini something of an in-house expert, since few others at Paulson & Co. were even vaguely familiar with the area.

"I was flabbergasted," Paulson recalls.

In the following weeks, Pellegrini asked a few more experts, including Arif Inayatullah, to come by and teach him and Paulson more about the market.

"When I found out there was a separate category of subprime, risky mortgages, it was a big lift," Paulson says. "The fact that they could be tranched into eighteen layers was the ultimate; I had never seen a capital structure with more than five layers."

He pushed Pellegrini to find the purest way to wager against the riskiest mortgages.

"Dig deeper, Paolo, dig deeper."

Pellegrini focused on buying protection for BBB-rated slices of securitization deals backed by collections of subprime mortgages, or those that credit-rating agencies viewed as just a bit safer than junk. He ignored the most noxious 5 percent of the deals, rated BBB− or even worse, figuring that it might cost too much to protect the absolute dreck of the mortgage market. The BBB slices seemed close enough to the bottom of the toxic-mortgage barrel.

Paulson agreed. If things go wrong, "these bonds don't have a prayer of getting paid," he told Pellegrini.

But it was difficult to buy CDS to protect these BBB slices, Pellegrini explained. There just weren't enough slices available in the market, the very problem that Lippmann at Deutsche Bank and his fellow bankers were busy trying to address. Pellegrini dug up figures showing that securitized subprime mortgages made up about 10 percent of the overall $10 trillion market, but there were only about $10 billion of BBB pieces outstanding. Much like Burry, Pellegrini guessed that tradable CDS contracts were soon on the way, to sate the appetite of investors for more BBB slices. He hired lawyers to complete the necessary paperwork so Paulson & Co. could be ready.

A month later, when Lippmann's gang finally rolled out its first batch of CDS to protect subprime bonds in the summer of 2005, Pellegrini rushed to Paulson's office, urging him to buy. Over the next two weeks,

Paulson turned to his old firm, Bear Stearns, to buy insurance protecting $100 million of subprime mortgages from defaults or losses, agreeing to pay just over $1 million for the coverage. It was such a pittance that Paulson couldn't figure out why others weren't also buying the cheap protection, if only for a rainy day.

As the summer heated up and the economy hummed along, Paulson's anxieties over the state of the economy and the housing market grew. Giddy investors were buying the BBB-rated mortgage-backed slices and all sorts of junk bonds without demanding much in return— interest rates of just 1 percentage point above those of supersafe U.S. Treasury bonds. It seemed absurd to Paulson. Who would buy a risky bond with a yield of 6 percent when Treasury bonds yielded 5 percent?

"This is like a casino," Paulson said of the market in a meeting with some of his analysts. "We need to sell everything and go short." He ordered his traders to close dozens of trades.

Paulson asked them to find the most dangerous investments to bet against.

"Where's there a bubble we can short?"

Over the next few months, Paulson trimmed holdings that seemed especially sensitive to the economy and shorted the bonds of others, such as Delphi Corp., the nation's largest auto-parts maker. He seemed prescient, at least at first. Delphi's bonds fell to sixty-five cents on the dollar, and in October the company's troubles became so severe that it sought bankruptcy protection. But Delphi's bonds suddenly began to climb in price, for no obvious reason, stunning Paulson. Seventy cents, then seventy-seven and all the way up to ninety cents on the dollar. Finally Paulson threw in the towel and ended his trade, buying back the bonds to return them to his broker and close out the short.

The experience was painful, one more of a series of aggravating moves that year. But it convinced Paulson of the advantages of using CDS contracts to express a negative view. Unlike shorting a stock or a bond, losses from CDS contracts were capped at the annual payment of the insurance, Paulson realized. He was fast becoming a convert to the benefits of derivatives trading.

In truth, CDS contracts weren't quite ready for prime time. One reason Delphi's bonds had soared was that investors holding CDS contracts protecting against a loss in Delphi's debt needed to get their hands on the company's bonds, to present them for payment to investors who had sold them the CDS protection. They scrambled to buy up Delphi's bonds, bidding up their price, despite the bankruptcy.

"What a waste—we're obviously too early," Paulson told another analyst. "The market's getting more wild."

Paulson's frustrations grew as he watched a series of leveraged-buyout firms make acquisitions at nosebleed levels during 2005. An $11.3 billion takeover of SunGard Data Systems became the biggest buyout since RJR Nabisco sixteen years earlier, while household names like Hertz Corp. and Metro-Goldwyn-Mayer also were gobbled up, thanks to cheap debt financing from generous lenders and investors.

"This is insane!" Paulson said, as he pulled up a chair next to Brad Rosenberg and they watched news of a new acquisition on a business-television channel. "There's so much money out there chasing things; they're lending too freely." Paulson told Pellegrini that they were up against a "wall of liquidity."

Paulson shook his head as he noted a surge of borrowing by Wall Street's banks, saying "Do you realize these guys are leveraged thirty-five to one?"

Rosenberg brought Paulson stories from the Internet about how borrowers were receiving mortgages without having to document their income or assets. Lending was getting out of hand in cities such as Phoenix, San Diego, and Las Vegas. The subprime frenzy seemed to be spreading. Paulson, Pellegrini, and Rosenberg held a series of conversations with Wall Street's top mortgage analysts, trying to understand why so few of them were worried. They were the experts, Paulson's team realized, and Paulson a rank outsider. Was there something he was missing? Paulson wondered.

"Our models say don't be worried," said Bear Stearns' Gyan Sinha, a top-rated analyst, on a phone call. "Home prices have never gone negative," another analyst said. Others emphasized that investment-grade mortgage investments had rarely defaulted. "They won't even go flat," one expert told Pellegrini.

"They thought we were crazy. They kept talking about 'our models,'" and said we didn't know what we were talking about," Rosenberg recalls.

F OR PELLEGRINI, a subprime trade that once was a mere sideshow to the fund's merger investments had become a potential lifeline, at least to him. Pellegrini's contributions to the merger team were negligible, and it was obvious how low in the pecking order he was. Most of the analysts reported directly to Paulson. Pellegrini, however, had to first run his ideas past Andrew Hoine, the firm's research director, as if he was a remedial student in need of a tutor.

In late summer, the young man he had replaced, Nikolai Petchenikov, returned to the hedge fund from a one-year stint in business school, adding to Pellegrini's anxiety. Paulson began to give the twenty-seven-year-old, rather than Pellegrini, key assignments in the international-merger area. Pellegrini's window of opportunity at the hedge fund seemed to be closing quickly.

Seeing the writing on the wall, Pellegrini approached Paulson, suggesting that he focus on the subprime and financial areas, an offer Paulson accepted with enthusiasm.

"This could be a gold mine for us," Paulson responded, encouraging him.

It was an enormous gamble for Pellegrini, despite his boss's enthusiasm. Merger investing was at the core of Paulson & Co. The CDS trade was a diversion, one that Paulson might drop at a moment's notice. The firm employed fewer than a dozen people; any deadwood wouldn't survive long. Pellegrini was forty-eight years old and on tap to earn about $400,000 that year. It was a substantial sum, although much of it went to pay his sons' private-school tuitions. His bank account still showed an embarrassingly small sum for a finance-industry lifer.

"It wasn't clear to me that I was a keeper at the firm," Pellegrini recalls. "John wasn't comfortable with my work, and I was just as frustrated with myself. Anyone else would have fired me, but John saw I was making an effort."

Pellegrini was confident the subprime trade would work; he just hoped he would be allowed to stick around long enough to profit from it.

"I had everything on the line," Pellegrini recalls. But he had been certain before in his career, only to have something foil him.

Rather than become nervous, however, Pellegrini was more excited than he had been in years. He came to work a bit earlier and stuck around later, unable to stop thinking about the housing market. Over the summer, on a second date with Henrietta Jones, who ran the retail division for the Donna Karan clothing label, Pellegrini spent the evening replaying a presentation he made earlier in the day about the state of real estate; over dessert, he encouraged Jones to sell her Manhattan apartment.

Interest rates and mortgage products weren't the most romantic topics of conversation, but Jones was taken with Pellegrini's passion.

Pellegrini soon realized that he and Paulson had missed something important, however. In November, Pellegrini joined a group of investors at a meeting at the Grand Hyatt hotel in Midtown Manhattan hosted by Robert Cole, the chief executive officer of New Century. Pellegrini sat quietly, listening to Cole's rosy presentation and a series of softball questions tossed by a group of upbeat investors, some of whom congratulated Cole on the low level of defaults among New Century's customers.

Pellegrini was convinced that his rivals were missing it.

Wait till rates reset, he thought.

He resisted speaking up, though, lest they figure out how bearish his firm was, and perhaps warm to the CDS protection that Paulson was becoming enamored with, pushing prices higher.

But Pellegrini had nagging concerns that he might be missing something. Was there a way to run his ideas past Cole?

After the speech, Pellegrini made a beeline to the lectern, grabbing Cole's attention before other investors had a chance.

"What will happen when the mortgages reset?" Pellegrini asked, thinking he had found the fatal flaw in Cole's bullish thesis. "Will there be defaults?"

Cole seemed remarkably unfazed.

"No, we'll just refinance the loans," he responded, matter-of-factly.

Cole explained that New Century, like other subprime lenders, earned so much in upfront fees from refinancings that his company was happy to refinance home mortgages before they had a chance to reset at higher interest rates even though it meant lower profits from new, lower-rate loans. That way New Century made sure that borrowers could still make their payments. They could keep refinancing their customers' loans as long as their underlying properties were worth more than when they took out their original loans, Cole said.

"Interesting," Pellegrini replied, meekly.

The Paulson team's original thesis, that a spike in interest rates would cause problems for home owners, seemed dead wrong. If rates moved higher, Pellegrini realized, lenders would just bail out borrowers, letting them refinance their homes at lower rates. Given that, a wave of defaults seemed unlikely, at least for homes that had climbed in price.

Pellegrini had a sinking feeling as he hustled back to the office to tell Paulson.

It wasn't the kind of news anyone at Paulson & Co. wanted to hear, and it couldn't have come at a worse time. The various hedge funds run by the firm gained 5 percent or less in 2005, trailing gains of 9 percent or more for other hedge funds. Chatter on Wall Street was growing that Paulson was falling behind the times.

"It was very frustrating," recalls Jim Wong, Paulson's point man with investors.

At Concord Management, LLC, an associate, Martin Tornberg, was grilled by the New York firm's investment chief about Paulson's disappointing performance.

"Why are we in this fund?" Tornberg's boss asked him about one of Paulson's funds. Tornberg suggested that they give Paulson some more time before pulling out.

By the end of the year, even friends were asking questions about Paulson's investing strategy. Visiting Paulson's office one day in November, Howard Gurvitch, his original investor, suggested that the firm's subpar performance might be due to the rush of easy money that was chasing every kind of deal, making mergers and other areas more difficult for conservative investors like Paulson.

"Maybe it's a new world, John?" Gurvitch asked his old friend, gently. Paulson told Gurvitch that he remained confident in his unpopular stance. His challenges soon would grow, however. Unbeknownst to Paulson, a few other investors were coming around to his view on housing and soon would be hot on his heels.

I N MAY, after Greg Lippmann had helped develop the perfect means to bet against housing, he and his colleagues began racking up commissions trading their new CDS contracts on pools of subprime mortgages. Lippmann, who also operated a trading account for Deutsche Bank, initially joined the pack, selling the CDS contracts to the few bearish investors like Burry in San Jose.

By June, though, Lippmann's contrarian instincts had kicked in. He decided to do his own research to make sure the bullish crowd had it right. Lippmann loved to boast about a research analyst at the bank named Eugene Xu, proudly telling colleagues that at just eighteen years of age, the Shanghai native finished second in a national math competition in China. Maybe Xu, who received a doctorate in mathematics from the University of California in Los Angeles, could test the bullish thesis.

Lippmann asked Xu to dig up as much data as he could about home-mortgage defaults, something Lippmann and most others in the business never thought to examine before, as housing seemed to be on an inexorable climb. Xu split the country into quartiles. He discovered that states with the lowest rates of default, like California, Arizona, and Nevada, also claimed the highest growth in home prices. The quartile with the highest rates of default had the slimmest growth in home prices. Florida and Georgia seemed similar in many ways, but Xu's numbers showed Florida had a much lower rate of default than its northern neighbor, which seemed due to its soaring home prices.

The clear relationship between home prices and mortgage defaults didn't seem to be a recent development, either. Xu found that home prices had been key to loan problems for more than a decade, including during the mini-downturn in real estate in the early 1990s.

"Holy shit," Lippmann exclaimed to Xu on Deutsche Bank's trading floor while reading over his work, "if home prices stop going up, these guys are done."

Lippmann's thesis seemed logical—but at the time it was quite a radical viewpoint. Most economists and traders figured that a range of factors, including interest rates, economic growth, and employment, determined the level of mortgage defaults. Sure, home prices had an impact, and they were bound to plateau at some point. But if the other factors all held up, then default rates shouldn't climb very much, according to the conventional wisdom.

Xu's data clearly showed those other factors didn't mean nearly as much as home prices. Indeed, California's employment rate was about the same as a number of states with much higher default rates, but which had more limited gains in home prices. The lesson to Lippmann was that hot real estate areas like California actually were poor credit risks, not good ones. If home prices ever leveled off, defaults would shoot up.

"Why hasn't anyone done this research before?" he exclaimed to Xu. A sudden convert, Lippmann wasn't shy about sharing his views within the bank.

"These things are gonna blow up!" he bellowed across the trading floor one day, as the other traders shook their heads.

Lippmann rushed to tell others at the bank, anticipating that they would appreciate his insight. He patiently explained to them that when home prices came back down to earth in California and other raging real estate markets, mortgage defaults and delinquencies would be as high as they were in states like Indiana, where about 6 percent of home owners were delinquent on their home mortgages, double California's rates.

His colleagues remained skeptical, however. Even veteran analyst Karen Weaver, who had been warning investors to avoid all kinds of aggressive mortgage-related investments, wasn't convinced. At weekly meetings, the other Deutsche Bank executives snickered or laughed at Lippmann's diatribes about the problems ahead.

"There goes Greg again," Weaver joked to the group one day. Others began poking fun at Lippmann, sparking a round of laughter.

"You'll see; I'll be right," Lippmann shot back.

Some at the bank insisted that Lippmann must be missing something—maybe the explosion in population in California and Florida helped keep defaults low. So Lippmann and Xu went back to their data, controlling for population changes and other factors. But they continued to find that housing prices alone were key to mortgage defaults. Nothing else seemed even close. To Lippmann, it was as if his colleagues and rivals were insisting that the earth was flat.

"All you need is for California [real estate] prices to start looking like Indiana's and you get twelve percent defaults, at least," Lippmann insisted to one colleague. Home prices in Indiana were growing about 5 percent compared with more than 15 percent in California. Lippmann argued that when prices stopped climbing, a rash of problems would result, in even soaring real estate markets.

By the late fall of 2005, Lippmann was even more convinced of this, but he needed permission from the bank to buy up CDS contracts and lay a big bet against housing. He took a deep breath and proposed to one of his bosses, Rajeev Misra, buying protection on more than $1 billion of risky mortgages.

"This seems like a great bet," Lippmann told him, holding twenty pages of documents. "If I'm right, I'll make a billion dollars for the bank and it will offset losses elsewhere; if I'm wrong, it's going to cost twenty million a year."

Lippmann suggested buying CDS protection on the BBB-rated slices of mortgage-bond deals, just as Paulson and Burry were doing. He noted that 80 percent of subprime mortgages adjusted to a higher rate after two years, so his trade wouldn't last very long—after four years or so, he'd know if it was working or not. The most he could lose the bank if he purchased insurance on $1 billion of BBB bonds was $20 million a year over four years, or $80 million, Lippmann argued. Their trade should be even larger, he argued.

"If we're right, we're looking at a sixfold gain," he told his superiors. But there wasn't a six-to-one chance that California real estate would keep going up, because it can't go up forever, he told them. The bank should take the risk.

He was showing so much enthusiasm for shorting mortgages that some at the bank thought he might have gone too far. Lippmann's approach at times seemed unconventional to Deutsche executives, and they weren't convinced his strategy would work. Grudgingly, however, they assented to his trade, though not in the size he hoped. The Deutsche Bank executives allowed Lippmann to pay $20 million or so a year to buy protection on $1 billion of mortgages. And they told Lippmann to make sure to update them on how the trade was going, keeping the leash tight on the thirty-seven-year-old trader.

It didn't help Lippmann's case that he had antagonized some at Deutsche Bank with his strong opinions and brash trades, resulting in various stories circulating about him. One tale that spread, despite no evidence that it actually took place, concerned the evening Lippmann exited the bank's building, running late for a business dinner. He couldn't find a cab. When he saw a long line of employees waiting for Deutsche Bank's car service, Lippmann went straight to the front of the line and told a woman about to be picked up that he was a senior trader and needed to grab a ride for an important dinner. The woman asked for his name, saying that she'd like to tell people that she'd had the privilege of meeting him. He proudly announced that he was Greg Lippmann, head of asset-backed trading. At that point, the woman said she was the head of human resources and that Lippmann had just taken his last ride in a company car.

Friends say the story didn't happen, but that didn't stop some at the bank from sharing it, a sign of the jealousy and resentment Lippmann had engendered among some at Deutsche Bank.

Indeed, for all his trading prowess, Lippmann had overlooked the huge personal risks he had assumed in making the most important trade of his life. He already was making several million dollars a year. If he got the subprime trade right, he'd surely make more millions, but it wouldn't change his life. If Lippmann was wrong, though, he jeopardized his career.

As mortgage prices moved higher, and the value of his protection dropped almost immediately after he put the trade on, Lippmann's move seemed especially misguided. When Lippmann told friends what he was up to, they began to worry about him. They warned Lippmann that he risked ruining his reputation at the bank by bucking the rest of the team. A colleague pulled him aside, asking, "Why are you doing this? . . . If you're wrong, they're not going to say thanks for having us buy this fire insurance we didn't need."

But Lippmann and Xu had picked up faint signals that housing already was moderating. Instead of pulling back on his trade, Lippmann was determined to find a way to grow it.

I F THE NEW CENTURY EXECUTIVE who had spoken with Paolo Pellegrini was right that borrowers would be able to refinance their mortgages and lower their payments, Paulson's insurance against $1 billion of subprime mortgages and corporate debt was unlikely to be worth much. In fact, while the value of his CDS protection rallied a bit in late 2005, the gains evaporated in early 2006, as some hedge funds sold their own insurance, convinced that housing would keep climbing.

Sensing a mistake, John Paulson sold his original CDS protection after concluding that it covered mortgages on homes that already had enjoyed so much appreciation that refinancings would be easy. But he continued to feel that the idea behind the trade was a good one. So he traded in his holdings for insurance on more recent subprime home mortgages—homes that wouldn't have appreciated in price yet, and which couldn't, therefore, get a refinancing if mortgage rates rose.

The moves did little for the fund, however.

"We weren't getting anywhere," Paulson recalls.

He and Pellegrini soon realized that the only likely scenario in which risky mortgages couldn't be refinanced, and a rash of defaults resulted, was if housing truly was in a bubble that eventually burst. Only then would it be impossible for lenders to bail out overleveraged borrowers by granting them refinancings, they reasoned.

Until that moment, in early 2006, Paulson's team hadn't put much thought or research into whether housing prices were bound to tumble. Sure, they seemed high. But consumers with heavy debt were at risk of missing their mortgage payments if interest rates rose, they figured, even if housing prices didn't fall.

Paulson wasn't even fully aware of how pervasive improper lending practices were until Rosenberg ripped a press release off a printer in January 2006 describing how Ameriquest Mortgage Co., then the largest maker of subprime loans, had agreed to pay $325 million to settle a probe of improper lending practices. The news seemed to startle Paulson.

"This is horrible," he told Pellegrini. That kind of aggressive lending was "crazy."

Paulson and Pellegrini concluded that the only way their trades would work was if the U.S. real estate market had reached unsustainable levels and began to fall, crippling the ability of borrowers to refinance their loans. The prospect seemed remote to many.

"At the time, everybody said home prices never had declined on a nationwide basis except during the Great Depression," Paulson recalls.

Paulson sent Pellegrini scurrying back to his cubicle to determine how overheated the real estate market was. It was a research project that seemed right up Pellegrini's alley. In the past, Pellegrini sometimes met criticism for spending too much time delving into an assignment. Paulson sometimes teased Pellegrini, saying that if he had to walk a block from their offices on 57th Street to 58th Street, Pellegrini likely would go across town, up the West Side, back to the East Side, and then downtown, to reach 58th Street. The direct route just didn't seem his style.

"Sometimes it's more fascinating for me to do everything on my own and re-create the wheel," Pellegrini acknowledges.

But an in-depth project was exactly what Paulson now wanted of Pellegrini. Each time he discovered new data, Paulson sent him back for more. Paulson asked probing questions: What happens to a home mortgage if there's a home-equity loan attached to the same house? How closely do mortgage losses track defaults?

An index produced by the National Association of Realtors showed that home prices had stopped rising in September 2005. But when Pellegrini and a colleague examined an index produced by the Office of Federal Housing Enterprise Oversight, it seemed to show prices were continuing to rise, stirring debate in the firm.

Paulson seized on signs of a slowdown in home sales. As bond prices raced to record levels in early 2006, Paulson became more concerned and sold all of his firm's debt holdings, which accounted for 30 percent of its portfolio. But the team still wasn't sure there was a housing bubble set to pop.

Then Paulson remembered how his old boss at Boston Consulting Group, Jeff Libert, had demonstrated that housing investments hadn't been especially attractive after inflation was factored in. So he asked Pellegrini to factor inflation into his calculations. Pellegrini learned to adjust his housing data using a barometer of inflation called the personal consumption expenditures price index. They were getting closer, but an answer wasn't yet clear.

Pellegrini would frustrate Paulson and others by sometimes re-creating sets of data that already were available, or getting bogged down in the details of his research. Pellegrini spent hours in Paulson's office, debating how to deduce a turn in the housing market. Tension between the two ran high and they sometimes clashed.

To relax, Pellegrini took his sons sailing or to the driving range, among the few moments he wasn't focused on real estate. Most weekends, he walked through Central Park trying to collect his thoughts and find a better approach to his research.

Pellegrini's colleagues still couldn't quite figure him out or why he was endlessly going over the data, but his ex-wife, Claire Goodman, had a sense of what he was up to.

"He's the kind of guy who will work on a problem until he finds what he would call the 'elegant solution,'" she said. "In the Italian culture, there's a difference between the practical solution and the elegant solution—you can't just make a couch; it has to be a beautiful couch. He has high standards and will push himself to find not only the practical solution but the elegant solution."

Tracking interest rates over the decades, Pellegrini concluded that they had little impact on house prices. That suggested that the Federal Reserve Bank's previous rate cuts didn't justify the recent housing surge, despite the arguments of the bulls. But as he reviewed academic and government literature and figures, Pellegrini grew frustrated. He couldn't quantify how excessive housing prices were or show when a bubble might have started. He couldn't even prove that the price surge was distinct from historic moves.

Grasping for new ideas, Pellegrini added a "trend line" to the housing data; the step illustrated very clearly how much prices had surged lately. Pellegrini took a step back to view things over a longer period, ordering up data on real estate all the way back to 1975. Late at night, hunched over his desk in his cubicle, Pellegrini painstakingly tracked annual changes in prices across the country. He then performed a "regression analysis" for the period, to smooth the ups and downs.

Suddenly, the answer was as plain as the paper in front of him: Housing prices had climbed a puny 1.4 percent annually between 1975 and 2000, after inflation was taken into consideration. But they had soared an average of 7 percent a year over the following five years, until 2005. The upshot: U.S. home prices would have to drop by almost 40 percent to return to their historic trend line. Not only had prices increased like never before, but Pellegrini's figures showed that each time housing had dropped in the past it fell *through* the trend line, suggesting that an eventual drop likely would be brutal.

Pellegrini sat upright, staring at his trend line, amazed at how simple and clear it finally was. When he placed the data on a chart, the visual effect was even more dramatic. The next morning, he raced in to show Paulson.

"This is unbelievable!" Paulson said, unable to take his eyes off the chart. A mischievous smile formed on his face, as if Pellegrini had shared a secret no one else was privy to. Paulson sat back in his chair and turned to Pellegrini. "This is our bubble! This is proof. Now we can prove it!" Paulson said.

Pellegrini grinned, unable to mask his pride.

The chart was Paulson's Rosetta stone, the key to making sense of the entire housing market. Years later, he would keep it atop a pile of papers on his desk, showing it off to his clients and updating it each month with new data, like a car collector gently waxing and caressing a prized antique auto. Pellegrini's masterpiece was a guiding light that told Paulson exactly how overpriced the housing market had become. He no longer needed to guess.

"I still look at it. I love that chart," Paulson says. "It's the first key piece of our research. Here was a picture of the bubble!"

To Paulson and Pellegrini, their discovery meant that housing prices were bound to fall, at least at some point, no matter what the moves in unemployment, interest rates, or the economy. And falling prices would put a quick end to all the mortgage refinancing by subprime borrowers, placing them in mortal danger.

Pellegrini's next assignment was to figure out how to make money from their thesis. The firm had been burned shorting various housing-related companies, so it seemed to make more sense to focus on subprime mortgages themselves. Paulson and Pellegrini remained convinced that CDS contracts provided the best risk-reward proposition for the fund, since they were insurance contracts that required Paulson & Co. to make set, annual payments, limiting any losses.

Looking for help, Pellegrini found Sihan Shu, a young analyst in Lehman Brothers's mortgage department, who claimed to be just as skeptical about real estate as the Paulson team and was eager to quit his firm to pursue the thesis.

Paulson, wary that Shu wasn't a true believer in the bear case and was just angling for a lucrative hedge-fund job, tested him in an interview.

"We think these securities are all junk," Paulson told Shu, referring to bonds backed by subprime mortgages, awaiting his reaction to what was then a radical stance. "They're going to go to zero."

Shu passed Paulson's test with flying colors, sharing overlooked research that Lehman had done showing that even flat home prices would
lead to huge losses for many slices of the mortgage bonds. Shu was hired.

Pellegrini and Shu purchased enormous databases tracking the historic performance of more than six million mortgages in various parts
of the country, hiring a firm named 1010data to make sense of it all.
They crunched the numbers, tinkered with logarithms and logistic
functions, and ran different scenarios, trying to figure out what would
happen if housing prices stopped rising. Their findings seemed surprising: Even if prices just flatlined, home owners would feel so much financial pressure that it would result in losses of 7 percent of the value of a
typical pool of subprime mortgages. And if home prices fell 5 percent, it
would lead to losses as high as 17 percent.

Pellegrini didn't know how much home prices would fall, or when a
tumble might begin. But if even flat home prices resulted in 7 percent
losses to pools of subprime mortgages it seemed to make sense to short
the slices that would be impacted by those kinds of losses, he argued to
Paulson—the BBB tranches of the mortgage pools. They were the obvious targets because they would be crippled if losses of even 6 percent
resulted.

"We knew that if home prices just didn't go up, the BBBs would be
extinguished and we'd be home free," says Paulson.

He ran Pellegrini's findings past analysts at a few banks. They tried to
undercut the bearish thesis, noting that home prices already seemed to
have plateaued, without the kinds of losses Pellegrini's data predicted.
Some of them, like Bear Stearns, Lehman Brothers, Merrill Lynch, and
Morgan Stanley, were anxious to increase their exposure to subprime
mortgages and didn't seem to appreciate Paulson's negativity.

"People said, 'Your work doesn't mean anything . . . you're wrong,'"
Paulson recalls.

But the analysts at the banks missed a subtle wrinkle in the Paulson
thesis. Loans from 2005 or earlier periods were for homes that already
had soared in value, so it was no surprise that big losses hadn't yet resulted, even though home prices had stopped soaring. These were
the mortgages that were easy to refinance. The losses Paulson was

predicting were for more recent mortgages on homes that wouldn't appreciate enough to be refinanced before resetting at much higher rates. Paulson didn't have any interest in refuting the arguments of the investment firms or banks, though—he was hoping they'd sell him mortgage insurance cheaply.

Excited by this new information, Paulson stepped up his buying of mortgage protection, purchasing insurance on $100 million, $200 million, and even $500 million of subprime mortgages a day. By the spring of 2006, Paulson's hedge funds had about as much protection on subprime mortgages as they could handle. He and his team told investors that the insurance was a perfect hedge to their existing portfolios, without getting into Pellegrini's chart and its troubling message about the housing market.

"We always told investors that we did not anticipate a meltdown in home prices, even though the chart implied a potential decline of forty percent," Pellegrini recalls. "We did not want to sound implausible at that stage."

Paulson was becoming even more convinced that CDS contracts on subprime mortgages would be a winner. The cost of the insurance remained dirt cheap—just 1 percent annually of the amount being protected. Paulson couldn't get over the potential upside—he was used to shorting a stock or bond and making 10 points if it went from 100 to 90; but if the subprime bonds backing the securitizations fell 10 percent, the lowest slices of the deals easily could become worthless, making Paulson a fortune.

"There's never been an opportunity like this," Paulson gushed to his research director, Andrew Hoine.

Pellegrini's team tracked millions of loans, becoming familiar with dozens of lenders around the country. They began to suspect that rating agencies were far too generous in their ratings. Subprime mortgages now made up 14 percent of the mortgage market, up from 1 percent a decade or so earlier. Housing prices were still rising, but the pace was slowing compared with the recent surge, one more sign that real estate was close to peaking. It was the perfect time for Paulson to put on his trade.

Traders at various investment firms told Paulson and his team that most of those selling mortgage insurance weren't investors who understood either the securities or the real estate market. Some weren't even especially bullish on housing. Rather, firms like Merrill Lynch, Morgan Stanley, and Credit Suisse were selling insurance to Paulson because they were eager to use the flow of CDS insurance payments from Paulson and other bears to create new investments for their clients. To Paulson, it was another reason to step up his buying of the insurance.

"We've got to take as much advantage of this as we can; it's just a matter of time," before the mortgages run into problems, Paulson told Hoine. "We really have to short as many securities as we can."

Paulson's funds already had committed to paying $100 million annually to buy insurance on $10 billion of risky mortgages. But it was always something of a stretch for the merger fund, or even some of Paulson's other funds, to turn to these mortgage derivative investments as a hedge, and Paulson knew he couldn't justify adding much more to the funds.

Paulson was tempted to use some of his own money to buy some mortgage insurance for his personal account and leave it at that. But he knew this was his chance to swing for the fences. To make a really huge score, he needed to sell investors on a new fund specifically dedicated to betting against these subprime mortgages. Earlier, Michael Burry had failed to convince investors to back a similar fund. Now Paulson would take his own shot.

History wasn't on his side, however.

6.

"Worldly wisdom teaches that it is better for reputation
to fail conventionally than to succeed unconventionally."
—John Maynard Keynes

MOUNTAIN CLIMBERS CONFRONT THE MIGHTY K2 IN THE HIMA-layas. Surfers brave Hawaii's Pipeline Surf. In the investing world, there's no more treacherous challenge than navigating a speculative mania; it can ruin amateurs and professionals alike.

History is littered with legendary investors who gave in to temptation and rode financial waves to their ruin, or attempted gutsy maneuvers to profit from what they viewed as inevitable crashes, only to suffer humiliating losses that sometimes haunted them for years.

In the early eighteenth century, Sir Isaac Newton, the man who discovered gravity as a fundamental force in nature and became the highest officer of Britain's Royal Mint, decried the growing passion for shares of the South Sea Company, a British company that gained a monopoly on trade in South America. Newton sold his own stock holdings of the company, worth £7,000, for a 100 percent profit, sure the shares would fall with a thud. But as the buying grew more frenzied, even Newton couldn't resist the pull; he bought more shares, only to lose £20,000 when the bubble finally burst.

"I can calculate the motions of the heavenly bodies, but not the madness of people," he later remarked.[1]

Benjamin Graham, considered the greatest modern-day investor, was so caught up in the roaring market of the 1920s that he embraced the fast-trading lifestyle of his day, taking up residence in the luxury Beresford Apartments on Central Park, hiring a manservant, and borrowing money to expand his investment portfolio. Graham failed to see a crash coming, and his investments lost roughtly two-thirds of their value between 1929 and 1931.[2]

Renowned trader Jesse Livermore fared somewhat better. He anticipated 1929's historic sell-off and scored $100 million of profits by shorting shares. The gains prompted threats on his life, and Livermore hired armed guards to protect him and his family. The stock market remained volatile, however, and by 1934 Livermore was bankrupt and suspended as a member of the Chicago Board of Trade. Six years later, he ordered two stiff drinks in the lobby bar of the Sherry-Netherland hotel, walked to the nearby cloakroom, and shot himself dead with a .32 caliber Colt automatic revolver. On a scratch pad attached to his wallet, he left a rambling note to his wife saying that he was "tired of fighting . . . my life has been a failure."[3]

Hedge-fund manager Michael Steinhardt, who rang up huge profits wagering against overpriced stocks in the 1960s, also bucked the market in the early 1990s, buying bonds as investors fled the market. Many of Steinhardt's own clients deserted him, doubtful his strategy would pay off. Bonds eventually rallied, however, leaving his fund $600 million richer.

"Betting against a bubble is dangerous, but it's one of the most rewarding things, it's truly a pleasure," Steinhardt says. "In your mind you're going to be right ultimately; there's a certain virtue in being alone."

Succumbing to hubris just a year later, however, Steinhardt lost 30 percent of his fund's assets.

In more recent years, those standing in front of Wall Street's rumbling herd were just as likely to be mauled. In the mid-1990s, when Jeffrey Vinik ran Fidelity Investment's Magellan Fund, the world's largest mutual fund, he increased the fund's bond holdings after becoming worried about the stock market. Many of his clients became upset about missing out on a soaring stock market, however, and directed their ire at Vinik, ignoring his enviable track record. In 1996, he finally quit his job to invest largely for himself. A senior colleague at Fidelity, George Vanderheiden, who managed $36 billion, came under intense fire just a few years later, this time for resisting overpriced technology stocks. He ended up retiring at the age of fifty-four, watching from the sidelines as those same shares finally tumbled, just as he predicted.

Julian Robertson was in a better position to buck the madness for tech stocks in the late 1990s. After all, Robertson, who ran his own hedge fund—the largest on record at the time—was among the celebrated names on Wall Street.

But Robertson stubbornly clung to airline shares and other value stocks instead of shifting into Internet companies, and his performance suffered. The tech craze went on years longer than he expected. In 2000 Robertson threw in the towel and closed his firm. Just weeks later, technology stocks finally crumbled, but he had been unable to hold on long enough to claim vindication.

The bursting of the Internet bubble even cost George Soros, considered a Midas of the markets. In the months leading up to 2000, Soros badgered his top lieutenant, Stanley Druckenmiller, to reduce risk and dump the technology stocks that he had become enamored with.

Druckenmiller, an accomplished investor in his own right, shared many of Soros's concerns. "I don't like this market," he told a colleague at the time. "I think we should probably lighten up. I don't want to go out like Steinhardt."

Despite these worries, Druckenmiller figured he was safe because the frenzy likely would go on a little longer.

He was wrong. By early 2000, technology stocks were in a sudden tailspin, shocking the Soros team. During the worst of this period, it happened that their offices were consumed by a powerful burning smell as electrical work on the floor above repeatedly started small fires, setting off deafening alarms. The smoke, the racket, and the dizzy headaches they caused seemed "like a divine message," one Soros executive said of the bizarre scene. "We almost wished it would burn down."

Facing losses of more than 20 percent over a few short months, Soros severed his long, profitable partnership with Druckenmiller and announced that he would cease managing money for others and take a more conservative stance.

"Maybe I don't understand the market," a reflective Soros said at a subsequent news conference. "Maybe the music has stopped, but people are still dancing."[4]

Fighting a runaway market can have more serious results. In 2008, German industrialist Adolf Merckle was among a group of sophisticated investors convinced that shares of Volkswagen were wildly overpriced. Merckle, who was estimated to be worth $9 billion at the time, sold Volkswagen shares short, but they kept soaring. It turned out that sports-car manufacturer Porsche was in the midst of a furtive effort to buy up Volkswagen shares, driving their prices higher. Losses of hundreds of millions of euros eventually became too much for the seventy-four-year-old Merckle. On a cold evening in January 2009, he lay down on railroad tracks near his villa in the southern German hamlet of Blaubeuren as an oncoming train took his life.

"The understanding of a bubble doesn't help you as an investor," says Soros. "Those that reach historic proportions go further than you would think."

JOHN PAULSON wasn't very concerned about the stumbles of previous investors. He was sure he had discovered proof of a housing bubble, and he was determined to profit from it. It was fortuitous that Paulson was a merger pro, and not a veteran of the mortgage, housing, or bond markets. He wasn't deterred by the dismal track record of those who already had bet against housing, and wasn't fully aware that his bearishness wasn't especially unique.

Two years earlier, in 2004, Professor Robert Shiller of Yale University produced data showing that U.S. residential real estate prices rose by only 66 percent between 1890 and 2004, or by just 0.4 percent a year. He contrasted that meager gain with the heady rise of 52 percent, or 6.2 percent a year, between 1997 and 2004. Shiller presented a series of lectures on the topic and included the charts and figures in an updated version of his best-selling book, *Irrational Exuberance,* in February 2005, trying to demonstrate how overpriced real estate had become.

Skeptical research on housing had been published in other countries as well. A report in early 2004 by Smithers & Co., a British consulting firm, said prices in the United Kingdom would have to fall by almost 30 percent to return to historic levels.

In fact, warnings were widespread that housing had gone off the rails. Between 2000 and 2003, there were 1,387 mentions of the phrase "housing bubble" in articles in U.S. publications. Over the next three years, there were 5,535 mentions of the phrase, including prominent stories in most major newspapers, some which sparked nervousness among major real estate investors.[5]

"Never before have home owners been so leveraged; and never before has the residential market been so speculative," said François Trahan, a Bear Stearns strategist, in May 2005.

Around the same time, a popular video made the rounds putting the housing market on a virtual roller-coaster ride that started at the beginning of the century and followed the ups and downs of actual historic prices as plotted on a track. The ride finished with a nerve-rattling ride to unprecedented heights, one that turned the stomach of even hardy viewers and hammered home the dangerous level the market had reached.

Even those betting on the housing market seemed to hedge themselves. By late 2005, Ralph Cioffi, who operated two big hedge funds at Bear Stearns and appeared to have an insatiable appetite for mortgage products, was steering clear of the riskiest subprime mortgage investments. Angelo Mozilo, CEO of Countrywide, sold more than $400 million of shares in Countrywide between 2004 and 2007, an unusual move for someone who professed to be unconcerned about a national housing bubble.

Still others expressed strong doubts privately. In an internal e-mail, a

Standard & Poor's executive told a fellow analyst that a mortgage deal the firm was rating was "ridiculous" and that they "should not be rating it." His colleague replied that "we rate every deal," adding that "it could be structured by cows and we would rate it." A manager of the collateralized-debt obligation group said, "Let's hope we are all wealthy and retired by the time his house of cards falters."[6]

"Does your brother-in-law, the real estate broker, owe you money?" asked financial-publication *Grant's* in a June 2005 issue. "Now is the time to collect."

A LTHOUGH INVESTORS long had been worried about housing, most were unable to profit from their stance, some failing quite miserably. Others already had dismissed the use of CDS protection that Paulson was warming to.

In 2002, William Ackman, a hedge-fund manager, argued that MBIA, the bond insurer, was heading for serious trouble, two full years before Paulson bought CDS protection on the company. But Ackman, a sharp-elbowed investor who relished telling corporate executives how to do their jobs, was too early, and he lost serious cash from the trade until late 2007.

"You can be totally right on an investment but wrong on the timing and lose a lot," Ackman says.

Another well-regarded investor, Palm Beach–based Otter Creek Partners, developed early concerns about mortgages and shorted financial companies, only to see the market race higher. It was a brutal lesson for others considering the same tack. Prominent hedge-fund managers with doubts about housing, such as Paul Singer of Elliott Management Corp. and Seth Klarman of Baupost Group, bought some CDS insurance contracts on risky mortgages but chose to buy small portions of it and not go overboard. No one wanted to be known for hurting clients by turning bearish too soon.

"Buying so much was a reputational risk," Klarman says. "It wasn't a no-brainer."

Others just didn't feel comfortable buying CDS contracts, some of the very kinds of "derivative" investments tainted by legendary investor Warren Buffett as "financial weapons of mass destruction" for their ability to inflict huge losses.

Bill Gross of Pacific Investment Management Co., the $800 billion gorilla of the bond business, took the pulse of the market from picturesque offices in Newport Beach, California. He became rattled in 2005 when two of his children, one of whom was a teacher, confessed to using aggressive mortgages to purchase homes they otherwise couldn't have afforded based on their limited salaries. After doing some research on real estate, Gross called an emergency staff meeting and began sending "shoppers" to key markets to pose as home buyers and glean intelligence about all the excesses. In 2005, Gross's own top mortgage trader, Scott Simon, advised clients about the huge upside possible from CDS insurance on mortgage bonds, putting him well ahead of the pack.

But Gross was uneasy with CDS contracts. Most of the money he oversaw was in dowdy mutual funds, and many of his clients couldn't own the derivatives contracts. Instead, Gross reworked Pimco's portfolio, buying things like safe, short-term Treasury bonds, dabbling just a bit in the CDS insurance. Even these small moves left Gross's newly conservative portfolio trailing the rest of the pack in 2006. It made Gross so miserable that he had to take an unplanned nine-day vacation midway through the year; he spent most of his break sitting around the house, sulking to his wife.

"I couldn't turn on business television, I couldn't pick up the paper; it was just devastating," Gross said at the time. "You can't sleep at night."[7]

When housing finally weakened, of course, Pimco's returns topped those of most competitors, a welcome relief to Gross. But Gross says he's not sure he would have aped Paulson's moves even if his investors demanded it.

"I'm a thirty-five-year veteran, an old fart, and the hedge-fund mentality is not me," Gross says. "We can't buy [derivative contracts] in a way to make it a slam dunk; we did the trade in a conservative, fall-asleep way."

Investment advisor Peter Schiff seemed in an ideal position to benefit from real estate troubles. For years, he had predicted that housing would stumble and that the financial system would implode. Schiff eventually was seen as something of a Cassandra of the markets, ridiculed unmercifully on business television networks. After one appearance in which Schiff issued his usual apocalyptic warnings, Neil Cavuto, an anchor on the Fox Business Network, asked Schiff if his next project would be an "exposé on Santa Claus." Commentator Ben Stein piled on, telling Schiff, "You're just wrong."

Schiff moved clients' money out of stocks and shorted risky mortgages, as did Paulson. But Schiff picked the wrong investments to shift into, choosing foreign currencies, commodities, and emerging markets, among other things, all big losers in 2008. Some clients lost half their money that year, underscoring the fact that an awareness of an investment bubble is only valuable when you know how to profit from it.

A key reason even experienced investors resisted buying mortgage protection: CDS contracts were a classic example of a "negative-carry" trade, a maneuver that investment pros detest almost as much as high taxes and coach-class seating. In a negative-carry trade, an investor commits to paying a certain cost for an investment with the hope of untold riches down the line. In the case of CDS contracts, purchasers usually agree to make an up-front payment, and to shell out annual insurance premiums, both of which bake in a sure cost.

If negative-carry trades don't work quickly, the cost piles up. An investor paying 5 percent a year to place a trade will face 20 percent cumulative losses after just four years. These losses grant a running start to competitors, an ill-advised move in a world where trailing a rival by even half a percentage point can lead to a swift dismissal. Mortgage and bond specialists were especially fearful of the costs of negative-carry trades because these investors didn't usually rack up big gains. Buying insurance at home is one thing; doing it at the office is something entirely different.

Bill Gross's star mortgage trader, Scott Simon, experienced the loathing of negative carry first-hand. In 2006, Simon tried to start a fund for Pimco to buy CDS contracts, pitching the idea to clients exposed to real estate, such as endowments, pension plans, and others. The insurance seemed custom-made for the investors. But they proved so unwilling to shell out money at the start of a trade that Simon and his team gave up, unable to sell the fund, thereby losing a chance to undertake the same trades as Paulson.

Even the most successful investors shun negative carry; it is like garlic to vampires. In the 1980s, when junior traders suggested that junk-bond king Michael Milken short especially risky bonds, he scoffed at the notion of paying high interest on the debt while waiting for it to fall in price. Trades that lock in instant payments in the hopes of a payday someday in the future make even the likes of George Soros queasy.

"I don't know if I would have done it myself, if I was in [Paulson's] shoes," Soros says. "I probably wouldn't have bet the house."

Instead, most traders prefer "positive" carry trades, or those where profits are immediate and clear. Banks, for example, borrow money at low interest rates and lend it out at higher rates. A borrower may go belly-up, of course, but on paper the move looks like a winner.

There didn't seem to be a more surefire positive-carry trade than selling insurance on even risky mortgage debt. Insurance companies like American International Group, huge global banks, and countless investors locked in instant gains from the premiums that Paulson and other bears paid for their CDS insurance. These profits sometimes meant the difference between hitting a profit goal and missing out on a huge bonus.

"Positive carry is the mother's milk for capitalism; it's ingrained and embedded in the minds of investors," says Gross.

JOHN PAULSON'S perspective was so vastly different from that of most others on Wall Street that it was as if he had landed from a different planet. For one thing, Paulson had periodically shorted bonds all along, and didn't see what the fuss was about. If an investment looked like a loser, he itched to bet against it, whether or not it might cost him a bit and allow a competitor to briefly pull ahead. To Paulson, CDS contracts on risky mortgage bonds were an investment with minimal downside and almost unlimited potential, a dream trade with a likely "asymmetrical outcome."

Paulson also had good fortune on his side: By the time he determined that the housing market was in a bubble in the spring of 2006, prices had begun to flatten out, making it the perfect time to bet against the market. Others who had come to a similar determination much earlier were licking their wounds because they had placed wagers against real estate too early and suffered as it climbed further.

Paulson flashed back to a book he had read years earlier: *Soros on Soros,* detailing George Soros's various insights. In the book, Soros urged investors to "go for the jugular" if they spotted a trade with huge potential.[8]

"That expression stood out for me," Paulson recalls. "As I became more convinced that there had been a massive mispricing of risk, we said, why just sit here with one billion of protection? Why not go for the jugular?"

Some at Paulson's firm noted that investors would have to be educated if these CDS trades were going to be the centerpiece of a dedicated new "credit" fund. A few clients already had indicated they were uncomfortable that the merger hedge fund purchased so much mortgage protection.

But Paulson was upbeat, predicting just a 10 percent chance of failure for his subprime trade. If housing cracked and it became difficult to refinance mortgage loans, borrowers surely would run into problems, crippling the collateral backing all those mortgage-backed bonds and rendering the BBB slices worthless. Even if real estate just leveled off, risky borrowers signing up for adjustable-rate mortgages in 2006 would be unable to refinance them in two years when the rates shot up, Paulson reasoned, because they would have little equity in their homes.

And if Paulson was wrong and housing somehow kept climbing? Most subprime borrowers probably would refinance their loans well before they had a chance to reset at higher rates, to avoid the increased monthly costs. Once the loans were refinanced, the protection Paulson purchased would expire, ending the trade with minimal losses—just the cost of the CDS insurance. Either way, Paulson was sure he would know by 2008 whether his trade would work.

"We found the El Dorado of investments," he said at one point to a colleague. "Are we going to just dip our toes in?"

Darker scenarios were possible, of course, but Paulson didn't focus on them. If the frenzy for risky investments grew and the BBB-rated bonds that he was skeptical of became even more popular, Paulson would certainly see losses.

But these bonds already traded at paltry interest rates close to those of the safest debt. Even investors with rose-tinted glasses were unlikely to accept yields on toxic mortgages unless they were greater than those of debt from the U.S. Treasury and other supersafe investments. To Paulson, it limited how much more expensive the mortgage bonds could become, reducing the dangers of wagering against them.

Sure, if the Fed slashed interest rates again, risky borrowers might be off the hook, as rates on their adjustable loans dropped, crippling the value of Paulson's insurance. But the Fed had been raising rates, pushing the key federal funds rate up to 5.25 percent from 3.25 percent a year earlier. The Fed was unlikely to start cutting them again unless the economy dramatically weakened. By then it would be too late to save home owners.

"There's never been an opportunity like this," Paulson gushed to Jeffrey Tarrant after an afternoon of tennis at Tarrant's Southampton home. Losses on pools of risky mortgages were running at almost 1 percent at the time. If they hit just 7 percent, the BBB slices "would be wiped out," Paulson said, excitedly.

So Paulson decided to go for the jugular. He figured that even his biggest fans wouldn't stomach losses of more than 25 percent over three years, or 8 percent or so a year. But if they could be capped at that level, Paulson might be able to raise a lot of money. He just had to figure out how to do it.

Paulson asked Rosenberg, his trader, for a quote. Rosenberg quickly came back with good news from the firm's Bear Stearns broker: There still was so much demand for bonds backed by subprime mortgages, and so little appetite for CDS insurance to protect them, that the cost of insuring the BBB pieces was still just 1 percent of the value of the bonds. If Paulson wanted to insure another $1 billion of BBB-rated slices, it would cost just $10 million annually.

At those prices, Paulson argued, his firm really should back up the truck to buy insurance on billions of risky bonds. If he could convince enough investors to back a new fund with $1 billion or so, it could purchase CDS insurance contracts on, say, $12 billion of bonds at a cost of just $120 million a year.

A 12 percent annual cost likely would seem too steep for many investors in any new fund. But because premiums on CDS contracts, like those on any other insurance product, are paid out over time, the new fund could keep most of its money in the bank until the CDS bills came due, and thereby earn about 5 percent a year. That would cut the annual cost to the fund to a more reasonable 7 percent. Since Paulson would charge 1 percent a year as a management fee, the most an investor could lose would be 8 percent a year, the exact figure he was shooting for.

"We looked at ten-to-one, twenty-to-one, even higher, but twelve-to-one seemed right to us, and we thought it would be right for investors," Paulson says.

And the upside? If Paulson purchased CDS contracts that fully protected $12 billion of subprime mortgage bonds and the bonds somehow became worthless, Paulson & Co. would make a cool $12 billion. Paulson and his team became more enthusiastic as they prepared to get in touch with prospective investors.

Paulson figured he could use some help running the fund, though, especially if it became as large as he hoped. He interviewed senior research executives at various Wall Street firms, dangling a top job at the fund. Some of the candidates had been recommended by Pellegrini, who scoured the industry for capable mortgage experts sharing a bearish bent.

But Pellegrini had mixed feelings about the assignment. He was thrilled that Paulson trusted him enough to help with the job search, and he was just as convinced as Paulson that the subprime trade would work. But Pellegrini had helped create the idea. He wanted Paulson to offer him a senior role at the fund; he was convinced he was up to the task. Instead, Pellegrini would have to work for the new hire, dropping down a notch on the hedge fund's totem pole.

"It was tricky for me," Pellegrini says. "If I resisted, it wouldn't have worked out. If I got credit for a great hire, that would be better than nothing, I figured."

For weeks, the response from the candidates Paulson approached was tepid, at best. Some analysts weren't nearly negative enough on housing. Others felt leaving well-paid jobs to help run a bearish fund that might not succeed was too risky. Moreover, abandoning a cushy Wall Street job for a hedge fund wagering against housing could brand the trader with a scarlet letter, a stain capable of preventing them from returning to an industry that generally made money when real estate rose, not fell.

"Everyone who might have been qualified said the strategy wouldn't work," Pellegrini recalls.

Privately, Pellegrini was elated by the response from Wall Street. He secretly hoped that it might improve his own chances for a senior role in the new fund. One day in the spring of 2006, after the latest disappointing interview, Paulson stopped Pellegrini in the hallway. Paulson was smiling warmly, filling Pellegrini with instant hope.

"I've thought about it," Paulson told Pellegrini. "We aren't going to hire anyone. We've decided you should be co-manager of the fund."

For a moment, Pellegrini was confused. He had no clue who the "we" was that Paulson was referring to and worried there might be someone else at the firm he had to impress. But when it dawned on him that he finally was getting the senior position he yearned for, Pellegrini turned ecstatic.

For the first time at the hedge fund, the terms of his compensation were put in writing. Pellegrini even moved into an office, in a corridor across from the firm's accounting bullpen. He proudly put his new title, "Co-manager of the Paulson Credit Opportunity Fund," under his name in his e-mails.

A few days later, however, Andrew Hoine approached Pellegrini. "You need to remove that new title from your e-mails," he said. "It might confuse investors." Later that day, Jim Wong, Paulson's investor-relations chief, relayed the same message. Clients might think Paulson wasn't running the fund, Wong said. Pellegrini turned ashen with embarrassment and agreed to drop the title from his e-mails. For all his valuable research and long hours, he hadn't yet achieved a position of security at the firm.

ALTHOUGH PAOLO PELLEGRINI understood the trade as well as anyone at the firm, his touch with potential clients was a little rough. At a Red Cross fund-raising event in Connecticut, hedge-fund investor Martin Tornberg stood with an executive of a university endowment during the cocktail hour. Pellegrini walked over, holding a glass of red wine, to join the conversation.

They quickly began discussing Paulson's new fund. The investors were intrigued. But as Pellegrini went on, they couldn't understand how he picked securities to short or how the firm was placing its trades.

"It was too hard to follow him," Tornberg recalls. "It was like torture."

Paulson's delivery was much smoother, and he proved expert at explaining his thesis and trade in simple terms. But some investors proved difficult to convince. Hoping to claim his alma mater, Harvard University, as a client for the new fund, an imprimatur that might encourage other investors, Paulson traveled to Boston to meet with Mark Taborsky, who helped pick hedge funds for Harvard's endowment. Taborsky already had met with Paulson and Pellegrini in their New York office and had come away impressed.

But the fund cost of 8 percent a year concerned Taborsky. He also thought Paulson might be excessively gloomy about the housing market. Moreover, Paulson's trade idea wasn't especially new, Taborsky felt.

"Look, guys internally are doing this already," Taborsky told Paulson, as he turned him down.

Afterward, Paulson shared his frustration with Howard Gurvitch. "They ought to be in," Paulson told him. "They should get it." (Harvard eventually purchased some mortgage protection, but focused on more inexpensive versions that didn't have a big payoff.)

Paulson reached out to his existing investors. Pellegrini's chart suggested that housing prices could plunge 40 percent, but Paulson and his team rarely expressed that view to investors. Even they didn't fully trust the chart. As a result, Paulson decided not to short the slices of the bond deals rated A or AA, the safest ratings, but instead to bet against the riskiest BBB-rated pieces, bonds with risks that Paulson and Pellegrini were convinced investors would recognize.

Some were skeptical, nonetheless. Richard Leibovitch, who invested in hedge funds for a Boston firm called Gottex Fund Management, grilled Paulson in a meeting, repeatedly telling him it would be a difficult trade to pull off. Leibovitch said he had spoken with Mike Vranos of Ellington Management, the preeminent mortgage trader, and he wasn't nearly as alarmed about housing.

"John, why do you think you know more than Vranos?"

"Look, you don't have to be a mortgage guy to read the tea leaves. I don't care if he's a mortgage genius," Paulson said. "Listen to the logic of my argument."

In the end, Leibovitch turned down the fund, though he stayed a client of Paulson's other funds. Before the meeting ended, he urged Paulson to meet with Vranos, but Paulson passed on the offer.

"Paulson was a merger-arb guy and suddenly he has strong views on housing and subprime," Leibovitch recalls. "The largest mortgage guys, including Vranos at Ellington, one of the gods of the market, were far more positive on subprime."

Paulson, Wong, and other members of the team described their investment thesis to Nolan Randolph, another client, who was an executive of a Texas firm called Crestline Investors. But Randolph kept shaking his head over and over again, unnerving the group. Randolph turned them down, arguing that the downside seemed too big if the trade didn't pay off.

"We don't think your fund will add alpha," Randolph said, using the industry lingo for value.

Even some investors who agreed with Paulson's bearish view doubted he would make much money because there was relatively little trading in the investments he was buying. They felt he might have a hard time selling them without sending prices tumbling, shrinking any profits.

"How are you going to get out?" asked one London-based investor.

Paulson patiently explained how the trade likely would play out, even predicting the dates at which nervous investors and banks would suffer housing-related losses and line up to purchase his mortgage protection. That would enable Paulson to sell it profitably, he argued. The investor wished him well, but passed on Paulson's new venture.

"It looked like a dangerous game, taking one single bet that might be difficult to unwind," says Jack Doueck, a principal at Stillwater Capital, a New York firm that parcels out money to funds. He, too, said no to Paulson's fund.

Still others grumbled that the new fund wouldn't let investors withdraw money until the end of 2008, a "lockup" that Paulson insisted on to ensure he wouldn't have to exit the trade due to client withdrawals before it began to work.

"Investors said, 'If you're so smart, why isn't everyone doing it, and why are firms in the mortgage business making a different argument?'" Paulson recalls. "I said, my job isn't to convince you."

Paulson's growing fixation on housing began to impact his business; some clients worried he was focusing on mortgages because opportunities were drying up in the merger area. Others thought he was becoming distracted. One longtime client, big Swiss bank Union Bancaire Privée, received an urgent warning from a contact that Paulson was "straying" from his longtime focus, and that it should pull its money from his firm, fast. The bank stuck with Paulson, but turned down his new fund.

Paulson even received flak from old friends.

"What could they do to mess with the trade?" Peter Soros grilled Paulson on regular phone calls and in meetings; he noted that politicians might feel compelled to aid mortgage holders. In the run-up to the election year, would Congress let two to three million home owners get thrown out of their homes? Soros asked.

Soros didn't give Paulson an investment.

Paulson wanted his fund to be big, so he could purchase the most mortgage protection possible. But he also felt pressure to raise the money quickly. Competitors might figure out the trade for themselves and buy the same insurance, driving up the cost. That made Paulson reluctant to provide many details of his trade. It was a stance that made it more difficult to raise money.

"It doesn't take much for hedge-fund managers to catch on, and it was such a glaring mispricing, I was afraid too much attention would cause it to disappear," Paulson says. "I didn't tell some potential investors the whole story, with all the details, because the more I discussed it, the more likely it would go away."

James Altucher, a writer who also invests money in hedge funds for clients, met the Paulson team and was shaken by their arguments. Coming out of the midtown New York offices, Altucher turned to a colleague and said, "We're screwed. The whole country is screwed."

Back at the office, though, Altucher called pros for their opinions. They said the insurance likely would drop in value before it began to rise, and that pension funds and other believers in the BBB slices wouldn't easily sell, limiting how much the bonds could fall in price. The advice dissuaded Altucher from investing in Paulson's fund.

"Only a little bit of asking was enough to put the gas on neutral," Altucher wrote in a column in *The Financial Times*. "It all made a lot of sense but I didn't invest . . . Who knew how long the irrational behaviour would last?"

Paolo Pellegrini honed his pitch and became smoother in presenting the trade to investors. But at one point, he couldn't bear all the dissing the firm received. In a meeting at the Ford Foundation, a Ford executive, Larry Siegel, said his organization wouldn't invest in the Paulson fund because it was wagering against home owners, something that Siegel said was "inconsistent with our social mission." To Pellegrini, the comment smacked of false piety; a colleague at Paulson & Co. had relayed an earlier conversation in which Siegel said he found a better trade to take advantage of housing weakness. After the meeting broke up, Pellegrini quickly approached Siegel outside the conference room, grabbing his attention.

"I heard you have a better trade . . . why is it better than what we're doing?"

Siegel said he didn't want to get into it, just that his was a more sophisticated approach than Paulson's. (Siegel now says he was just trying to get out of the meeting, and that his bosses never would have approved an investment in a fund that wagered against mortgages.)

Paulson wasn't getting much more respect from Wall Street's establishment. Rosenberg invited two Morgan Stanley traders, John Pearce and Joseph Naggar, to visit the office, hoping to learn more about the market and include Morgan Stanley as one of its brokers on the trade.

Pearce and Naggar showed up in khaki pants and polo shirts, saying they didn't have much time to talk because they were late for a golf outing with other clients.

"Let's try to make this as brief as we can," Naggar said.

Pellegrini and Rosenberg, in suits and ties, handed the Morgan Stanley traders a list of subprime mortgage–backed bonds that the firm was hoping to bet against.

"Here are the names we'd like to put more shorts on," Pellegrini said.

Pearce and Naggar didn't seem to have much interest in trading with Paulson's team, though, or in spending much time on their questions.

"It sounds like a good trade; maybe *we'll* do it," Pearce said, with a laugh. Pearce was just humoring them, Rosenberg thought.

As they ended the meeting, Pearce said, "Well, if we get more capacity, we'll put it on for you."

Pearce and Naggar already had placed a few bearish subprime trades for their own firm, though they didn't want to let that on in the meeting. To the Paulson team, it was another exasperating experience.

"That was a waste of time," a glum Pellegrini said to Rosenberg as they walked out of the room.

By June, Paulson hadn't raised much money. Jeffrey Tarrant wanted to invest for his firm, Protégé Partners, but he faced complaints from clients.

"One of our investors said, why would you agree to a trade with negative carry?" Tarrant recalls. "People on trading desks warned, 'He doesn't have expertise in the area,' or 'He doesn't know what he's doing.'"

Every day, Paulson walked into the office of Jim Wong showing unusual urgency, as if a clock was ticking on his trade.

"Lemme see the latest list" of investors, Paulson said to Wong insistently. After looking it over, Paulson asked in frustration, "Where *are* we with these people?"

On another occasion, passing Philip Levy in the hedge fund's hallway, Paulson stopped the marketing executive, asking for an update of the level of interest in the new fund. After Levy delivered the latest disappointing news, Paulson complained, "I don't know why they don't get it . . . this is the trade of a lifetime," before walking away, abruptly.

Paulson was thrilled to hear from Jeffrey Greene when he called in the spring of 2006. Greene, an owner of millions of dollars of real estate properties, was eager for a way to protect them from the downturn he was sure was coming. And he and Paulson were longtime friends. Greene was an obvious candidate for the new fund, someone who could write a big check and help get it off the ground.

Greene was one investor that Paulson would come to regret hearing from, however.

7

J EFFREY GREENE CAME ACROSS AS SOMETHING OF A HOLLYWOOD CLICHÉ. A lifelong bachelor in Los Angeles, Greene dated would-be starlets and wannabe models. When he wasn't hosting parties for friends like Mike Tyson, Heidi Fleiss, and Paris Hilton, Greene was relaxing at one of his spectacular homes, including an estate on five acres overlooking the Malibu shore, where he had enough space for his miniature horse, Winston, to run free. Gracious and down-to-earth, Greene stood out in the Hollywood scene with his easy laugh, Harvard education, and winning touch in business.

But by the spring of 2006, Greene's laid-back image masked growing concerns. The six foot tall, youthful-looking fifty-two-year-old, sporting thick brown hair and arched eyebrows, had spent over a decade accumulating more than seven thousand apartments and a handful of office buildings in Southern California, as if they were properties on a Monopoly board. They were valued at more than $500 million, according to the overheated prices of the time.

But as he woke one morning in his Malibu home and opened the *Los Angeles Times,* Greene's face tensed. Reading fresh details of the raging local housing market, Greene was reminded that another downturn could leave him broke. He was too old to go through that again. Somehow, he had to protect himself from a collapse.

Greene called everyone he knew, from stockbrokers to business associates, asking what to do. Sell some properties and wager against shares of home builders? That wasn't nearly good enough. Finally, Greene reached out to his longtime friend John Paulson. Paulson told him he was working on an interesting idea, something to do with shorting mortgage bonds. He invited Greene to come to New York to discuss it.

Shortly afterward, Greene walked into Paulson's offices, excited to see his old friend. They had first met back in 1990, introduced by a mutual acquaintance over dinner at a popular Southampton restaurant. When Greene asked Paulson to join him and some young women at a barbecue the next day, Paulson eagerly accepted the invitation, riding his bicycle thirty miles to the Amagansett home where Greene was staying. Over the years, they remained close; Greene served as an usher in Paulson's wedding; John and Jenny stayed at Greene's Malibu home during their honeymoon. The two were a contrast in styles—Greene relaxed and outgoing, Paulson more serious and reserved. But Greene was drawn to smart people and he got a kick out of Paulson's dry humor and expert storytelling.

As Greene patiently waited for his friend in the main conference room at the hedge fund, he glanced around the office and was impressed. Greene always had been the wealthier and more successful of the pair. When Paulson came to the West Coast, Greene usually would ask his chef to prepare a gourmet meal; when Greene was in New York, Paulson lugged bags of groceries from an upscale market before making dinner. Paulson's firm's previous offices had been a simple, 2,000-square-foot space.

This time, though, Paulson had new, expansive digs. On one wall of the conference room was an abstract painting by Louisa Chase of disembodied hands and feet in a swirl of blue and white; in the corner were assorted drinks and a shiny ice chest. The glass paneling provided a view of young, well-dressed traders and analysts walking briskly through the halls. As Paulson walked in, Greene was about to compliment his friend on the look of his operation. But Paulson had an intense look on his face, and a colleague was a step behind him. Paulson closed the door firmly and extended a hand to Greene, who responded with a warm hug. Paulson seemed uncomfortable with the display of affection, surprising Greene.

Sitting across a long, polished wood conference-room table from Greene, Paulson launched into an overview of the housing market, a speech he had given endless times to prospective clients. Greene was dressed casually, in a jacket, an open-collar dress shirt, and slacks; Paulson wore a full suit and tie. Greene realized Paulson was making a business presentation, not greeting a good friend.

A few minutes into the pitch, Greene tried to offer a point of his own, but Paulson cut him off.

"Just *listen*," Paulson said sharply, his voice rising.

Greene wasn't sure what to make of Paulson's bizarre behavior. He offered no smile, leavened his speech with no humor, and maintained a strange formality. Why weren't they chatting in Paulson's private office, as they usually did?

It's as if he doesn't know me, Greene thought.

Paulson spoke for twenty more minutes, leafing through an elaborate marketing document that featured Pellegrini's housing data. He described how Paulson's new "credit" fund would buy protection on subprime mortgages. Greene, shrugging off his friend's odd behavior, tried to keep up with him.

Although Greene didn't know it, Paulson was in a difficult position. An investment from Greene would help Paulson get his new fund off the ground. But once again Paulson felt torn; if he shared too many details of his moves with his friend, others might hear of the trade and ape him, reducing any gains.

"It doesn't take much for investors to catch on, and I had just a fixed amount I could spend" on the insurance, Paulson says, explaining his behavior.

Greene was intrigued by the presentation but remained noncommittal about the fund. He was more than a bit confused about how it all would work. Moreover, he wasn't sure why he needed to pay to invest in a special fund to short the market, rather than just doing the trades himself as he had with previous tips from Paulson.

"Can I just do it on my own?"

Paulson looked disappointed. "There's no way you can get ISDAs," he responded, referring to the formal documentation from the International Swaps and Derivative Association necessary to trade the sophisticated CDS contracts.

They met again Friday night for dinner. Paulson seemed friendlier this time and more himself, putting Greene at ease.

"Jeff, this trade could be huge," Paulson confided in Greene. "This could take me to another level."

Greene still didn't quite follow Paulson's idea, though.

"I didn't know what the hell J.P. was talking about, tranches and credit-default swaps," Greene recalls. "It was hard to understand. You're not shorting, exactly; it's a derivative that mimics the bond . . . I figured I needed a tutor or something."

Greene asked an old friend, Jim Clark, to join them for lunch the next day. He hoped that Clark, a mathematician and Ph.D. in computer science who helped found pioneering Internet company Netscape Communications, among others, could give him some guidance. But after lunch at Nello's, a popular Upper East Side restaurant owned by one of Paulson's friends, Clark told Greene that he couldn't quite follow Paulson's idea either.

Back in Los Angeles, Greene couldn't stop thinking about Paulson's trade. Buying cheap insurance on other people's risky mortgages sounded too good to be true. Paulson said Greene couldn't do the trades by himself. But Greene had built a fortune on his own; maybe he could protect it with these mortgage investments.

G REENE HAD BEEN BORN in Worcester, Massachusetts, in a blue-collar community that seemed a galaxy removed from jet-set Los Angeles. Greene's father, Marshall, worked in the textile-machinery business, much like his own father before him, reselling machinery parts. Jeffrey sometimes tagged along as his father visited mills around New England, selling knitting spools, parts, and other machinery.

The Greene family owned a three-bedroom, one-bathroom home in a close-knit, mostly Jewish neighborhood. His mother, Barbara, taught Hebrew school three days a week. He had a sister who was two and a half years older, and a younger brother, eight years his junior. The family couldn't afford to send their three children to summer camp, but they rented a cozy two-bedroom house near Nantasket Beach on Massachusetts's South Shore, two blocks from the ocean.

Jeff was close to his maternal grandfather, a peddler from Eastern Europe who sold needles, thread, and other household items. Spooked by crime in the area, he had closed his store and gone door to door, extending credit to his neighborhood customers for their purchases. He often took his grandson along on his rounds.

Studious and clean-cut, Greene was on the verge of nerdy. He didn't touch drugs and he played the trumpet in his high-school band. He never had a serious girlfriend. Slow dancing to the Bee Gees in a friend's wood-paneled basement was as wild as it got for Greene.

Marshall Greene's business deteriorated in the late 1960s, as mills moved south seeking cheaper labor. So he followed his customers, traveling to cities like Chattanooga, Tennessee; Spartanburg, South Carolina; and Fort Oglethorpe, Georgia. When Marshall called home, his son could detect disappointment in his voice; it was a dramatic change for the normally affable salesman.

"He'd try to sound optimistic, but I could sense things weren't going well," Greene recalls.

His mother, a child in the Great Depression, was a genius at stretching the family's dollars, becoming a regular at Filene's Basement, the local discount giant. One year she fitted her children with irregular velour shirts; the stitching was a bit off but not so much that Greene's friends noticed. Marshall Greene had a very different perspective on money from his wife, spending whatever he made as quickly as it came in, leading to growing tension in their marriage.

"My parents always argued when I was growing up," Greene recalls.

Marshall bought a rubber stamp business for a time, and then became an auctioneer. Eventually he acquired a soda-vending business in West Palm Beach, Florida. Nothing really worked, though.

Making money came more naturally to his son. On snow days, Jeff Greene was the first up in the neighborhood, grabbing a shovel to clear neighborhood walkways, beating the better-off kids with their snowblowers. He mowed lawns, had a paper route, made $5 playing trumpet at Memorial Day parades, and caddied for the wealthy, saving enough money to eventually buy a used yellow Datsun 510.

When Marshall decided to move his family to Florida to be with him, Greene resisted, unwilling to leave his friends. So his parents let Greene, just fifteen at the time, move into a spare bedroom at a great-aunt's home.

"I didn't drive yet and she didn't, either," Greene says, "so I got a lot of rides."

During vacations, Jeff flew south to help with his father's business. They would load a van full of soft drinks to restock vending machines in local motels, businesses, and farms, sometimes donning long boots to walk through mud and around snakes.

"My dad was always proud," Greene recalls. "But he struggled the rest of his life."

When she wasn't teaching nursery school, his mother worked as a waitress at Palm Beach's storied Breakers Hotel.

In high school, Greene didn't particularly stand out. But he was part of a competitive class, many of whom gained acceptance to some of the top schools on the East Coast. Greene received a partial scholarship to attend Johns Hopkins University in Baltimore, a halfway point between his Boston home and his parents' in Florida. He took extra courses and graduated in three years, partly to save money.

One day in 1973, Greene spotted an advertisement in a local newspaper for "telephone sales positions." Few had heard of telephone marketing at the time, but Greene was intrigued. The pay, $2.50 an hour or commission, beat the $1.60 an hour minimum wage at the time. The job was to sell circus tickets to local business groups. Customers assumed the proceeds went to local police, firefighter, or other nonprofit groups, putting them at ease. But the businessmen running the telephone-sales operation usually took a healthy cut of the action.

On his first morning, Greene took a spot in a long row of seats and began making calls, using the standard pitch he was given.

"Hi, I'm calling for the Fraternal Police Association. We're sponsoring the circus at the Hippodrome this year. Care to buy some tickets?"

Greene barely made any sales. He wasn't much of a morning person, and he quickly became bored and frustrated.

After lunch, though, Greene returned in a better mood. He decided to improvise on the canned speech.

"Hey, how are you doing?!" he'd start, with great enthusiasm, as if he was a friendly neighbor. "The Fraternal Police are bringing the circus to town. Can we count on you?!"

By the end of the day, Greene was making six times more than anyone else in the office. He claimed a commission as his pay, forgoing the hourly rate.

"It wasn't much of a circus," Greene recalls. "The only elephant was the one on the ticket. But I was making a hundred dollars a day, and I realized I loved sales."

Greene stayed with the business and continued to work on his delivery. Soon he was making $500 a week, more than his father's salary. One day, the operation's manager pulled Greene aside, asking if he wanted to quit school and run his own circus-sales office in Virginia. Greene initially turned him down. But he noticed that his boss, just a year older than Greene, drove a Cadillac El Dorado. Clearly, much greater profits came to those running the operation. So he approached his boss. "Yeah, I'm ready to be a promoter."

His parents urged Greene to drop the idea, trying to convince him that the job was too risky and the flight south too expensive. But Greene grabbed the opportunity and proved a natural.

"We're bringing the holiday circus to town! Can we count on you again to buy a book of tickets? Great! Is it okay if we round that up to fifteen tickets?"

Greene spent the rest of the summer selling tickets. He found he could quickly read his customers, determining who might buy big blocks of tickets and who would be resistant, and he adopted unique methods to put customers at ease. When Greene dialed a family with an Irish-sounding surname, he introduced himself as Jeff O'Hara. With an Italian family, he'd adopt an Italian surname. Sometimes he'd even slip in an ethnic accent, mimicking whoever answered the phone, perhaps working in some Yiddish or even an Irish lilt.

"Just from their tone and pauses I could tell how hard I had to push," Greene recalls.

He traveled to Savannah, Georgia, to set up another office, hiring eighteen young people, including someone to run the operation and report to Greene. Twenty percent of the profits went to the local Knights of Columbus, 40 percent went to the company, and 40 percent went to Greene, out of which he paid his crew. In just three weeks he made $1,000.

The next summer, after finishing his final exams, Greene picked up where he had left off, pocketing $10,000 working out of the back of a small local business and living in an Econo Lodge, eating buffet dinners at Pizza Hut or Sizzler.

"All my friends were drinking and having a good time," Greene says, "but I'd hit the road."

After finishing college in 1974, Greene managed phone operations in small cities like Rome, Georgia; Jamestown, Virginia; and Gettysburg, Pennsylvania; racking up thousands of miles on his Grand Am. Local businesses remembered Greene fondly from previous circus seasons, and Greene soon was making almost $1,000 a day.

After a few years, Greene had banked $100,000, a remarkable sum at the time for a young man his age. It was enough to pay his way at Harvard Business School, which he entered in September 1977.

A serious student, Greene nonetheless continued to run the circus business. His first year, he made $50,000, more than most graduates of the school, and became eager to invest his growing profits. Real estate was one obvious possibility; Greene chatted about housing with businessmen at local Kiwanis Clubs when he called to pitch circus tickets, and sometimes discussed it with the owners of the circus business.

A few friends of Greene's were profiting by buying three-decker apartments in the Harvard area; they would live in one of the apartments rent-free, and rent out the other two. Greene got in touch with an agent in nearby Somerville, a blue-collar community, and agreed to buy a three-decker apartment for $37,000, using $7,000 as a down payment. Days later, Greene was offered inexpensive student housing on campus, but he decided to go through with the purchase and to rent all three of the apartments.

"My parents said it's a headache, don't do it," Greene says. "But I really liked real estate."

Greene made hundreds of dollars each month and was quickly bitten by the real estate bug.

I've gotta own more of these! he thought.

So he bought more three-deckers, charging graduate students $750 a month for each apartment, a bargain compared with the rent in nearby Cambridge. He fixed up dilapidated properties and rented those, too. By his second year at Harvard, Greene was buying homes, refinancing them, and purchasing still more; by the end of the year, he owned eighteen properties. He convinced a classmate, Jeffrey Libert, later John Paulson's first boss at Boston Consulting Group, to buy properties for himself.

Greene was constantly on the phone with circus promoters, tenants, and mortgage lenders. He wouldn't miss a class, but sometimes he had little time to read the required case studies.

"He doesn't read—it's an attention-deficit issue—so he'd call me up and say, 'How much have you read?'" recalls Libert. "But he could spot the smartest guy in the class and pick his brain and pump him for information. That's Jeff's skill."

Greene had taken advantage of the moribund real estate market of the mid-1970s to buy properties inexpensively. Soon the market raced back, sending the value of his properties climbing. It left the twenty-six-year-old wealthier than the parents of some of his classmates.

In 1979, his father, a two-pack-a-day cigarette smoker, suffered a massive heart attack, dying at the age of fifty-one. It was a sad end to an often frustrating business career, and it left a deep impression on his son.

"I realized I didn't want to lose a career like my dad did, and struggle week to week," Greene recalls.

After graduation, Greene set out for Los Angeles, staying in a month-to-month rental in Sherman Oaks, close to a few relatives. Later he bought a one-bedroom condominium in the upscale Brentwood neighborhood.

Greene had never had much of a social life up to this point. He was younger than most of his classmates in high school and college, and his summers had been spent on the road selling circus tickets.

But Greene took to the Los Angeles party scene like a bear coming out of hibernation. He bought a silver Mercedes convertible and a 3,000-square-foot, $385,000 home in the mountains of Bel Air, with a pool and a Jacuzzi. At the age of twenty-six, his real estate was worth well over $1 million. He quickly became known as the Harvard-educated boy wonder and was coveted at parties and at the hottest clubs. Even his Worcester accent, marked by his dropped r's, helped him to stand out.

"Out there I was considered a genius because my background was different," he says. "All of a sudden I had this amazing social life and—oh my God—there were all these hot girls everywhere."

Invited to a backgammon tournament, he found himself facing off against Lucille Ball, a childhood idol. Later in the evening, he spotted Frank Sinatra.

Greene assumed he would continue to invest in real estate in Los Angeles, just as he had in Boston, but he couldn't quite figure out the West Coast market. He was accustomed to buying a property only if he could make a profit renting it, a straightforward calculation. In Los Angeles, however, Greene kept getting outbid; owners seemed happy just to break even with their rental properties. They were much more focused on flipping properties and taking a profit than charging monthly rent.

Uneasy playing that game, Greene decided to branch out. He already had a crew of one hundred people working for him making circus calls. Maybe they could sell tickets to other events that Greene could organize?

He searched for wholesome, family-oriented music groups, signing the New Christy Minstrels, which once had included John Denver and Kenny Rogers and was best known for the song "This Land Is Your Land." They committed to forty dates around the country and made Greene an immediate profit.

Next, Greene hired acts like the Serendipity Singers, Gary Lewis and the Playboys, Glenn Yarborough, and Rick Nelson, one-time wonders thrilled to extend their careers. Together they netted Greene more than $1 million in 1984.

Attorneys general around the country were cracking down on misleading telephone sales, however, and Greene received a warning letter that his callers didn't fully disclose how much of the tickets' proceeds went to charity. He didn't want to push his luck, so in 1986 he closed down his company to focus exclusively on the local real estate market.

If he had to buy high and sell even higher in Los Angeles, Greene decided to buy aggressively. He started with an eight-unit apartment building in the Brentwood area. Soon, he held $15 million of properties. As the market soared, his properties grew in value to about $110 million over the next six years. Minus the $80 million Greene owed to the banks, that gave him a net worth of roughly $30 million. He ran a thirty-five-person company to manage all the properties; lenders shoveled money at him.

"I was buying aggressively, using crazy, short-term loans," Greene says.

The collapse of the California real estate market in the early 1990s caught Greene flat-footed. He figured there might be a slowdown, eventually, but everything seemed to crumble at once, even his best properties. His holdings—five office buildings and about 350 apartments—suddenly were worth just $50 million while Greene was facing debt of $60 million. His lenders threatened to foreclose on Greene's properties, leaving him broke. He had to find a way to pay them back in full. It was the first crisis in a charmed business life.

"I was blindsided; I didn't see it coming," Greene says. "It was like someone flipped a switch—there were no yellow lights. Every day I said, 'What do I do?'"

Greene had built a 10,000-square-foot home for himself in Brentwood, with dramatic views of the Pacific Ocean to the south, views to the west of the Santa Monica mountains, and a hundred-year-old pine forest to the southwest. Desperately needing cash, he was forced to rent it out, making as much as $50,000 a month from the likes of singer Diana Ross. But a dispute with one tenant, actor and director Ron Howard, put still more pressure on Greene's finances.

Greene held his lenders at bay, waiting for a recovery he was sure was just around the corner. Things only got worse, though; soon each of his properties was worth less than their debt. Loan payments were coming due, but Greene couldn't find any buyers. It got so bad that Greene was afraid to answer his door, thinking he might be served with a lawsuit.

Greene owed Glendale Federal more than $50 million. He agreed to give the bank a few of his buildings, trimming his debt to $35 million. But Greene's cash flow was dropping even faster. He stayed up all night, making projection after projection, trying to find a way out of the mess. After all his years of hard work and success, he had nothing to show for it. Worse than that, Greene owed more than he was worth.

One day in 1994, Greene asked to meet a Glendale senior vice president. Sitting across from the VP and several of his staff members in a small conference room, Greene launched into an upbeat analysis of his holdings, detailing a plan to make a few sales, refinance some loans, and pay his debts.

After outlining each step in his plan, however, he received the same response from the VP: "Nyet."

At the end, the VP gave it to him one last time: "Nyet. Nyet. Nyet."

"I didn't know how I would get out of it," Greene recalls.

In 1995, just as Greene was ready to throw in the towel, the Los Angeles market slowly began to improve; a year later, his properties were valued at several million more than their debt. Greene sold a building to the Getty Museum for $12 million, allowing him to breathe a little easier. Rather than pay down his loans, though, he bought three buildings that sellers were unloading at what seemed like bargain-basement prices.

Over the next few years, Greene bought all he could, taking advantage of those who were licking their wounds and eager to dump properties at prices that were a fraction of their replacement costs.

Greene used fixed-rate, ten-year, nonrecourse mortgage loans, eschewing the supercheap, adjustable-rate mortgages that he once relied on. As quickly as he could, Greene refinanced his loans at lower rates, keeping the cost of his debt low.

Once again, Greene was a favorite of local brokers. They knew he'd pay top dollar if he liked a new property, just based on its description.

"I would refinance a building and fifteen minutes later use the cash for another closing," Greene says. "It was a fast-moving train and I didn't want to get off."

By 2003, Greene owned real estate that by some accounts was worth $800 million. He lived large in a grand, 15,000-square-foot home in the Hollywood Hills once owned by comedian W.C. Fields and hosted late-night parties with models, celebrities, and other new friends. He was named by *Vanity Fair* magazine as a top figure in Los Angeles's after-hours scene. Heidi Fleiss, the Hollywood madam, spent a year in Greene's guesthouse after leaving an abusive relationship, joining Greene for Passover dinner with his mother. Greene rented his Brentwood home to stars including Angelina Jolie, 50 Cent, and Mariah Carey.

He had few serious girlfriends, playing a game of sexual catch-and-release with an assortment of willing women, including Russian models new to Los Angeles.

"I would always jump ship because there was always a busload of new women coming into town," Greene acknowledges.

His mother grew worried that he'd never settle down.

"You have all these beautiful chicks, why don't you go with one that's wife material?" she would ask on visits to Los Angeles.

"What's wife material?" Greene responded, noting that several of his friends had divorced. Privately, though, he began to ask the same questions.

For all the wheeling and dealing, Greene's wealth existed largely on paper, based on the assumed value of his properties. And it made him nervous.

"In the back of my mind I always remembered the earlier period," Greene says.

As Greene traveled around the country, he couldn't quite figure out why real estate was soaring. Friends in Miami, where real estate was on fire, said an influx of South Americans was buying up homes in the region, an explanation that seemed far-fetched to Greene.

"How many rich South Americans are there? And do they need thousands of condos?"

Greene sold some buildings, but the market climbed still higher. He decided his caution was misplaced and began buying properties once again.

By 2005, however, his travels made him warier. Greene and a girlfriend had boarded his 145-foot yacht, *Summerwind,* for a two-month cruise starting in Spain and visiting Istanbul and cities along the Black Sea, stopping at Kiev, Odessa, and Yalta. At various stops they were joined by an assortment of friends and acquaintances, including Mike Tyson; David Baron, Greene's rabbi at the Beverly Hills Temple Shalom for the Arts; and Ali Karacan, a friend from Turkey. Two Ukrainian strippers made cameo appearances, and Greene hired stewardesses from coastal towns to serve as his crew.* Some doubled as massage therapists, which came in handy after a day of scuba diving, Jet Skiing, or kayaking.

By day, they viewed half-finished real estate projects dotting the coast. At night, they partied with locals. Sometimes local dignitaries came aboard to dine with Greene, feasting on baby lamb chops grilled to order by his chef or dipping into big bowls of caviar. In each city, the Communist-era political figures pitched real estate projects they were developing; the mayor of Constanta, a Romanian port city, tried to sell Greene a multimillion-dollar coastal development.

"This is crazy," Greene said to Ali. "Everyone wants to be a developer—is the whole world trading real estate? Who would buy at these prices?"

Back home, the pilot of Greene's Gulfstream jet peppered him with questions about getting into the real estate market. Greene shook his head in growing disbelief.

By the spring of 2006, Greene stopped buying real estate, convinced that things had gotten out of hand. He was unsure what to do, though. Greene didn't want to sell his properties and write a huge check to the government to pay the tax bill. But he had to protect himself from an-

---

*Greene later would say, "Maybe some on board thought they were strippers, but they weren't. They were just cute girls."

other real estate collapse. John Paulson's trade seemed the best one he had heard.

After returning from New York, Greene spoke with Gary Winnick, a former top bond trader, and Fred Sands, a major local Realtor; neither had much insight into Paulson's trade, and neither wanted to invest alongside Greene.

"I like to go in on investments with others, to give me validation," he says. "But no one wanted to do the trade with me."

Greene kept asking why anyone would sell insurance on iffy mortgages so cheaply. Who was on the other side of Paulson's trades?

Greene asked Sands to call his friend Angelo Mozilo, Countrywide's CEO, to see what he thought of the subprime trade. Sands relayed a message from Mozilo: "You'll never make money, it's a bad idea.... You'll keep paying out the insurance premiums because everything will be fine."

A broker at Goldman Sachs told Greene it was like earthquake insurance, a waste of money. "Don't touch this stuff," the broker said.

But articles in local newspapers and business magazines claimed few could afford to buy a home at present-day prices. Greene figured he must be missing something.

He got in touch with Jeffrey Libert, his classmate from Harvard Business School who was running a successful real estate investment firm after leaving Boston Consulting Group, where he worked with John Paulson.

"Jeffrey, I was a subprime lender in the 1980s; it's a horrible business," Libert told his friend.

"Well, it's a trillion-dollar business now on Wall Street."

"You're kidding me!"

"We have to short it," Greene said emphatically, hoping his friend would do the trade with him. "CDS seems to be the way."

Greene considered giving Paulson a $20 million investment. But he wasn't sure he was ready to tie up so much money in an idea that still seemed confusing. Perhaps he could figure out which derivatives Paulson was buying and just do the trade himself.

"Part of me is thinking I should tell him," Greene recalls. "But who knows if I'll even stick with it?"

He called a contact at Countrywide, trying to understand some of the aggressive loans they were making.

"So how do these 'stated income' loans work? How do people get loans without any verification?"

The Countrywide representative told Greene that lenders weren't allowed to ask an employer for proof of an employee's salary.

"So we just go to salary.com, look up a job, see what the highest salary is," and place that on the loan application, she explained.

Greene immediately realized the implication: An architect, teacher, or accountant in Nevada or Texas might not make half the salary of someone in the same profession in New York or a few other high-income states. But on a mortgage application, they'd be able to claim the same high compensation to buy a home they couldn't really afford.

"How else do you think they can afford these homes?" a friend in the mortgage business asked Greene, after sharing a few more secrets to getting a huge mortgage.

Greene drove to Riverside County and other areas in Southern California to meet mortgage brokers. He discovered that the only way some subprime borrowers were able to keep up with their payments was by refinancing their homes, sometimes as many as three times a year.

"It was like, 'Aha, so that's how it's done!'" Greene recalls.

Some in the bond business warned Greene that if he agreed to pay millions a year to buy insurance on mortgages and housing held up, he'd go broke. But if most subprime borrowers refinanced their mortgages in three years or so, he realized he likely only would be on the hook for a few years of payments on the CDS insurance.

Greene was convinced Paulson was onto something with his trade. Greene had set out simply to find protection for his holdings. But he became convinced he had uncovered a superhot trade. He phoned his broker at Merrill Lynch, Alan Zafran, telling him about John Paulson's idea. He asked Zafran to do the same trades for him.

"I gotta tell you, this isn't bread and butter for a retail brokerage account," Zafran told him.

Zafran had heard of John Paulson and his firm, and the idea behind the trade made some sense to him. But Zafran, who claimed some of the largest accounts at the brokerage firm, doubted Merrill Lynch would let him make these kinds of complicated trades for an individual like Greene.

Days later, Zafran's bosses confirmed they wouldn't allow the trades. On paper, Greene's net worth was several hundred million dollars, but the vast majority of it was tied up in real estate. He had $50 million in his Merrill account—a huge sum for an individual, but tiny compared with the big firms that traded credit-default swaps.

Zafran heard rumors that Paul Allen, the cofounder of Microsoft, had been turned down by his Goldman Sachs broker after requesting to do the same trade. It seemed an even longer shot that Greene would get a green light.

"You're a two-legged individual; you're not a hedge fund. It can't be done," Zafran said.

Greene hardly flinched.

"You're a smart guy—figure out a way."

Greene kept pushing Zafran, day after day, needling him that he might take his business elsewhere. Zafran searched for other executives at his firm who might approve the trade, but they kept turning him down. Derivative trades were too complex for most individuals, the Merrill officials said. The firm didn't want to open itself up to a lawsuit if big losses resulted. Zafran didn't tell Greene about all of the slammed doors at the firm, wary of how he'd react.

"You're not trying hard enough," Greene would tell Zafran. "Keep trying."

In early May, Zafran finally found a few sympathetic executives at his firm who were looking for a way to help individuals buy housing protection. They said they would do their best to help Zafran as long as Greene signed a form saying his trade was an "unsolicited transaction" and a one-time event. More than a dozen Merrill Lynch executives had to sign off, but Greene was thrilled—he had become the first individual to buy CDS contracts.

Greene already had cherry-picked thirteen BBB-rated slices of mortgage bonds backed by what seemed to be especially risky mortgages, all from borrowers with poor credit history in areas such as California and Nevada. Most had low teaser rates that would climb after two years and bought homes with no equity. The bond slices were worth $15 million each, or $195 million in total. Greene purchased CDS insurance contracts on them all at an annual cost of about 1.25 percent for each contract. His derivative investments would cost about $2.4 million a year. But if the mortgage debt ever became worthless, Greene's insurance could be worth $195 million.

Days later, Greene got the go-ahead from Zafran to buy insurance on $75 million more BBB mortgage bond slices. By the end of May, he had purchased protection on $350 million with mortgage bonds, as well as CDS protection on another $250 million of various ABX indexes, developed by a group of banks to reflect the value of a basket of subprime mortgages made over the previous six months. Greene even bought some protection on seemingly safer A-rated mortgage slices. It was so cheap, he couldn't say no.

He kept on buying, finding a broker at J.P. Morgan Chase also willing to sell the investments to him. After a flurry of trades, Greene agreed to pay about $12 million annually in insurance premiums for CDS contracts protecting just over $1 billion of bonds backed by subprime mortgages.

He worried that he was missing something, though. A month or so later, Greene was invited to sit with Jamie Dimon, the chief executive officer of J.P. Morgan Chase, in the bank's private suite at the U.S. Open in New York. Greene was excited. Finally, a pro could weigh in on his moves and tell him if he was missing anything.

I'm just a beginner figuring it all out. He's the expert!

Dimon bounded over, a warm smile on his face. This was Greene's chance. He could hardly contain himself.

"Hey, Jamie. My biggest position is shorting subprime credit through credit-default swaps. I've done four hundred million with you guys."

Dimon had a blank look on his face. "What's that?" he asked.

Greene was taken aback. Dimon was among the most important players in the financial markets. But he didn't seem to know much about credit-default swaps. Even the $400 million figure didn't grab his attention. Dimon kept glancing at the tennis match below, where Roger

Federer was fending off Novak Đjoković in the finals. Then Dimon looked around the suite, smiling at his other guests.

Greene thought maybe he just needed to explain it better. He outlined his trades to Dimon as best he could, speaking quickly and growing more excited with each detail. Greene was sure J.P. Morgan was buying the same derivatives. Or maybe the bank had discovered a hidden flaw in the trade. Greene was on pins and needles to hear Dimon's reaction.

Dimon had little reaction, though. *He's either bored or doesn't understand the trades,* Greene realized. *How could that be?*

Dimon soon excused himself to greet other clients.

Back in Los Angeles, Merrill Lynch's Alan Zafran called a handful of his best customers, pitching trades similar to Greene's. A few liked the idea and told him to go forward. But Merrill Lynch's head of compliance put his foot down, allowing only one client to place a trade, on a much smaller scale than Greene.

Greene had gotten in just under the wire.

A S GREENE EDUCATED HIMSELF about the mortgage market, he continued to stay in touch with Paulson, e-mailing him insights about the market that he gleaned from conversations with various mortgage brokers. Paulson never followed up, though. Greene figured he was too busy, or just didn't find his musings and tidbits of news that interesting.

In June, Greene made plans to sail his yacht to the Hamptons and New England. He was excited about seeing Paulson and a few other friends, as well as hosting a fortieth-birthday bash for Mike Tyson in Sag Harbor.

Before leaving, Greene sent Paulson an e-mail saying he now was interested in investing in his new fund. He mentioned that he'd done some of the trades by himself and had some questions.

Paulson fired an e-mail back.

"What trades?"

"The ones we discussed."

"I can't believe you did the trades; you went behind my back," Paulson wrote. Greene, caught off-guard, could tell Paulson was fuming.

"Should I unwind it, J.P.?"

"Yes, unwind it."

Greene spent a few days thinking about whether to exit the trades. He didn't want to anger his friend and thought he might not have done them properly.

It's so fucking complicated, maybe I should just let him do it.

But Greene had done so much research, and the investments were hard to unwind because they didn't trade very frequently. So Greene decided to hold on to his trades. It was a decision that would cost him dearly.

8.

JOHN PAULSON WASN'T FINDING MANY INVESTORS WILLING TO TAKE A chance on his new fund. If it was going to get off the ground, he'd have to turn to friends and family. Jeffrey Tarrant, his tennis buddy, finally convinced his partners to pony up $60 million from their investors. A few of Tarrant's clients put several million dollars of their own into Paulson's new fund. The parents of Andrew Hoine, one of Paulson's executives, pitched in a few hundred thousand dollars. And Paulson drained a personal savings account at his local bank, J.P. Morgan Chase, to invest about $30 million of his own, almost all of the money he held outside his firm.

The total was just $147 million, a puny sum in an era when new funds sometimes launched with billions of dollars. Even some of those who signed up weren't true believers. A few were real estate pros seeking to protect their holdings. Privately, they confided that they wouldn't mind if Paulson flamed out because that would mean good things for their real estate portfolio.

Like hunters waiting on their prey, Paulson and his team eyed home prices, searching for a sign of weakness as a signal to pull the trigger on their trade.

One morning in early June, Brad Rosenberg raced into Paulson's office clutching a news release fresh off the printer: Data from the National Association of Realtors showed that home prices had risen a paltry 1 percent over the previous twelve months. Paulson flashed a grin—this was just what he was hoping for. His team already had anticipated that if housing prices went flat the BBB-rated slices of all the mortgage bonds would start to see losses. That time seemed at hand.

It was "a defining moment," Paulson says.

Every trader up and down Wall Street pored over the same data that morning. Paulson worried that his window of opportunity was in danger of closing. And yet he sat on his hands. His other funds had purchased mortgage insurance, but Paulson hadn't made a single trade for his new "credit" fund dedicated to betting against housing. He realized that if he was going to swing for the fences, it was now or never. Any more delay and he risked missing it all.

The $147 million would have to be enough, he decided, at least to start. So Paulson formally launched his fund and told Rosenberg to start buying.

A short, bespectacled thirty-four-year old, Rosenberg had worked at the hedge fund for four years. He sat right outside Paulson's office, close enough to share market intelligence throughout the day. He tended to get to work early, usually greeted Paulson around 8 a.m., and often wished him a good-night after 6 p.m.

But Rosenberg still didn't know what made his boss tick. They exchanged few pleasantries. Paulson had never met his wife or family, and Rosenberg couldn't remember having a single personal conversation.

That was true of most of Paulson's staff. Rosenberg didn't mind the lack of camaraderie, though. The son of a Long Island shoe-sales executive and a graduate of Tulane University, he was focused, serious, and bookish. The only adornment on his desk was a faux turtle made of two rocks and cardboard, a present from his young son. He didn't wish for a high five after a successful trade—he was just as uncomfortable with that kind of celebration as Paulson.

From the moment Paulson gave him the green light, the pressure was on Rosenberg to buy as much mortgage protection as possible before it rose in price. At the same time, he had to avoid tipping off competitors to prevent them from copying the idea and driving up prices of the CDS contracts. Rosenberg began working the phones, placing orders with major banks up and down Wall Street to spend the $147 million on insurance for mortgage slices with BBB ratings, trying to be as casual about it as possible.

"So what's the level here?" he asked one trader, as calmly as he could,

fishing for a price quote. Later, Rosenberg placed a contact on hold, trying to convey marked indifference, before getting back on the line to do
some buying. Rosenberg's customary lack of emotion came in handy—
few of the brokers seemed to have a clue how desperate he was to buy
boatloads of the CDS insurance. Paulson often stood over Rosenberg's
shoulder, a slightly intimidating presence; Rosenberg ignored him and
kept on calling.

He hit immediate pay dirt. Each time Rosenberg asked to buy protection, as many as a half-dozen banks offered shockingly inexpensive
prices. The reaction confounded Paulson—it was as if the bull market
for housing was just beginning, rather than showing signs of age.

Didn't anyone else see the news today about housing prices?

Paulson raced to do even more buying.

"It was like a vacuum, people just sucked it up," Paulson recalls. "We'd
send lists of what protection we wanted to buy and it would get snapped
up. I couldn't believe it."

When the ABX index tracking subprime mortgages was introduced
in July 2006, Paulson's team immediately bought CDS protection on
that, too. It was yet another arrow in their quiver. The cost was a bit
more expensive than for the CDS contracts he had been buying on slices
of selected mortgage bonds, but the ABX was more heavily traded,
promising Paulson an easier exit later on. The fund even purchased a bit
of insurance on the index tracking supposedly safer, A-rated slices of
subprime mortgage bonds.

At first, traders were happy to sell CDS insurance to Paulson, thrilled
at the mounting commissions. By selling Paulson mortgage protection,
they also could create product for bullish investment vehicles to buy.

At Morgan Stanley, a trader hung up the phone after yet another
Paulson order and turned to a colleague in disbelief.

"This guy is nuts," he said with a chuckle, amazed that Paulson was
agreeing to make so many annual insurance payments. "He's just going
to pay it all out?"

Soon, however, the traders began to wonder when all the buying
would stop. The more CDS insurance they sold Paulson, the more they
were on the hook to find bullish investors willing to take the other side

of the transactions. Some worried that they might be stuck with Paulson's trades if they couldn't find enough investors to take the contracts off their hands, a dangerous position if housing crumbled.

Others seemed to be making the trades for their own banks' investment vehicles, relying on mathematical models that deemed it safe to sell protection to Paulson. If he bought much more, though, the price of the insurance investments the banks were selling might go up, dealing losses to their own investment vehicles.

Josh Birnbaum, Goldman Sachs's top trader of CDS protection on the ABX index, kept calling Rosenberg, asking how much protection Paulson ultimately planned to buy. When Paulson and Pellegrini got wind of Birnbaum's inquiries, they told Rosenberg to keep him in the dark. They worried that Birnbaum might raise his prices on the CDS insurance if he knew more buying was on the way.

Birnbaum persisted, asking to come by the office. A slim thirty-four-year-old who looked several years younger despite streaks of silver in his hair, Birnbaum came alone. Sitting across from Paulson, Pellegrini, and Rosenberg in a small conference room, he quickly got to the point.

"If you want to keep selling, I'll keep buying," he said. "We have a few clients who will take the other side of your trades. And I'll join them."

Birnbaum was trying to tell Paulson he was making a big mistake. Not only were Birnbaum's clients eager to wager against him, but Birnbaum was, too. He urged caution if Paulson's team was going to stay bearish on even safer parts of the subprime market.

"Look, we've done the work and we don't see them taking losses," Birnbaum said.

Some on Paulson's team couldn't figure out what Birnbaum was up to. Was he truly looking out for them or did he want to discourage the firm from shorting more of the ABX index? Was he afraid their trading might cost Goldman?

"It felt foolishly presumptuous to suggest we knew better than Goldman," with its army of professionals and sterling reputation, Pellegrini recalls.

After Birnbaum left, Rosenberg walked into Paulson's office, a bit shaken. Birnbaum was the expert on the market—should they change their stance?

Paulson seemed unmoved. "Keep buying, Brad," Paulson told Rosenberg.

Almost as soon as Birnbaum returned to Goldman's trading floor, Rosenberg phoned him to place more bets against the ABX.

"Really??" Birnbaum responded, apparently surprised that he hadn't persuaded them to stop.

Paulson invited mortgage experts from Bear Stearns to challenge his team to make sure they weren't missing anything. The group walked into the "Park" conference room, next to Pellegrini's office. The room featured a long set of windows looking north. In past meetings, the view sometimes proved distracting. Inside a gleaming, glass building across the street was a huge showroom with a long runway where female models sometimes gathered, wearing revealing Christian Dior swimsuits.

This afternoon there was less to ogle. The Bear Stearns team, among the most bullish on Wall Street, began by saying that subprime-mortgage losses of more than 3 percent were highly unlikely and that BBB slices of mortgage deals wouldn't fall much.

"You guys are good customers and we're concerned about you," one Bear pro said. "You guys need to do more research on historical price appreciation."

"What are your models based on?" Paulson responded. "The market has changed—now you can get a loan without any documentation. Are you including that in your models?"

"Our models are fine," the Bear Stearns expert responded, polite but self-assured. "We've been doing this for twenty years."

Scott Eichel, a senior Bear Stearns trader, chimed in that buying a huge amount of mortgage protection on a few mortgage pools was misguided. Don't concentrate your bets, he warned.

Eichel was struck by the thesis of the Paulson team. It sounded too simple for a firm that he suspected had placed billions of dollars of trades. Didn't they understand the complexities of the mortgage market?

Pellegrini listened closely to the conversation, displaying little emotion. He became convinced that some of the executives didn't fully believe their own arguments. They simply were aiming to stop Paulson from shorting so much and causing trouble for Bear Stearns, Pellegrini concluded. He quietly seethed.

Two could play this game, Pellegrini eventually decided. He started to act as if he was having second thoughts about his bearish stance, pretending he was being swayed by the arguments of the guests.

As the meeting wrapped up, Pellegrini turned to the Bear Stearns executives with a smile. "We really appreciate the help; thanks, guys." He didn't dare reveal what really was on his mind.

"We said, 'Oh, thank you for your help,' but really we were saying 'Fuck you,'" Pellegrini recalls. "We were both pretending."

Paulson remained poker-faced during most of the firm's meetings with the Wall Street pros. He digested their points and made doubly sure he hadn't missed anything, but he didn't hint at how bearish he truly was. If he wanted to keep buying at inexpensive prices, Paulson couldn't reveal his true appetite for the insurance.

"They concluded that I was an inexperienced manager," he recalls. "I had to play dumb. But I got tired of people saying I was stupid or wrong."

Although the new fund wasn't large, there weren't many others doing much buying of mortgage protection, so Paulson's activity quickly became the buzz of the market. Over the next few months, he received checks from new clients who sensed that housing might be peaking. He put the money to work, placing even more trades. Paulson's team soon became more fearful about rivals catching on. When some of his investors shared details of the fund's tactics, Paulson turned furious, installing technology to prevent clients from forwarding his e-mails.

Paulson called on Hank Greenberg, the founder of insurance giant American International Group, to see if his investment firm, C.V. Starr, wanted to invest in the Paulson fund. AIG had spent the last few years selling tens of billions of dollars of CDS contracts on subprime mortgages, and Paulson knew AIG could be at risk if housing crumbled. An investment in Paulson's fund might be a good way to offset that position, he argued.

Greenberg and his team didn't know Paulson, though, so they asked an outside specialist, Anauth Crishnamurthy, to vet the idea. Visiting the firm after the close of trading one day, Crishnamurthy grilled Pellegrini and Jim Wong, Paulson's head of investor relations, pushing for details of their moves. When Paulson dropped by the meeting, Crishnamurthy asked why C.V. Starr should pay the hedge fund to invest in the ABX index when it could do that on its own.

"What's your trading advantage?"

"That doesn't matter," Paulson responded. "The bonds are going to zero."

Listening to Crishnamurthy's detailed questions, the Paulson team worried that he might steal the trade and teach his bosses to do it themselves.

After the meeting broke up, Pellegrini pulled aside Wong, saying, "Don't waste your time with him."

Paulson pored over mortgage-servicing reports and noticed rising delinquencies among borrowers. The Fed already had raised its short-term interest rate back to 5.25 percent from 4.25 percent at the beginning of the year. Borrowers surely would come under more pressure.

In July 2006, Paulson got more enthused. Option One Mortgage Company, a subprime lending unit of H&R Block that was accounting for about half of the profits of the tax-filing company, reported poor earnings and acknowledged problems with loans it had issued. So many customers were skipping even their first payments that the company was being forced to take mortgages back from banks to which it had sold them.

"It was one of the first signals that something was wrong with the business," Paulson recalls.

As Paulson's confidence grew, he couldn't resist bidding on a 6,800-square-foot, seven-bedroom home in Southampton with an indoor glass-enclosed pool, agreeing to a $12.75 million purchase.

In the summer of 2006, Paulson and his wife and daughters joined Bruce Goodman and his family at the fashionable Southampton Bath and Tennis Club for lunch. After their meal, the old friends walked to the beach to watch Paulson's daughters play on the sand. As they chatted about work, Paulson seemed cagier than usual, as if he was hiding some big secret.

Finally, Paulson opened up: "I'm working on a situation where I've made a major investment of my personal funds," Paulson confided. "Bruce, if this works out, it will be extraordinary."

Paulson beamed—Goodman hadn't seen his friend this excited in years. He pushed for details of what Paulson was up to but all he got was an impish smile.

"I'd love to tell you, Bruce, but I can't," Paulson said.

Paulson's trade started off with a thud, however, as the price of his protection slipped in August. Complicating matters, the Federal Reserve stopped raising interest rates, worried that if they got too high, home owners would feel pressure. Some investors expected the Fed to lower rates at some point, and mortgage costs fell in anticipation. It seemed that housing might survive. Paulson's trade might be a bust.

At home, Paulson's wife, Jenny, expressed concerns, asking her husband if he was having second thoughts.

"It's just a matter of waiting," he reassured her, before heading out to Central Park for his three-mile run.

Friends phoned to see if Paulson was going to cut his losses and exit some of his positions.

"How are you holding up?" Peter Soros asked. "What are you going to do?"

"I'm adding to the bet," he responded.

The way Paulson saw it, it wasn't bad news that these CDS investments remained unpopular and he was losing a bit of money. Instead, it was an "absolute gift" because it allowed him to buy even more, he told a friend.

Peter Soros was so impressed by Paulson's conviction that he invested in the fund, after months of sitting on the fence. Soon, Paulson's fund was up to $700 million, and he made plans to start a second fund to make additional wagers.

Paulson and Pellegrini soon realized that they had made a major mistake in their trade, however. Data emerged that home prices had dropped almost 2 percent in 2006. But most of the subprime mortgages that the firm had bet against were handed out before 2006, and were for homes that already had appreciated in value. These borrowers were unlikely to run into problems because they easily could refinance their mortgages. Paulson had taken aim at the wrong target.

"We were too early," Pellegrini acknowledges. "Even though home prices were down over the previous year, people in the market didn't care."

Paulson walked out of his office toward Rosenberg's desk, a new plan in hand. "We've got to roll everything," he told his trader. "We need protection on the latest vintages"—in other words, on houses that had not enjoyed any appreciation; those owners would not be able to refinance because they had no equity in their homes.

Quietly, Rosenberg traded the firm's CDS protection for similar insurance on more recent mortgages. Once again, Paulson and Pellegrini chose the riskiest subprime bonds to insure. Not only were they made to borrowers with sketchy histories but they were made at a time when home prices no longer were rising.

Rosenberg called every contact he had to get his hands on more mortgage protection.

"What do you have, what do you have?" Rosenberg asked trader after trader. He made himself something of a pest. On Fridays in the summer, when some senior traders took their time getting back to him, hoping to push off the transaction to Monday and get an early jump on the weekend, Rosenberg kept after them, prodding them with repeated calls.

Luckily for Paulson & Co., the exchange for insurance on the latest mortgages proved relatively painless because the ABX index tracking the most recent mortgages remained around 100, close to the level where it began trading, reflecting continuing enthusiasm for housing. Because the index was so high, the cost of the CDS contracts on the mortgages remained cheap. Paulson had dodged a bullet.

O UT ON THE WEST COAST, Jeff Greene was experiencing more serious setbacks. He had placed his own trades a few months before Paulson launched his fund. As the market continued to rally in the summer of 2006 and the cost of mortgage protection fell further, it caused Greene deeper losses than Paulson was experiencing. By the summer, Greene was down about $5 million.

He ached to reach out to his old friend, to discuss the market and ask whether he should hold on to his trades. And Greene still remained interested in Paulson's fund. But Greene's account was down so much, he was even less eager to exit his trades and lock in the losses. He knew he had to confess to Paulson that he had kept his investments, despite Paulson's demand that he sell them.

Sitting in his Malibu home, the wind chimes playing a gentle tune, Greene booted up his computer and wrote a new e-mail to Paulson. When he had finished, he took a deep breath and pressed the send button. In his e-mail, Greene had written that he was looking forward to getting together when he was back on the East Coast. He asked if he could still invest in Paulson's fund. Then Greene casually mentioned that he still held his own subprime trades.

Greene quickly got a sense of Paulson's reaction: He was livid.

"I don't want you in my fund," Paulson fired back in an e-mail. "You're not an honorable person."

Paulson stormed out of his office to alert his staff not to have anything more to do with Greene.

A few days later, Paulson called Jeffrey Tarrant, sounding hurt: "You build a relationship with someone and this is what happens?"

"We really could have used Greene's money at the time," Paulson said later, explaining why he felt so betrayed. "And he said he unwound the trade after I asked him to and he didn't."

Greene felt some regret over his actions, and his friend's reaction. But a part of him also wondered what the big deal was. Paulson had given him dozens of investment tips over the years. He had acted on most of them. And Paulson had told dozens of investors about the trade; he already owned billions of insurance protection. Surely the word was out. *It's not like it's a secret*, he thought to himself.

"He never told me 'Don't do it,'" Greene says.

For Greene, the dustup was a downer, especially since few of his other friends managed to find brokers willing to place the trades for them.

"It was lonely," Greene says.

Greene never did see Paulson on his trip back east. Well after midnight on a warm Saturday night, he anchored off Sag Harbor to check out another party. There, at the back of a room crowded with people, Greene met an attractive woman, Mei Sze Chan, a Chinese refugee from Malaysia who had grown up in Australia. Like Greene, Chan was in the real estate business and was a fixture in the late-night scene, sometimes attending a half-dozen parties a night in the Hamptons or New York. The thirty-two-year-old also had begun to wonder whether she would ever find Mr. Right.

Greene and Chan hit it off. She touched his shoulder. He held her hand. Then they found a quiet spot in the back of the room and began to discuss mortgages.[1]

A few months later they were engaged.

Greene was less successful with his short trade, however, and his frustrations began to boil over. Every day at 11 a.m., soon after rolling out of bed, he called his broker, Alan Zafran, to ask, "What's the pricing today?"

Most mornings Zafran came back with data showing that Greene's protection was worth less than the day before. Demand for subprime mortgages was growing, not shrinking, Zafran told him.

"It doesn't make any sense to me," Greene responded one morning. "It just doesn't make any sense."

Zafran visited Greene's Hollywood Hills home to go over the results of the trade, and they pored over a giant spreadsheet of figures together.

Soon Greene's calls to Zafran became more heated. Greene couldn't even get a quote on his investments without asking a bond dealer for an estimate, feeding his frustrations. He also couldn't figure out why the insurance wasn't rising in price, even as housing seemed to falter. The Merrill traders seemed reluctant to lower the value on all those subprime mortgages, he decided.

"How can you justify this price?!" Greene asked at a rapid-fire clip, his voice rising with anger. "It doesn't make any sense to me. Does it make sense to you!? Call me back!"

After Greene read a newspaper article about growing difficulties at

Countrywide Financial, he called Zafran, who patched in a Merrill executive in New York, Cliff Lanier.

"I *have* to be in the money, right?" Greene said, bitterly.

Lanier retrieved a fresh quote for Greene from a trader, along with an update on the market: The ABX index tracking subprime mortgages indeed was falling. But Greene held insurance on a range of mortgage bonds, not just the ABX, and those positions showed even more losses for Greene.

"Come on!!" Greene responded. "Countrywide's on the front page of the paper. I don't understand it!"

With each call, he noticed that the quotes were getting a little better. That pleased him, but it also sowed suspicions about how Merrill was coming up with its quotes. The Merrill team said it was merely passing along the latest quotes.

Greene had spent millions investing in an obscure, opaque market. Now, as housing was slipping, his mortgage insurance wasn't budging. He couldn't even be sure what they were worth.

"I don't understand it, Alan. Explain it to me," Greene pleaded to Zafran.

MICHAEL BURRY was under even more pressure. He'd become bearish on housing a full year ahead of Paulson & Co., buying protection against mortgage securities and financial firms when no one else wanted it. But by mid-2006, his investments, too, were falling in value. And unlike the previous year, Burry couldn't find many winners with his stock picks to offset the losses. His trade was dealing his fund its worst setback ever.

Before long, he began to get calls from concerned clients. They weren't nearly as skeptical as Burry about real estate; in fact, many were openly dubious about his housing investments. A few advised him to stick with stock investing. What do you know about mortgages? he was asked.

In August 2006, Burry's brokers called to tell him that someone was buying up every piece of subprime mortgage protection out there, CDS on RMBS (residential mortgage-backed securities), CDS on the

ABX, anything and everything. Huge chunks of credit-default swap contracts were flying off the shelf, sometimes more than a billion dollars of protection in a single day. Angela Chang, his broker, told Burry the buying was so lightning-quick and overwhelming, "it was like a drive-by." Another trader passed on chatter that an investor named John Paulson was doing the buying.

Burry was thrilled. He was sure all the activity would boost the value of his firm's positions. But Burry's brokers refused to adjust the value of his investments, making it impossible for him to show any gains. Sometimes, the prices seemed dated or inconsistent. Brokers gave him different prices for the same protection on the very same day. Other times, they wouldn't update a quote for a full week.

Burry couldn't believe it—Paulson was buying protection every day, housing prices finally had flattened out, the ABX index was dropping, and shares of home builders were weakening. But Burry was being told by his brokers that the value of his firm's protection on over $8.5 billion of mortgages and corporate debt was barely budging. Some brokers explained that Burry's positions didn't trade frequently, making it hard to prove they had risen in value.

Burry fumed. He started to come home late at night, creeping up the stairs of his luxury home and going straight to bed, to avoid his family. He was afraid his kids might see him bristling with anger.

Fed up, Burry finally decided to pull the mortgage investments out of his hedge fund and place them in a separate account, called a sidepocket. There they'd sit, frozen in price, until Burry was ready to sell them. That way he could place a more exact value on the fund himself and treat his investors more fairly, without relying on quotes from unreliable brokers.

Hours after he announced his move to his investors, however, Burry's firm was in turmoil. His clients already were skeptical of his housing investments. Now Burry was telling them that they were stuck with the housing protection until he decided it was time to exit. The fine print of his agreements with his investors allowed Burry to undertake this kind of move. But it seemed like a money grab—a heavy-handed way to prevent the investors from fleeing, and to stop the mortgage protection from weighing down his fund.

In October, Joel Greenblatt, Burry's original supporter, demanded a face-to-face meeting. Several days later, he and his partner, John Petry, flew to San Jose and rented a car to drive to Burry's office for a late-afternoon sit-down. Months earlier, Greenblatt had told a financial-television network that Burry was among the world's top investors. But now, as Greenblatt grabbed a seat across from Burry in his small office, he fumed.

Greenblatt told Burry how foolish he was to set up the side account; it was harming Greenblatt's reputation, as well as his own, he said.

"Cut your losses now," he told Burry, and advised him to get out of his mortgage positions before clients revolted and his firm was ruined. Greenblatt could barely contain his anger. The trades could be "a zero in the making."

For Burry, it felt like an uppercut to the jaw. One of Wall Street's most respected investors—the first to show any faith in him—was ordering him to cut short the biggest trade of his life, one that he had spent more than a year crafting. Like the rest of his investors, Greenblatt and Petry didn't even bother to try to understand his trade, or to read his letters that mapped it all out, Burry felt. Now, in the first rough period of Burry's career, they were turning on him.*

Sitting behind his desk, Burry shifted in his seat, growing increasingly uncomfortable under the onslaught. As he listened to Greenblatt and Petry, he realized he might not have enough support to keep his firm going if he held on to the positions and was proved wrong.

Then it dawned on Burry that Greenblatt wasn't saying anything new. He had no information that in any way negated or changed Burry's original investing premise.

Looking past his guests through a window just behind their chairs, he could make out the red roof of a condominium, one of countless overpriced units recently erected in an area already teeming with new supply.

If Greenblatt wants proof, he thought, *it's just a rock's throw away!*

---

*Greenblatt says he didn't disagree with Burry's housing bet, but he was frustrated with how large it had become, and how many investments Burry had placed in the side account.

Greenblatt was facing his own pressures. His firm, Gotham Capital Management, which made investments but also placed money in various hedge funds for clients, had received withdrawal requests from 20 percent of its investors. If Burry refused to sell investments and hand money back to Greenblatt and Petry, they would be in a bind.

Greenblatt tried to compromise with Burry, suggesting that he cash in some of his trades, rather than freeze them all. But Burry wouldn't budge.

"I can't sell any of them," Burry responded. "The market's just not functioning properly."

"You can sell *some* of them," Greenblatt responded, his anger rising again. "I know what you're doing, Michael."

To Burry, Greenblatt seemed to be suggesting that he was clinging to the trades to avoid handing back cash to his clients. Burry turned livid.

"Look, I'm not going to back down," Burry told his visitors. He was going to put the mortgage investments in the side account, as planned.

Greenblatt and Petry stormed out of the office, ignoring Burry's employees on their way to the door. Days later, Greenblatt's lawyers called Burry, threatening a lawsuit if he went through with his move.

Other investors, angry that Scion now was down about 18 percent on the year, also turned on Burry, withdrawing all the money they could from other accounts at the firm, pulling out $150 million over the next few weeks. A few potential clients, learning about the squabble, suddenly lost interest in Scion.

Burry turned sullen, stress obvious on his face. His wife began to worry about his health.

Late in 2006, Burry felt he had to do something to save his firm and his reputation. So, reluctantly, he began selling some of the CDS insurance, raising money to hand back to disgruntled investors. Over three weeks, he sold almost half of the protection he held on $7 billion of corporate debt of companies like Countrywide, Washington Mutual, AIG, and other financial players that seemed in dangerous positions.

Burry couldn't have picked a worse time to sell. At that point, Wall Street still held few worries about housing. The protection on $3 billion of debt, which originally cost Burry roughly $15 million or so a year, now cost new buyers only $6 million a year. In selling the insurance, he took a substantial loss. To Burry, it was like giving away a collection of family jewels, accumulated with loving care over two long years.

Money continued to flow out of the fund, though. Burry scrambled to cut his expenses, slashing salaries and firing employees. He flew to Hong Kong to close a small office there.

"Mike, you can't do this," a recently hired trader told Burry, his anger growing.

Burry tried to calm him down, explaining that he had no choice. But the trader turned even more agitated.

"You owe me the difference between what I would have made" at his previous job and the severance Burry now was promising. He demanded $5 million.

"I can't do that," Burry replied meekly.

His cost-cutting moves destroyed the morale of his remaining employees back in San Jose. In a tailspin, Burry withdrew from his friends, family, and employees. Each morning, Burry walked into his firm and made a beeline to his office, head down, locking the door behind him. He didn't emerge all day, not even to eat or use the bathroom. His remaining employees, who were still pulling for Burry, turned worried. Sometimes he got to the office so early, and kept the door closed for so long, that when his staff left at the end of the day, they were unsure if their boss had ever come in. Other times, Burry pounded his fists on his desk, trying to release his tension, as heavy-metal music blasted from nearby speakers.

The growing toll the trade placed on Burry seeped into an unusually frank letter that he sent his clients at the end of 2006: "A money manager does not go from being a near nobody to being nearly universally applauded to being nearly universally vilified without some effect."

GREG LIPPMANN had convinced his bosses at Deutsche Bank to let him buy protection on about $1 billion of subprime mortgages. But as the trade stalled in the summer of 2006, the Deutsche Bank executives became impatient, expressing doubts about his tactics. They seemed tempted to close Lippmann's trade.

"Just give me four years," Lippmann asked Rajeev Misra, his boss. Most subprime borrowers refinanced their mortgage loans after just a few years, Lippmann reminded him, so his trade surely would be over by then. "Give it a chance to work."

"Show me the research," Misra responded.

When he did so, Lippmann's bosses reluctantly gave him a green light to continue with the trade. The regular payments he was making for all the CDS insurance were slowly adding up, so those above him at the bank weren't thrilled. Yet for all his bluster and self-confidence, Lippmann wasn't prepared to quit Deutsche and go off on his own. Instead, he had to figure out a way to keep his trade alive and hold on to his job.

Lippmann managed a group that placed bond trades for investors. He realized that if he could convince enough investors to do the same trade he was undertaking, he might be able to rack up sufficient commissions to offset the costs of his bearish housing trade and placate his bosses. And if new investors could be convinced to buy the same CDS contracts that he owned, the price of these investments was bound to climb, which also would help Lippmann.

He traveled uptown to the offices of a hedge fund called Wesley Capital to meet two senior executives, to try to sell them on the idea. At first, they seemed impressed. Then they asked a friend who happened to be in the office, Larry Bernstein, who once managed a powerhouse bond-trading team at Wall Street firm Salomon Brothers, to weigh in on the trade.

Bernstein was dubious. "Coase Law says you'll be wrong," he said, dismissively.

The executives looked at each other. Lippmann had no clue what Bernstein was talking about. Neither did the Wesley executives. Coase Law turned out to be an economic theorem—but it didn't seem to have much to do with the trade. Then the meeting turned contentious. If problems arose, Bernstein argued, the government likely would step in to bail out troubled borrowers. Even if you're right and the price of the mortgage protection rises, when investors began to sell their insurance, the price would be pushed down, sinking the trade, Bernstein said.

Ultimately Lippmann walked out with nothing.

Jeremy Grantham's GMO LLC seemed like a certain client. The Boston money-management firm had been cautious about the market for years, and Grantham was among the most vocal doomsayers, writing downbeat op-ed columns for various newspapers warning of "a sensational bust."

But when GMO executives consulted their resident bond expert, Allen Barlient, he shot down the idea, arguing that most mortgage deals had so much protection that they likely would be fine.

Some investors he met with leveled abuse at Lippmann. "My brother works for Fidelity and he's buying this stuff," one said, referring to subprime-related investments. "You're either an idiot or a liar" trying to wring trading commissions.

Behind his back, some on Wall Street called Lippmann names, such as "Chicken Little" or "Bubble Boy," chuckling at his quixotic effort. At conferences, some traders teased him, saying "Your crazy trade is losing money." Others repeated an industry maxim: "A rolling loan gathers no moss."

Lippmann began avoiding investors with deep knowledge of mortgages or complex bond investments. They understood his maneuver but were lost causes, wed to their markets and reliant on sophisticated models that suggested everything would be fine. Instead, Lippmann asked salesmen at his bank who catered to investors in the stock, junk-bond, and emerging markets worlds if they would help arrange meetings for clients with a potential interest in his idea.

He sometimes stumbled onto tough questions—why were the rates of mortgage delinquencies so different in North Dakota and South Dakota?

"You're missing it, you have to take a look at employment," an investor said.

Lippmann was stumped. North and South Dakota sure seemed the same; the fact was that Lippmann didn't know why the rate of delinquencies was so different. He had never even visited those states. So he and Xu went back to the data. Sure enough, the two states had similar levels of employment and seemed alike in other ways, but home prices were rising much more rapidly in North Dakota, explaining why delinquencies were lower. It confirmed that the biggest factor on default rates was whether or not houses were rising in value. It made Lippmann more certain than ever of his thesis.

Slowly, he began to win converts. A number of investors signed up in London, eager to profit from a U.S. economy they viewed as fragile. It took less than an hour for Lippmann to convince Phil Falcone, a hedge-fund manager in New York, who seized on the limited downside and huge potential windfall of the trade. Falcone didn't even ask about the technical aspects of the mortgage market. The next day, he called Lippmann's team to buy insurance on $600 million of subprime mortgages. Later he made even more purchases.

By September, Lippmann had pitched the trade more than a hundred times and had his spiel down pat.

Lippmann won over dozens of investors, and CDS contracts began to fly out the door of Deutsche's Lower Manhattan office, $1 billion of protection a day. One investor even made a T-shirt that he gave to Lippmann and others saying "I shorted your house," a joke that seemed amusing at the time.

"What Lippmann did, to his credit, was he came around several times to me and said, 'Short this market,'" says Steve Eisman, a hedge-fund manager. "In my entire life, I never saw a sell-side guy come in and say, 'Short my market.'"[2]

A few hedge funds were such eager converts that they became as evangelical as Lippmann after doing their own research.

"You better get up to speed on the mortgage market . . . fast," Alan Fournier, founder of New Jersey hedge fund Pennant Capital, wrote to a journalist in an e-mail in the summer of 2006. "All these crappy loans have been gobbled up by investors and they're gonna get burned . . . the credit unwind is really just getting started."

In all, Lippmann bought insurance on $35 billion of subprime mortgages, keeping about $5 billion of CDS protection for his own firm's account while selling the rest to eighty or so hedge-fund investors. A few others who already had placed the trade, like John Paulson, compared notes with Lippmann, shared intelligence, and then did some buying through Deutsche. The growing commissions enabled Lippmann to buy even more subprime insurance for his own account.

Nonetheless, by the end of 2006, most of Lippmann's clients had lost money on the trade. He shared with a friend that his career would be affected if his scheme didn't work out. Within his bank, Lippmann had become an object of derision. When Paulson's trader, Brad Rosenberg, called to ask for him, a salesman answering the phone let out a loud laugh: "Why do you want to talk to him? That guy's crazy!"

Others at Deutsche Bank resented Lippmann. Yes, he was generating commissions, but his trade also was costing the bank about $50 million a year, reducing the firm's bonus pool, some traders grumbled.

B Y LATE 2006, housing prices finally had leveled off. Subprime lenders, including Ownit Mortgage Solutions and Sebring Capital, had begun to fail. John Paulson, Lippmann, Greene, and Burry should have been making oodles of money. But their positions barely nudged higher.

Late one afternoon, following another day of lackluster gains, Paulson picked up the phone to dial Lippmann, his subprime consigliere. To his investors and employees, Paulson showed absolute faith that the protection his firm owned on $25 billion of subprime mortgages would pay off.

With Lippmann, though, he could share his fears.

"Is there something I'm missing?" Paulson asked Lippmann. "Don't these people realize this stuff is crap? This is absurd!"

Paulson sounded like he might be wavering, surprising Lippmann.

"Relax, John. The trade will work."

Lippmann remained cocky because he was on the trading floor, buying and selling mortgage protection all day long. He knew better than almost anyone who the mysterious investors were on the other side of all the trades, a group so eager to sell insurance on all of those risky mortgages. And he knew their time would come to an end.

9

Never get high on your own supply.
—Al Pacino in *Scarface*

A SIMPLE, THREE-LETTERED ACRONYM EXPLAINED WHY PAULSON, Lippmann, Greene, and Burry weren't making much money in late 2006, even though housing was stalling out and home owners were running into problems: CDO.

A 1980s invention of some of the brightest financial minds, collateralized debt obligations, or CDOs, were investment vehicles that seemed to make the world a safer place—that is, until they fell into the wrong hands, not unlike other weapons of mass destruction.

Mortgage-backed bonds gave investors a claim on the cash flow of a group of mortgage loans; CDOs took it one step further. They were claims on giant pools of all kinds of debt that could include slices of loan and bond payments made by companies and municipalities, and even monthly payments by those leasing aircraft, cars, and mobile homes.

Investors were sold a set of securities with claims on all that flow of cash, each bearing a different degree of risk, like any securitization. The riskiest pieces of a CDO paid investors the highest returns but were first in line to suffer if the CDO received slimmer cash payments than it expected. Pieces with lower risk had lower returns but received the first income payments.

By the middle of the 2000s, the financial engineers were convinced that securitizations had spread the risk of all those loans, all but eliminating the chance of any big economic disaster. So they went back to the laboratory and concocted something called a mortgage CDO, featuring claims on a hundred or so mortgage-backed bonds, each of which in turn was a claim on thousands of individual mortgages.

The investments proved popular but their returns left something to be desired, spurring the bankers to craft CDOs that used the seemingly plentiful cash flow from slices of mortgage bonds rated BBB− and BBB—the ones backed by loans to borrowers with sketchy or limited credit histories—along with a sprinkling of other mortgages and loans. This investment was named a "mezzanine" CDO, after those dangerous BBB tranches.

The new CDO investments were an instant hit because they had juicy returns, thanks to all those high-interest subprime mortgages. Some slices promised annual returns of nearly 10 percent. Just as important, rating companies were convinced that most of the pieces of these CDOs should receive sky-high AAA ratings, or close to it, even though they simply were claims on huge stacks of risky home loans. The bankers argued that more cash was coming into the CDO than it needed to pay out, and that the mortgages came from all over the country and from more than one mortgage lender, making them safe. They had taken the straw of the mortgage market and spun gold: It was modern-day alchemy.

Lending by these CDOs powered the real estate market, ushering in the music, wine, and women chapter of the housing surge. In 2006, about $560 billion of CDOs were sold, including those using the cash flows from risky mortgages, almost three times 2004's levels. The "CDO system" had replaced the banking system, in the words of writer James Grant.

Few were as good at concocting CDOs as Chris Ricciardi. Growing up in affluent Westchester County, north of New York City, the son of a stock salesman, Ricciardi tagged along with his father to the floors of Wall Street firms and the New York Stock Exchange, captivated by the fast pace and huge sums of money changing hands.

Ricciardi couldn't find a job as a stock trader or an investment banker when he graduated during the economic slump of the early 1990s, so he started trading mortgage bonds. A few years later, as Wall Street pushed for ways to drum up higher fees and investors searched for better returns, Ricciardi was among the first to bundle the monthly payments from groups of dicey home mortgages with other debt to back securities with especially high interest rates.

Other bankers came up with their own CDOs but Ricciardi stayed a step ahead. As he moved from Prudential Securities to Credit Suisse Group, his groups always towered over competitors, as Ricciardi pushed his staff to churn out still more CDOs. Lured in 2003 to Merrill Lynch, a firm eager to take more risks under then-chief Stanley O'Neal, Ricciardi pushed Merrill to first place in the business, vaulting over bond powerhouse Lehman Brothers. New Century and others who made risky loans knew that Merrill Lynch was eager for their product so it could sell more CDOs—the more the better.

Soon Merrill was the Wal-Mart of the business, producing CDOs at a furious pace. By 2005, the firm underwrote $35 billion of CDO securities, of which $14 billion were backed mostly by securities tied to subprime mortgages.

Every quarter, Ricciardi taped rankings near Merrill's trading desk, highlighting in yellow the firm's top-place finish. Staff members were pushed to grow sales by 15 percent a year. They hopped the globe to Australia, Austria, Korea, and France, selling CDOs to pension funds, insurance companies, and other investors. Back in the United States, they pitched hedge-fund investors such as Ralph Cioffi of Bear Stearns on the manicured lawns of the Sleepy Hollow Country Club in Westchester, New York, the ski slopes of Jackson Hole, Wyoming, and elsewhere.

For each CDO Merrill underwrote, the investment bank earned fees of 1 percent to 1.5 percent of the deal's total size, or as much as $15 million for a typical $1 billion CDO. Soon Merrill's CDO profits topped $400 million a year or more.

Ricciardi's bosses cheered the activity, convinced profits would roll. "We've got the right people in place as well as good risk management and controls," Merrill's CEO, Stanley O' Neal, said in 2005.

But as the CDOs became increasingly risky, some of Merrill's troops grew so uncomfortable selling certain products that they began lying to Ricciardi, telling him that clients had no interest in his group's latest creations, even before testing the waters. Ricciardi bolted Merrill in early 2006, after pocketing an $8 million paycheck for his work the previous year, to join Cohen & Co., a small firm that managed CDO deals. He continued to champion CDOs.

"These are the trades that make people famous," he told staff at his new firm that year, trying to drum up enthusiasm for CDOs, according to *The Wall Street Journal*. His new firm eventually would manage CDOs with the most defaults.[1]

By the time Ricciardi left Merrill, the investment bank was hooked on profits from risky CDOs. Dow Kim, then head of markets and investment banking at Merrill, vowed to do "whatever it takes" to stay number one in CDOs. In 2006, the firm pushed even harder to get these deals out the door, racking up $700 million of fees and issuing $44 billion subprime CDOs, up from $14 billion in 2005. That year, O'Neal was paid an $18.5 million cash bonus and $48 million in total pay.

Investors who bought the CDO slices often believed in their safety, or were assured by the top-notch investment ratings they received. Like firefighters going into yet another burning building, they had survived for so long, they began to see their work as routine.

Ralph Cioffi, a twenty-two-year Bear veteran who ran two hedge funds at Bear Stearns, first became worried about subprime borrowers in early 2006. But the military-history buff put almost all of his funds' cash in high-rated slices of CDOs, borrowing so much money that the funds owned $20 billion of these investments. Cioffi, who was personally worth $100 million at one point that year, didn't buy blindly; he also owned CDS contracts insuring other, lower-rated mortgage bonds, a strategy that seemed more conservative to him.

His investors had utmost confidence in Cioffi and his partner, Matthew Tannin.

"I often bragged about the fund because it didn't have a single down month in three years, and that was just amazing to me," says

Ted Moss, a sixty-seven-year-old real estate developer from Cleveland, Tennessee, who invested about $1 million in one of Cioffi's funds at Bear Stearns.

It seemed like investors hungered for these CDO slices because housing was rising. But in reality, many were taking advantage of a slick accounting maneuver. When a bank purchased the AAA piece of a CDO while simultaneously buying credit-default swap insurance on that same slice, it often could immediately book as profit the present value of the future cash flows from that CDO as long as it had a higher interest payout than the cost of the CDS. Traders buying a CDO slice yielding 5 percent a year, e.g., while at the same time paying 4.8 percent a year to purchase a CDS contract on that same slice, could boast an easy 0.20 percent annual profit. They sometimes even claimed an immediate windfall based on the *expected* profit of these trades over the subsequent ten years.

Borrow enough money, repeat this trade frequently, and a huge bonus was in store for the traders, a windfall that even those harboring suspicions about housing found hard to turn down. Eventually, these "negative basis" trades led to a major percentage of the losses on CDOs, according to UBS Securities.[2]

THROUGHOUT 2006, Greg Lippmann was eager to find evidence of cracks in housing. Most mornings, after taking a cab or bus from his downtown loft to Deutsche Bank's Wall Street–area office, he uncovered fresh proof that real estate was weakening. But the subprime mortgages he had bet against were not dropping. Sometimes colleagues would see Lippmann shake his head, a bemused smile on his face. He knew the CDOs were still buying, propping up the market.

It didn't make much sense to Lippmann. He got on the phone, urging investors to short the very same mortgage bonds that the CDOs were purchasing, reassuring those with losing trades that the CDO buying would have to stop, at some point.

Demand only grew, however. In fact, there weren't enough subprime mortgages to meet the rabid interest for the high-return "mezz" CDOs.

So investment bankers turned ingenious, creating CDOs with claims on the income of other CDOs, calling these "CDO squared." They crafted other CDOs from the cash generated by selling CDS protection to investors like John Paulson. These "synthetic" CDOs, in fact, became the dominant form of CDOs by late 2006.

Investment banks favored synthetic CDOs because they were easier to construct, a quick way to generate fees. They didn't require the purchase of actual mortgage bonds, a process that typically took months. A billion-dollar CDO could be assembled in mere weeks by selling enough CDS contracts on home mortgages. By the end of 2006, there were $1.2 trillion of subprime loans, about 10 percent of the overall mortgage market. But by introducing so many CDOs, more than $5 *trillion* of investments had been created based on all those risky loans, according to some estimates. This is the secret to why debilitating losses resulted from a market that seemed small to most outsiders, unaware of the breakneck growth of CDOs.[3]

There was just one hitch: The top-rated slices of these CDOs could be hard to sell, since they had lower yields than riskier CDO slices. So the banks often kept or bought these "supersenior" pieces for themselves. Giant insurance company AIG stopped selling insurance on these investments by 2006, but the banks kept piling them on, eager to get CDOs out the door. (At the time, AIG Finance, an arm of AIG, still had perhaps the most exposure to these investments.)

Merrill Lynch, Citigroup, Morgan Stanley, and UBS, the same investment banks creating CDO deals from toxic mortgages, all placed these supersenior CDO slices in their own accounts, like butchers bringing home noxious sausage to share with the family. Top management either approved the process or were clueless it was happening, assured by underlings that the securities were safe. Yes, the CDO investments they held shared AAA ratings with the debt of the U.S. government. That's where the similarities ended. They were both AAA rated the way that Miley Cyrus and Meryl Streep both get high marks from audiences. In other words, they were worlds apart.

Some bankers had vague worries, but they felt pressure to get as many CDOs completed before it all ended, like a giant game of musical chairs.

Charles "Chuck" Prince, chief executive of Citigroup, the largest bank in the world, who received a $13.2 million cash bonus and $25.6 million in overall pay in 2006, captured the sentiment in an unusually frank statement: "When the music stops, in terms of liquidity, things will be complicated. But as long as the music is playing, you've got to get up and dance. We're still dancing," he told the *Financial Times*. (By June 2008, Prince would resign from his job as the bank dealt over $15 billion in losses, much of it from CDO investments.)

Others believed in the safety of the high-rated debt slices, or relied on brainy quants and their whiz-bang computer models, which deemed the CDO slices safe, like illusionists fooling even themselves with a trick they had performed.

JOHN PAULSON already had purchased billions in CDS investments that would pay off if the home mortgages of borrowers with sketchy credit ran into problems. And he bought insurance contracts that would rack up profits if groups of subprime mortgages tracked by the ABX index suffered.

But if he was genuinely going to make the trade of a lifetime, he needed more. Like a cocksure Las Vegas card-counter, he was eager to split his winning blackjack hand, again and again.

"Given where the credit markets were, we had to find short opportunities," Paulson says.

As Paulson eyed the raging CDO market, he realized it, too, was bound to collapse. He decided he had to get his hands on insurance for these investments as well.

Pellegrini and the rest of Paulson's team searched the market for especially bad CDOs, like a shopper picking through a fruit bin. Rather than find the healthiest and ripest of the lot, though, Pellegrini and his team searched for the most rotten. Then they bought CDS insurance contracts on those CDO slices. A CDO with a lot of loans made by

New Century? Throw it in the basket. One dominated by liar loans and interest-only mortgages? Definitely. A CDO with lots of mortgages from the superheated real estate markets of California and Nevada? Grab two handfuls.

But as Paulson's shorting became an open secret in the business, Pellegrini noticed that the Wall Street pros were treating him less warmly, as if he was throwing a wrench in their well-oiled machine. At one point in 2006, Pellegrini was eager to learn about a group of CDOs filled with mortgage bonds put together by Carrington Capital Management LLC, run by hedge-fund manager Bruce Rose. Pellegrini recognized that he remained an amateur in this world and he was worried that he might miss something if he didn't see the "tape" detailing the actual mortgages in the CDOs. He told his broker at Bear Stearns that if he sent the tapes of Carrington's mortgage-bond deals, he might consider buying safer slices of the CDOs.

After a few hours, the broker called Pellegrini with some bad news.

"I'm sorry," the broker said, sheepishly. "The issuer doesn't want you to see it."

"What do you mean? How is that even possible!?"

Later that day, Pellegrini got Bruce Rose on the phone to express his displeasure at the unusual blackballing.

"I've seen your investment presentation," Rose replied. "I find it amusing. But I don't want anything to do with you."

Rose then hung up, leaving Pellegrini boiling.

"They were closing ranks on us," Pellegrini says.

The activity began to wear on Rosenberg, the firm's only debt trader. Sometimes Paulson wanted him to *buy* protection on mortgage bonds. Other times he'd *sell* the ABX index of subprime bonds—it was another way to be bearish on housing. None of the investments was traded on public exchanges or had clear pricing, making it harder to know if it had been a good deal. Rosenberg also bought protection on a few financial companies. And once in a while, Paulson asked him to buy some bonds, too.

Each morning before 10 a.m. Rosenberg e-mailed seven or eight Wall Street dealers an "OWIC" list, or Offers Wanted in Competition, a list of the names of mortgage slices that Paulson & Co. wanted to buy CDS protection for. At 2:30 p.m. he'd receive a spreadsheet of their best offers. Pellegrini took the list to Paulson, and they'd huddle in his office, speaking in undertones. Rosenberg would emerge an hour later for a new round of furious phone calls.

There was no time for breaks. Paulson ordered lunch in for his staff, and Rosenberg ate at his desk.

Rosenberg left the office exhausted, although he claimed the pace didn't faze him.

"I'm from Bear Stearns, the toughest firm on the Street. I didn't need a pat on the back," says Rosenberg. "They ranked everyone and fired the lowest guy on the desk each year."

Rosenberg didn't know exactly how much mortgage protection Paulson wanted, but he knew Paulson hungered for more.

"We had to get on as many trades as possible before it was too late," Rosenberg says.

JOHN PAULSON, focused on creating a huge trade, soon took a controversial step that would lead to some resentment for his role in indirectly contributing to more toxic debt for investors.

Paulson and Pellegrini were eager to find ways to expand their wager against risky mortgages; accumulating it in the market sometimes proved a slow process. So they made appointments with bankers at Bear Stearns, Deutsche Bank, Goldman Sachs, and other firms to ask if they would create CDOs that Paulson & Co. could essentially bet against.

Paulson's team would pick a hundred or so mortgage bonds for the CDOs, the bankers would keep some of the selections and replace others, and then the bankers would take the CDOs to ratings companies to be rated. Paulson would buy CDS insurance on the mortgage debt and the investment banks would find clients with bullish views on mortgages to take the other side of the trades. This way, Paulson could buy protection on $1 billion or so of mortgage debt in one fell swoop.

Paulson and his team were open with the banks they met with to propose the idea.

"We want to ramp it up," Pellegrini told a group of Bear Stearns bankers, explaining his idea.

Paulson and Pellegrini believed the debt backing the CDOs would blow up. But Pellegrini argued to his boss that they should offer to buy the riskiest slices of these CDOs, the so-called equity pieces that would get hit first if problems resulted. These pieces had such high yields that they could help pay the cost of buying protection on the rest of the CDOs, Pellegrini said, even though the equity slices likely would become worthless over time, as the debt backing the CDO fell in value. And if their analysis proved wrong and the CDOs held up, at least the equity investment would lead to profits, Pellegrini said.

"We're willing to buy the equity if you allow us to short the rest," Pellegrini told one banker.

To try to protect themselves, the Paulson team made sure at least one of the CDOs was a "triggerless" deal, or a CDO crafted to be more protective of these equity slices by making other pieces of the CDO more likely to take early hits. Paulson's goal was to make the equity piece a bit safer, but this step made the other parts of the triggerless CDO even more dangerous for anyone with the gumption to buy them.

He and Paulson didn't think there was anything wrong with working with various bankers to create more toxic investments. Paulson told his own clients what he was up to and they supported him, considering it an ingenious way to grow the trade by finding more debt to short. After all, those who would buy the pieces of any CDO likely would be hedge funds, banks, pension plans, or other sophisticated investors, not mom-and-pop investors. And if these investors didn't purchase the newly created CDOs, they'd likely buy another similar product since there were more than $350 billion of CDOs at the time.

However, at least one banker smelled trouble and rejected the idea. Paulson didn't come out and say it, but the banker suspected that Paulson would push for combustible mortgages and debt to go into any CDO, making it more likely that it would go up in flames. Some of those likely to buy the CDO slices were endowments and pension plans, not just deep-pocketed hedge funds, adding to the wariness.

Scott Eichel, a senior Bear Stearns trader, was among those at the investment bank who sat through a meeting with Paulson but later turned down the idea. He worried that Paulson would want especially ugly mortgages for the CDOs, like a bettor asking a football owner to bench a star quarterback to improve the odds of his wager against the team. Either way, he felt it would look improper.

"On the one hand, we'd be selling the deals" to investors, without telling them that a bearish hedge fund was the impetus for the transaction, Eichel told a colleague; on the other, Bear Stearns would be helping Paulson wager against the deals.

"We had three meetings with John, we were working on a trade together," says Eichel. "He had a bearish view and was very open about what he wanted to do, he was more up front than most of them.

"But it didn't pass the ethics standards; it was a reputation issue, and it didn't pass our moral compass. We didn't think we should sell deals that someone was shorting on the other side," Eichel says.

For his part, Paulson says that investment banks like Bear Stearns didn't need to worry about including only risky debt for the CDOs because "it was a negotiation; we threw out some names, they threw out some names, but the bankers ultimately picked the collateral. We didn't create any securities, we never sold the securities to investors. . . . We always thought they were bad loans."

Besides, every time he bought subprime-mortgage protection, someone had to be found to sell it to him, Paulson notes, so these big CDOs were no different.

Indeed, other bankers, including those at Deutsche Bank and Goldman Sachs, didn't see anything wrong with Paulson's request and agreed to work with his team. Paulson & Co. eventually bet against a handful of CDOs with a value of about $5 billion.

Paulson didn't sell any of these products to investors. Some investors were even consulted as the mortgage debt was picked for the CDOs to make sure it would appeal to them. And these deals were among the easiest for an investor to analyze, if they so chose, because they were "unmanaged" CDOs, or those in which the collateral was chosen at the outset and not adjusted later on like other CDOs. It wasn't his fault that others were willing to roll the dice.

A few other hedge funds also worked with banks to create CDOs of their own that these funds could short—so Paulson wasn't doing anything new. Nor did Paulson's moves create more troubled mortgages or saddle borrowers with additional losses—the deals were CDOs composed of CDS contracts, rather than actual mortgage bonds.

"We provided the collateral" for the CDOs, Paulson acknowledges. "But the deals weren't created for us, we just facilitated it; we proposed recent vintages of mortgages" to the banks.

But some investors later would complain that they wouldn't have purchased the CDO investments had they known that some of the collateral behind them was chosen by Paulson and that he would be shorting it. Others argued that Paulson's actions indirectly led to more dangerous CDO investments, resulting in billions of dollars of additional losses for those who owned the CDO slices when the market finally cratered.

In truth, Paulson and Pellegrini still were unsure if their growing trade would ever pan out.

They *thought* the CDOs and other risky mortgage debt would become worthless, Paulson says. "But we still didn't know."

10.

ANDREW LAHDE WAS OUT OF WORK IN THE SUMMER OF 2006, HE had little left in his savings account, and he was stuck in a cramped one-bedroom, rent-controlled apartment. But Lahde was convinced he had at least one thing of value: a trade that was sure to make him a fortune. He just couldn't get anyone to believe in him.

The thirty-five-year-old had been let go by Los Angeles investment firm Dalton Capital after a series of clashes with his boss and an abrupt shuttering of the hedge fund that Lahde was working on. He wasn't very concerned, at least initially. Young traders were launching hedge funds with ease, from coast to coast. Lahde figured he'd just do the same. But investors turned him down cold. The only nibbles came from those offering very little money but demanding a huge chunk of his new firm. That was something Lahde wouldn't consider, though in truth his firm amounted to little more than a glass desk and a simple chair in his Santa Monica living room, as well as an unyielding conviction that the housing market was about to crater.

It didn't help that Lahde looked more like a chilled-out surfer than a budding hedge-fund titan. Six-foot-two with tousled blond hair, chiseled features, and sleepy, deep-blue eyes, Lahde seemed to have just rolled out of bed, more than a bit upset at having been awoken. He didn't seem comfortable around people, fidgeting in his seat during most meetings, and the slow, deliberate tone of his voice was so deep and muted, it sometimes was hard to make out what he was saying.

Lahde's mother, Bonnie, back home in Michigan, kept calling, badgering him to find a real job. His best friend, Will, insisted that his trade

idea wouldn't pan out because the Fed and the government would ensure that housing held up, at least through the 2008 elections. It had
been years since Lahde cared very much about the opinions of family
members and friends, but their lack of confidence grated on him. It's
not like he didn't at least apply for some jobs at nearby firms, but they
didn't pan out, partly because Lahde, brimming with a confidence not
yet reflected in his résumé, was uninterested in junior positions.

"Dude, I stopped looking for a job, full on," he told Will after one
more irritating call.

Lahde's deep suspicions and bitter resentments always lay just below
the surface. He grew up in a religious home, the son of a mechanical engineer and a physician's assistant, in the mostly white, wealthy Detroit
suburb of Rochester, Michigan, Madonna's hometown.

His father, Frank, worked for Ford Motor Company and then for
various auto suppliers in the area, but he was occasionally out of
work as the industry's troubles grew. Nonetheless, the Lahde family
stretched their finances to buy a 2,000-square-foot home, among the
smallest in the neighborhood, adding to the tension in the home.
Sundays were spent at St. John, a local Lutheran church, and all three of
the Lahde boys attended the church's school from fourth to eighth
grades.

But at fourteen, Lahde, hoping to generate some cash for himself
amid the family's strain, began selling marijuana to wealthier kids in
town, after starting with fireworks sales. Once, when he was caught
dealing pot, Lahde argued to his parents that alcohol was a gateway drug
and a far greater evil than cannabis.

"I figured out that the only way to have security was to have a business with good cash flow, or to be wealthy enough so you didn't have to
work," Lahde recalls.

At Michigan State, where Lahde majored in finance and graduated
with honors, he began subscribing to The Wall Street Journal, impressed
with stories of traders making millions. Math courses came easily to
Lahde, though he had little patience for much else. After college, and a
few years making less than $30,000 a year as a broker at TD Waterhouse,
Lahde was rejected by every business school he applied to. It happened

again, a year later—Stanford University, the University of Chicago, the Wharton School, and Yale University all turned him down. Finally, he gained acceptance to UCLA's Anderson School of Management, the last student taken off their waiting list.

At UCLA, Lahde bristled at his more privileged classmates, some of whom graduated from prep schools and Ivy League universities but didn't seem especially bright to him. When he told them that he had graduated from Michigan State, rather than its more prestigious rival, the University of Michigan, he felt they looked down on him. Things didn't go any more smoothly inside the classroom. Lahde almost was kicked out after receiving an F in a Human Resources class. He blamed the grade on his repeated challenges to the professor's weak arguments during class discussions. The F drove Lahde nuts because he was paying his own way at the expensive school, draining savings from his earlier jobs and extracurricular activities while many classmates were enjoying a free ride courtesy of their families.

"He almost took away everything I had worked for," Lahde recalls, referring to his professor.

Placed on probation after the failing grade, Lahde graduated in 2002 to a discouraging job market. In his spare time during business school, he had taken courses to become a chartered financial analyst, helping to distinguish him in the market. Through a UCLA contact, Lahde landed a job at Roth Capital, a third-tier investment bank in nearby Newport Beach known for raising money for small, usually obscure companies. He was miserable from day one, itching to invest money rather than sell securities to investors. But Lahde quickly found his niche, picking a number of winning stocks for clients and learning to pitch the firm's various products.

In the fall of 2004, Lahde latched on as an analyst at Dalton. Steve Persky, the owner of the growing, $1 billion hedge fund on Wilshire Boulevard in Los Angeles, judged Lahde the hungriest of the job candidates he met. But Lahde soon began to clash with his demanding boss, unhappy when Persky publicly criticized employees in regular group meetings when they overlooked details in their work. On the other hand, Lahde's work impressed Persky, who named his firm after the prestigious New York prep school he had attended. But Lahde rankled his boss by overdramatizing investment opportunities, sometimes calling a promising company "another Microsoft," while referring to a problematic company as "the next Enron."

At the time, both Persky and Lahde were novices when it came to real estate. When he first joined Dalton, Lahde told his boss that he was thinking about buying a $600,000 condominium by paying $30,000, or 5 percent of the price, as a down payment. Persky seemed shocked.

"Are you serious, that's all they want?" Persky said.

"Yeah, that's the standard," Lahde replied. "I think I can even get a mortgage with no down payment at all."

One day, after Persky's wife told him that she wanted to start investing in the white-hot Los Angeles real estate market, despite the fact that she had no background in the business, Persky began to get concerned. Weeks later, he read a negative article in *Barron's* magazine about a big subprime-mortgage lender in nearby Orange County called New Century Financial and asked Lahde to check it out.

Lahde had a vague awareness of the company from his time at Roth Capital and spoke with an old friend who was still an analyst at the firm, Rich Eckert, who had a "Buy" rating on New Century's shares. But Lahde had been developing his own misgivings about housing and had recently convinced his parents to sell their second home, on a lake in Michigan. Lahde spent weeks studying New Century, quickly realizing the company had little cash of its own—only by selling its mortgages to Wall Street banks to be used in mortgage pools could New Century get the financing to make new loan commitments. If that securitization market ever disappeared, Lahde figured, New Century's business would disintegrate.

Lahde dug into the world of securitizations, telling Persky that it didn't seem like many slices of the mortgage pools would hold up if borrowers ran into problems. Even if housing prices just flattened out, the riskiest slices of the pools could be in trouble, because home owners wouldn't be able to refinance their mortgages.

Lahde walked into Persky's office one day and said the firm should short "the entire Orange County," where real estate development and aggressive lending were running rampant. It was Lahde's usual hyperbole, and obviously impossible, but Persky fully agreed with his sentiment. Betting against shares of New Century seemed to be the next best thing, though Lahde warned Persky that it might take a year or two before things slowed and the trade worked.

By early 2005, New Century was Dalton's biggest short position; it soon would be joined by fellow subprime lender Accredited Home Lenders. Lahde and Persky visited another Orange County financial company, Downey Savings and Loan, and were amazed to realize that so much of their business was extending so-called option ARM loans, or loans that allowed borrowers to make monthly payments that didn't even cover the interest cost of the loan. They quickly began to short Downey as well.

But the stocks kept climbing throughout 2005, as respected hedge-fund investor David Einhorn established a big position in New Century and then joined the company's board of directors. Adding salt to Dalton's wounds, New Century paid its shareholders a hefty annual dividend that amounted to 13 percent of the value of its shares. By shorting, or borrowing and selling the shares, Dalton had to pay that dividend to the investors it had borrowed from, adding to the firm's losses.

But Dalton wouldn't give up, adding to its bearish positions in 2005 and into 2006, even buying CDS insurance contracts on a number of housing players and mortgage-related debt. The losses piled up, month after month. With each bad day, and each furious call from his investors, Persky became more frustrated.

"I was doing what I thought was prudent, but my performance was modest, and many of my investors had short leashes," Persky says.

Tempers simmered, and the bickering between Persky and Lahde escalated. When Persky criticized Lahde, who was on edge because his recommendations were losing money for the firm and his bonus was in jeopardy, he often fired back at his boss, even in public meetings. By April 2006, Persky had had enough. He began to sell all the fund's bearish housing bets, handing cash back to his clients, even though he remained convinced a real estate collapse was inevitable. He just couldn't take it anymore. The decision shocked Lahde, as did Persky's subsequent decision to fire him and give him just three months' severance pay, or about $30,000.

Lahde remained convinced that housing was set to crack. New Century and other lenders were starting to come under pressure because as interest rates rose, their borrowing costs were approaching those of the loans they were making to customers, crimping profits. It was a sure sign that their business couldn't last.

His unpleasant experience at Dalton weighed on Lahde. As he gazed out his window at the beach next to his apartment, he was tempted to give up on the financial business, find a girl, and go on a long vacation. But Lahde figured that if he could set up a hedge fund of his own dedicated to wagering against real estate, the payoff could be huge.

"It was always going to be a two-year thing," Lahde says. "I knew they couldn't hold it together longer than that."

He set up Lahde Capital in his 800-square-foot apartment, angling his chair to get a good view of the blue water glistening just a few hundred yards away. Some days the weather was so warm that Lahde took a break from his steamy apartment, which lacked central air-conditioning, to jump in the nearby Pacific Ocean.

All summer, the sun shone brightly outside the apartment while darkness grew within. Lahde was sure that housing was on its last legs, but he worried that all kinds of financial firms would be devastated by the fallout. The way he viewed it, he was about to get on a surfboard ahead of a tsunami. The wave would be huge but it could turn out at the last second, knocking him cold before he reached shore.

To avoid that, Lahde decided to buy only CDS protection on the ABX index of subprime residential mortgages, rather than on various MBS pools like other bearish investors. He figured the ABX was more actively traded and would be easier to exit on a dime when things surely crumbled.

In truth, Lahde didn't really know much about the ins and outs of trading CDS contracts. At Dalton, he had focused on New Century and other lenders. Persky didn't let him tackle the firm's CDS moves. So

Lahde asked advice from the few traders he knew who were willing to spare him some time.

Lahde began to pitch potential investors on his two-year strategy of betting against risky mortgages, asking for minimum investments of $5 million, aiming to start with at least $100 million. But every meeting was another strikeout. No one was interested in Lahde or his bearish arguments. Pressure grew; Lahde felt he had only several weeks to place his trades before it all unraveled.

In a desperate moment, Lahde even tried Persky, who also turned him down. Lahde began leaving his tie and suit at home, wearing a polo shirt to meetings with investors, and adopting a jaded attitude; it was as if he had given up.

"Andrew's not a perfect guy to persuade you to invest," says Dr. Norman Zada, one of those who received a call from Lahde asking for an investment. Zada, founder of *Perfect 10*, an adult magazine featuring women willing to pose nude but unwilling to undertake cosmetic surgery, ignored Lahde's entreaties for months before finally giving him some cash. "He's a youngster and a little strange . . . and he seems sort of nervous around people."

At first, Lahde couldn't convince brokers to enter into ISDA (International Swaps and Derivatives Association) agreements with him and serve as counterparties to his new firm, making it impossible for Lahde to buy the CDS contracts he so coveted. The brokers said his firm was too small. Lahde didn't even have much of his own money to invest, compounding matters. He was worth only about $150,000 and needed most of it to pay the firm's bills, not to mention his own living expenses.

After weeks of frustration, Lahde sweet-talked brokers at Lehman Brothers and Bear Stearns into considering selling him CDS contracts, telling them that big money was on the way and soon he'd be managing $100 million or more. They were skeptical but began working on complicated trading agreements just in case the money came through.

By November, Lahde had managed to raise $2 million from a few investors, but he was exhausted from the chase, and it didn't seem like he'd be able to turn up other investors. Holding his breath, he asked the Bear

Stearns and Lehman brokers if he could begin putting his trades on with the money he already had. He reminded them that his firm was sure to grow quickly and pointed out how much work they'd already done on the complex agreements. Why put it all to waste, Lahde argued.

He picked an opportune time to ask. By late 2006, Wall Street firms were squeezing every last drop from the housing market. After hemming and hawing, his contacts at Lehman Brothers and Bear Stearns agreed to sell him CDS contracts, as long as the paperwork was approved by their superiors. But they insisted that their credit departments approve Lahde before each trade he made, much like a parent insisting on accompanying a new driver.

One day in November, just after 5:30 a.m., the phone rang in Lahde's bedroom, startling him. His broker at Lehman Brothers called to say the paperwork was complete and Lahde could begin trading. Not only that, but the CDS insurance contracts he wanted were so unpopular that Lahde actually would be paid an up-front fee if he agreed to pay regular premiums on this insurance for risky mortgages. Lahde fumbled with the phone in the dark, trying to make out the implications of the quote.

Do you want the trade, the broker asked?

"Do it," Lahde responded, before he rolled over and went back to sleep.

Over the next few weeks, Lahde accumulated more protection on slices of the ABX index, ranging from those rated BBB− all the way up to AA, focusing on mortgages handed out during the first half of 2006, when the market was at its most exuberant.

But Lahde's stress level was building as the new year approached. He'd hired an associate for his firm, legal bills were due, and Lahde was down to $100,000 of savings. Even after raising another $1.5 million and buying more CDS contracts, he owned protection on just $17 million of risky mortgages, a figure so puny by Wall Street's standards that it was embarrassing. The trade of a lifetime was slipping through his fingers. Unless Lahde could quickly raise some serious money, he would have to shutter the firm and look for a job.

A friend called to level with Lahde: The brochures with the summary of his investment thesis that he'd been sending out to prospective investors made him look like a rank amateur. Lahde had to concede the point.

A week before Christmas, Lahde sat down at his circular, glass desk, which doubled as his apartment's dining-room table, to rework his marketing materials. He kept at it, writing and rewriting the presentation, again and again. He canceled Christmas plans. Pretend I'm in a submarine and out of touch, he told his mother. Lahde put in a series of all-nighters, including one on New Year's Eve, finally finishing on January 7. The marketing materials now looked impressive. But he wasn't sure he had enough time left to pull off his trade.

I N LATE 2006, Paulson stayed upbeat. He was waiting for his trade finally to begin to work. In November, he closed his fund, the Paulson Credit Opportunities Fund, to new investors. He had raised $700 million and spent it all on various mortgage protection. Paulson immediately launched a sister fund to make the same bets, even though his trade, though profitable, wasn't clicking.

To let off stress, he spent hours swimming and sailing in Southampton, and playing tennis with his friend Tarrant, displaying a nasty serve. To keep his employees loose and upbeat, Paulson sometimes adopted a faux British accent, keeping the ruse going during an entire dinner with one client. Paulson started one meeting about the mortgage business with a spot-on imitation of a current television commercial:

"You just filed for bankruptcy? No job? No problem! No money down!"

For all his equanimity, however, his concern was growing. What if the subprime market really did collapse—who would be on the hook for the billions of insurance he was buying?

"We didn't know who was selling it all to us," recalls Rosenberg, who traded with investment banks, not directly with those who sold Paulson & Co. insurance. "But if the sellers got in trouble, it would hurt the investment banks."

Concerns about the health of his brokers led Pellegrini to set up separate accounts for the firm at various banks, and to settle positions with his trading partners on a daily basis.

Paulson's outlook for the financial system became downright glum as a new advisor gained his ear. Paulson came across a newsletter published by an obscure economist in suburban New Jersey named A. Gary Shilling that predicted dour things for the economy. Paulson was so taken with the forecast that he asked Rosenberg to call Shilling and invite him to come by, to discuss his views. Shilling had spent more than a decade publishing a newsletter and periodic articles, usually with a single theme: The bad times were around the bend—sell everything! Most dismissed Shilling's warnings, sometimes with a laugh. The end was never as near as Shilling predicted.

Paulson was a merger guy—he didn't know Shilling was Wall Street's version of the Boy Who Cried Wolf. When Shilling met with Paulson and predicted a collapse of home prices and a sharp rise in mortgages foreclosures, Paulson took notice.

Shilling, a septuagenarian with bushy eyebrows and a balding pate, favored bright-red pocket handkerchiefs in his blue blazers. He emphasized to Paulson's team that the subprime market wasn't a fringe area, but rather a key underpinning to the entire real estate market. When it went, so would housing, bringing down much more.

"Boy, if you're right, the financial system will fall apart," Paulson said to Shilling, after one more dire forecast to a room of Paulson's analysts.

"Yes, John, it will."

Shilling, who vividly recalled the tears in his father's eyes during the Great Depression, predicted that housing prices would fall 37 percent.

"Do you really think it's going to get that bad?" Paulson asked, after another dire forecast.

"As sure as you can be."

Paulson began to focus on the linkages, and how troubles for subprime borrowers could topple housing, which might in turn bring down the financial system and the global economy.

This could really get bad. We need to broaden the trade.

But even Paulson didn't realize how quickly his prediction would come true.

P AOLO PELLEGRINI RECEIVED AN URGENT PHONE CALL IN EARLY 2007 from a trader at a major bank eager to lend him a hand. The prices of some home-mortgage bonds had weakened a bit, helping Paulson & Co.'s positions. But the trader reminded Pellegrini that those same subprime investments had dropped in price in late 2005, before quickly snapping back. It could happen again, costing Paulson the small profits it had achieved from its trade, he warned.

"Why don't you sell us back your positions so you can buy them back cheaper in March?" the trader advised Pellegrini.

Pellegrini was convinced his counterpart was trying to sow seeds of doubt. If Pellegrini followed his advice and exited positions, the trader might be able to get out of CDS insurance he had sold Paulson & Co. Or maybe he was trying to discourage Paulson from buying more protection, given the pressure it put on mortgage investments owned by the trader's bank.

"I actually don't know how much we have," Pellegrini replied. "We may have sold already."

Pellegrini was playing coy. He knew his boss was quietly raising the stakes of his bet, rather than cashing in his chips, putting to work money that was arriving daily from new investors. Paulson even had Rosenberg buy CDS insurance on mortgages with a high A rating— investments that others saw as relatively safe—not just BBB bonds.

To Paulson, it seemed obvious that housing was about to crack. Borrowers with spotty credit were running into trouble paying their loans. HSBC and others were dealing with problems, and subprime lenders, worried they were running out of borrowers, dropped already-low underwriting standards to hand mortgages to those with even weaker credit.

Despite those concerns, investment banks were fighting with one another to acquire subprime lenders, as if they were picking over the last jewels of a treasure chest. In January 2007, Stanley O'Neal and Merrill Lynch proudly unveiled an agreement to pay $1.3 billion to buy First Franklin Financial, one of the largest subprime lenders; Merrill now had more than $11 billion of such loans, even though the firm's own economists predicted a decline in housing prices of up to 5 percent. Morgan Stanley and Deutsche Bank, with billions of their own loans to borrowers with sketchy credit, also purchased subprime-lending companies.

Reading about it all on his Bloomberg computer terminal, Paulson shook his head, bewildered. He picked up the phone to speak with his old friend Howard Gurvitch.

"It just doesn't make sense. . . . These are supposedly the smart people."

But so far the prices of mortgage bonds hadn't fallen very much and CDOs built on risky BBB-rated loans were barely moving, preventing Paulson from making much money.

When will the market catch on? he thought.

Paulson was particularly aggravated by New Century Financial. The nation's second-largest lender to borrowers with iffy credit was smashing earnings records and enjoying a climb in its share price, even as other subprime lenders reported growing problems. Some home buyers weren't even making their first payments. Yet New Century claimed its performance was getting better. New Century executives explained that its underwriting was more thorough than its competitors', allowing it to grab business as the rivals faltered.

Paulson wasn't buying it. He asked an analyst to track loans made by New Century; he found its mortgages were running into *more* problems than those of its rivals, not fewer, feeding Paulson's suspicions.

"They're lying through their teeth. It's just not possible!" Paulson told Pellegrini, displaying unusual emotion after another aggravating day of watching New Century's shares rise. "These guys are preying on poor people!"

In early January, when Paulson shorted the company's shares, betting that they would go down, competitors snickered. New Century's largest shareholder was David Einhorn, the frequently praised investor and poker-tournament champ who counted actor Michael J. Fox among his loyal clients.

A salesman called Rosenberg expressing caution.

"Do you realize that Einhorn is on the board of New Century?" he asked. "He does serious due diligence."

The respect New Century commanded on Wall Street grated on Paulson. Every few hours, he got up to walk by Rosenberg's desk and check on his trades or receive an update on market chatter. Sometimes Paulson pulled up a chair and put his feet on the desk, watching CNBC on a nearby monitor.

Paulson's apparent calm reassured his staff. But in fact he was impatiently counting down to February 7, the day New Century was scheduled to release its 2006 results. You can lie about first-quarter, second-quarter, and third-quarter earnings, Paulson theorized, but year-end results are audited by an accounting firm, forcing a company to come clean.

Sitting at his desk late in the afternoon on February 7, a paper bag of red cherries nearby, Paulson looked up to see Andrew Hoine almost running toward him. Hoine placed a press release from New Century on Paulson's desk and watched him digest the news: New Century had reported an unexpected loss for the fourth quarter of 2006.

"John, these guys are blowing up!" Hoine blurted excitedly.

Paulson, peering over his tortoiseshell bifocals, read on: So many of New Century's borrowers were running into problems paying their loans that the company was forced to take back loans it had sold to various banks, reducing the company's previously reported profits for almost a full year. It turned out that New Century *was* just like the other subprime lenders.

Paulson looked up at Hoine, a look of relief across his face.

"Finally."

The news was a glass of cold water to the face of investors. The next day, New Century's stock plunged 36 percent on huge trading volume, Paulson's first big score.

As bond trading got under way in the morning, Rosenberg dialed a broker to get the latest quote on the ABX index. The response left him agape.

"Repeat that?! Did you say it's down five points?!"

Paulson held insurance on $25 billion of subprime mortgages. So a 1 percent move in the ABX index—or each single point drop—meant a 1 percent profit for the firm. That worked out to about $250 million. The 5-point move meant Paulson & Co. had just pocketed $1.25 billion— $250 million more than George Soros scored with his legendary bet against the British pound. All in a single morning!

Watching the ABX on the screen in his office, Paulson was transfixed by the figures flashing by.

"This is unbelievable," he muttered.

As the ABX plunged further over the next few weeks, Paulson kept his emotions under wraps. Employees sometimes caught glimpses of his building excitement, though. Leaving at the end of the day, he often had a big smile on his face. Instead of snapping at the small mistakes of his staff, Paulson became patient with them.

One afternoon in February, after the close of trading, Paulson wandered into Hoine's office and sat in a chair near him, crossing his legs and flashing a mischievous grin. Slowly, he raised then dropped his hands on the armrest, without saying a word, his grin turning into a broad smile. Hoine didn't have to ask—it was another good day.

Paulson and a few staff members followed the ABX index on their computer screens. His other investments, such as those betting against select subprime mortgage bonds and various CDOs, were harder to track because they didn't trade as frequently and weren't tracked with an index.

To get a sense of how the entire portfolio was doing, the firm's risk manager, Adam Katz, came around twice a day to deliver a printout of each position to Paulson. The mere sight of Katz rounding the bend, making his way to Paulson's office, sent the hearts of Paulson's team aflutter, just as the bells of an ice-cream truck get a child's heart racing. They knew the better the firm did, the larger their bonuses would be. Some staff members squinted to try to see Paulson's reaction to the printout, but he usually maintained his poker face.

Many of Paulson's clients were unaware of the growing troubles for subprime mortgages, news that didn't yet grab many headlines. A few weeks later, after they received a letter describing the fund's results for February, Jim Wong, the head of investor relations, received a call from a major client who sounded bewildered.

"Is this a misprint?? It's 6.6 percent, right, not 66 percent??"

But it wasn't a mistake—Paulson's credit fund had climbed 66 percent that month alone. Investors were incredulous. Paulson never before had gained anywhere near 66 percent, even in a full year. Some investors remained so dubious that Wong and his staff had to reiterate that the figure was indeed accurate.

"They wanted to hear it again, to make sure it was real," Wong recalls. "They were shocked."

Wong became uneasy delivering the results, sure investors wouldn't believe him or would think the firm had done something incredibly risky to produce those kinds of profits.

"It was just so off-the-wall that I felt uncomfortable," he recalls.

Panic soon swept the rest of the financial world. On Morgan Stanley's huge trading floor in Midtown Manhattan, hedge funds made urgent calls to their brokers, desperation in their voices.

"We missed it!" one bellowed into the phone, frustrated that he hadn't purchased any mortgage insurance. Some barely knew what a CDO or a CDS was, pleading for immediate tutorials. Calls also came from traders at big banks like Citigroup, Merrill Lynch, and UBS, who were frantic to get their hands on CDS insurance. The buying sent the price of the ABX still lower, adding to the angst.

Paulson's trade finally was working. His two credit funds had spent about $1 billion to buy CDS protection on $11 billion of assorted subprime mortgage investments. His merger and other funds together spent another $1 billion or so for insurance on $14 billion more mortgages. Already he was sitting on extraordinary gains of about $2 billion.

Banks and others now owed Paulson an amount of money that rivaled any sum owed in a financial trade. Some of them balked at forking all that cash over to Paulson before the CDS contracts were ended. Pellegrini and his team insisted, though, citing terms of their agreements, and the money was handed over. One bank dared Paulson to cause a default but ultimately backed down and posted the required collateral, a huge reverse margin call. The amateurs were putting the screws to the pros.

Paulson sold a bit of his CDS protection, to lock in some profits, but he clung to most of it, convinced that much worse was ahead for housing. The trade had become much riskier, however. When the cost of mortgage insurance was dirt cheap, Paulson was able to pay very little for protection, limiting his risk. But now that the ABX had tumbled from 100 to 60, Paulson had a lot more to lose—the index easily could snap back to 100. If the mortgage investments recovered in price, Paulson would be known as the investor who let the trade of the year slip through his fingers. For days, Pellegrini grew increasingly anxious about this prospect. Finally, he walked into Paulson's office with a recommendation.

"We should probably do some selling here, John."

Paulson looked Pellegrini straight in the face before giving him a curt reply: "No."

Pellegrini knew he wasn't going to get anywhere by protesting. He walked out, disappointed.

Pellegrini's fears soon proved well placed as it became clear that the industry was rallying behind subprime mortgages. Those with the most at stake, such as Bear Stearns, seemed the most eager to race to the defense of the market. The firm was the fifth-largest underwriter of subprime mortgages and generated a big chunk of its profits trading this debt. Bear also operated two large hedge funds run by investor Ralph Cioffi that owned all this debt.

Gyan Sinha, Bear's top mortgage analyst, convened an urgent conference call for clients to discuss the ABX index. Paulson and Pellegrini were among those who listened closely as Sinha addressed nine hundred investors. Most were hanging on his every word, eager for guidance in dealing with the crumbling market.

Sinha's advice was blunt: "It's time to buy the index," according to a participant on the call. Based on Bear's models, "the market has overreacted" to the news from HSBC and New Century. There was nothing fresh out there for investors to react to, Sinha repeated.

Paulson couldn't believe what he was hearing. During the question-and-answer period, he was tempted to argue with Sinha, but he held back, still unwilling to let others know much about his moves.

Paulson recalls, "[Sinha] said, 'My duty is to tell people how oversold the market is.' I had to bite my tongue."

Sinha blamed the sell-off on selling by inexperienced investors with no background in mortgages. It seemed to be a direct shot at Paulson's team.

"Almost the entire price movement can be blamed on nothing other than pure sentiment-driven selling," Sinha continued. "Maybe I'm naive and really I should stop thinking about fundamental valuation in all these markets."[1]

To Paulson, Sinha was a hopeless bull. Pellegrini had a less generous appraisal.

"He was full of shit," Pellegrini says.

Others also came to the defense of subprime mortgages, helping the ABX stage a rebound. At an industry conference in late February at the Roosevelt Hotel in New York, both Cioffi and Ricciardi made comforting comments about the market. Some snickered that Paulson and the other shorts were "tourist investors" who really didn't understand their market.

Then Sam DeRosa-Farag, the president of New York hedge fund Ore Hill Partners, stood to give an address, urging the crowd of hundreds of fellow investors to step up their buying. Though rough times were ahead, the short-term outlook looked rosy.

"We're not taking enough risk," he said. "We are all really a bunch of wimps."

At his desk, Rosenberg fielded calls from traders passing along gossip about rival funds that were gearing up to buy mortgage investments.

"Cerberus is going to be a buyer," one trader told Rosenberg, referring to the huge New York hedge fund. "There's a ton of money on the sidelines."

Rosenberg turned nervous—perhaps the traders were right about all the money ready to pounce. If Paulson didn't sell now, it might be too late later.

"I'm hearing about a lot of buyers out there," Rosenberg told Paulson as he pulled up a chair one morning. Paulson seemed amused by the chatter. Picking up a stack of papers in his hands, he pointed to a figure on one sheet.

"What's the average home price last month, Brad?"

The point was obvious: Home prices were still too expensive, and finally were falling. Now was not the time to get cold feet.

The ABX kept rallying, though. It rose past 70, hit 75, and rose as high as 77 in mid-May, slicing Paulson's gains by half. The climb came even after New Century announced that it couldn't pay its creditors and then filed for bankruptcy protection. The worst seemed over for the mortgage markets.

BEHIND THE REBOUND were investors like John Devaney, who once swore off subprime mortgages but now saw value and rushed to get in. As a teenager, Devaney was thrown out of a boarding school for partying and had had his ups and downs in the wake of his parents' divorce.

But in 1999, he started a Key Biscayne, Florida–based trading firm, United Capital Markets, which soon became among the largest traders of "asset-backed" bonds—bonds backed by streams of cash from credit cards and leases. While others ran for the hills, Devaney excelled at buying unloved investments, including the debt of mobile-home makers and aircraft leases after the September 11 terror attacks.

By 2007, Devaney boasted of a $250 million fortune. When he wasn't flying in his Gulfstream jet or sitting around his 16,000-square-foot Victorian mansion in Aspen, Devaney entertained guests on his 140-foot yacht, *Positive Carry*, named after the bond-market term for borrowing money at a low rate and investing it at higher rates. At conferences, he sponsored performances by comedian Jay Leno and bands such as the Counting Crows and the Doobie Brothers. At a 1970s-themed benefit he sponsored for the local Boys & Girls Club, Devaney made his entrance dressed as a rhinestone-studded Elvis Presley, while his wife, Selene, played a disco diva.

Devaney placed paintings by Renoir, Cézanne, and others on his mansion walls. He donated money to a range of causes, from literacy programs to the Republican Party, becoming a player in the Florida social circuit.

In the financial world, some positively gushed about his trading prowess.

"I don't think there is anyone in the business who wouldn't want to be John Devaney," Mark Adelson, then a senior analyst at Nomura Securities in New York, told the *New York Times*, "to have the insights and guts to do what he did, as well as the managerial skills, the analytic skills to pull it off."

By 2006, Devaney had a $600 million hedge fund that was on a roll, scoring heady annual gains of 60 percent. But he resisted purchasing risky mortgage investments, going as far as to tease those doing the buying.

"I personally hate subprime—and I'm kind of hoping the whole thing explodes," Devaney said on a panel discussion at an industry conference in early 2007.

As investors turned nervous after New Century's collapse, however, Devaney sensed bargains. Over the spring, he spent about $200 million to buy what he considered to be higher-quality subprime-mortgage investments. Not all subprime mortgages were dangerous, he argued, no matter what investors like Paulson were saying.[2]

"'Oh! Oh! Another news tidbit of New Century news. Oh, my god!'" Devaney said in a mockingly hysterical tone to a reporter, poking fun at the worrywarts.[3]

. . .

BACK IN JANUARY, at a conference devoted to subprime securities at Las Vegas's Venetian hotel, Rosenberg was chatting with a banker outside a conference hall when an investor approached and relayed a troubling conversation he had had the previous evening with some Bear Stearns traders.

"It's not so simple to short mortgages," one of the Bear Stearns traders allegedly told the investor. "A servicer can just buy mortgages out of a pool, so you guys never will be able to collect" on the insurance contracts.

It turned out that Bear Stearns owned a "servicing" company called EMC Mortgage Corp. that collected the monthly loan payments of home owners. If EMC exchanged poorly performing home loans within a mortgage pool for healthier loans, or added cash to the pool, it could ensure that the pool had sufficient cash flow to pay off all its investors, rendering Paulson's insurance worthless.

Later at the conference, another bearish investor, Kyle Bass, shared with Pellegrini a similarly ominous comment that he said he had overheard Bear Stearns' head mortgage trader, Scott Eichel, make in a crowded bar.

Eichel later denied boasting of any such maneuver, saying he was simply warning bearish investors of something they should be wary of. But Pellegrini already was on high alert. For months he had fretted about how the firm's big gains might be stripped by a player in the market, and he wondered whether investment banks might take steps to bolster pools of mortgages.

"I got concerned because I thought I would have done it myself if I was in Bear Stearns' shoes," Pellegrini says.

On a vacation in Jackson Hole with his elder son over Christmas, Pellegrini, atop a ski slope, held a conference call with executives at Markit Group, which developed the ABX index, suggesting that they clarify what would entail manipulation of the index. But they passed the buck to an industry group, the ISDA, that represented traders of these complex market instruments, and the group never addressed Pellegrini's concerns.

Back in New York, as Rosenberg finished another purchase of mortgage protection, a Bear Stearns trader added an unusual comment: "There's a document we want to send you."

Uh-oh, that can't be good, Rosenberg thought.

Reading it carefully at the fax machine, Rosenberg saw that Bear Stearns was reserving the right to work with EMC to adjust mortgages. Rosenberg immediately showed the document to Pellegrini. Unnerved, he and Rosenberg got on the phone with Eichel, warning him not to mess with the mortgages.

"A trading desk shouldn't be telling a servicer what to do," Pellegrini said flatly.

"But Paolo, we *are* allowed to," Eichel replied. "Read the documents."

A senior trader said Bear Stearns was proposing the new language to ISDA. Adjusting loans that borrowers were having difficulty paying could be effective public relations for Bear Stearns—the firm already had created what it called the EMC Mod Squad, a team working with local community groups to modify the home loans of delinquent borrowers.

Pellegrini and Rosenberg brought the document to Paulson, who seemed just as shaken. He called in Michael Waldorf, a lawyer on Paulson's team. In most firms, the traders are demonstrative and the lawyers more reserved. It worked in reverse at Paulson & Co. After quickly reading the document, Waldorf, an animated thirty-seven-year-old with close-cropped hair, stormed out of Paulson's office, his pink hue turning a beet red as he shook with anger.

"They're going to manipulate the market!" he bellowed. "They could take away" all the firm's winnings.

Waldorf had spent months watching Paulson and Pellegrini plot their moves; now was his chance to help the big trade.

Waldorf called others betting against subprime mortgages, including Greg Lippmann and Kyle Bass, and then hired former Securities and Exchange Commission chairman Harvey Pitt to spread the word about the alleged threat from Bear Stearns. He and Waldorf held a series of meetings in Washington, D.C., and elsewhere, arguing that EMC could modify all the mortgages it wished—slicing a home owner's mortgage payments actually might help Paulson because it would reduce the cash coming into mortgage pools. But, they argued, EMC couldn't discuss its moves with Bear Stearns or switch mortgages just to keep a pool of sub-prime loans from running into problems.

Pitt and Waldorf seemed to cause enough of a fuss: Bear Stearns soon withdrew its proposal. Paulson had avoided catastrophe. But he was having other difficulties. Each time Rosenberg called a trader to buy protection on subprime mortgages, he seemed to get an expensive price. Now that the market was weaker, the hedge fund would have to pay more, the trader said. But when Paulson's brokers gave him their daily "marks," or valuations of the holdings of its portfolio, the prices were much lower, sometimes for the very same investments.

As Rosenberg relayed the various quotes to him, Paulson became increasingly agitated, sometimes picking up the phone to speak with a broker himself.

"Why can't you give us the same pricing?!" one of the other brokers heard Paulson saying on the phone. "You're selling to us at ninety-five and we're buying at seventy-five!"

"Well, we can't," the trader replied.

At other times, Paulson was struck by the unrealistically high prices being quoted for slices of CDOs, even though he knew that no one was offering anywhere near those prices. Because the CDOs and other investments weren't dropping in price, Paulson's protection wasn't rising in value, keeping a lid on his returns.

Paulson was uncharacteristically blunt with investors and friends, lambasting Bear Stearns for giving him marks that understated how much his insurance was worth. But he stayed a Bear Stearns client, loyal to his former employer.

The more he thought about it, the more Paulson began to suspect that the brokers weren't picking on him. Instead, they were relying on faulty models spitting out prices that bore little resemblance to what he was seeing in the market. If they were quoting Paulson prices for toxic investments that were higher than they should be, he knew they must be placing excessive values on similar investments the banks held on their own books. It provided another valuable hint that the banks weren't nearly as healthy as they seemed.

TWO BIG HEDGE FUNDS operated by Ralph Cioffi soon provided Paulson with more reasons to be suspicious of Bear Stearns' health. Cioffi's funds, which held about $2 billion in capital but borrowed so much money that they owned nearly $20 billion of mortgage-related investments, scored early gains in 2007. Cioffi and his partner, Matthew Tannin, owned various slices of CDO positions, including those with the safest ratings, as well as considerable protection on the ABX. So when the ABX dropped, his two big hedge funds rose in value.

Privately, though, Cioffi was beginning to show signs of nervousness.

"I'm fearful of these markets," Mr. Cioffi wrote in an e-mail to a colleague on March 15, 2007, according to court documents. "Matt . . . said it's either a meltdown or the greatest buying opportunity ever. I'm leaning more towards the former."

In the spring, CDO prices finally began to fall, even as the ABX index snapped back. Cioffi's funds lost 15 percent or so in March and April, and his lenders became increasingly nervous—withdrawing their lending lines and putting pressure on Cioffi and Tannin.

In late April, Tannin e-mailed his more senior colleague Cioffi that he feared the market for complex bond securities in which they had invested was "toast." He suggested they discuss the possibility of shutting down the funds, according to the e-mail, which was sent from Mr. Tannin's private account. The pair decided their caution likely was misplaced, however, and they soon reassured their investors about the health of the funds.

But market conditions turned still worse and they scrambled to sell $8 billion of CDO investments. The air finally was coming out of the CDO market, as investment banks, stuffed with billions of CDO investments of their own from the previous several years' excesses, dumped their own holdings, pushing prices down.

At first, Bear Stearns' chief executive, James Cayne, seemed unconcerned about growing problems at his firm's hedge funds. Bear Stearns' money wasn't at stake, he reasoned. Rather, big institutions, wealthy individuals, and lenders, all of whom knew the risks going in, stood to lose their money from their dealings with the funds. Cayne, a gruff seventy-three-year-old former scrap-iron salesman with a penchant for cigars, golf, and cards, took off many Thursday afternoons and Fridays that summer to play golf near his New Jersey vacation home. As prices of various mortgage investments fell further in the summer and the funds ran into more losses, Cayne spent more than a week in Nashville, Tennessee, competing in a bridge tournament, seemingly confident that Cioffi's funds wouldn't have much of an impact on Bear Stearns.[4]

Soon, though, lenders forced Bear Stearns to extend one of the hedge funds' portfolios $1.6 billion to keep it afloat. A huge red flag had been raised, warning investors to Bear Stearns' own problems.

By July, the Bear Stearns funds had collapsed, leading to billions of dollars of losses for clients and throwing financial markets into chaos. Investors suddenly shunned mortgages. Brokerage firms could no longer avoid reducing the value of slices of all kinds of CDOs and subprime mortgage bonds, sending the price of all of Paulson's insurance shooting higher. He now was up more than $4 billion in profits, at least on paper. But until he exited the positions, he had no realized gains.

As investors and banks scrambled to buy protection, Paulson decided it was a good time to sell some of his positions. But Rosenberg, his only bond trader, was with his wife, Lisa, who was in labor with their second son. In a corner of the delivery room of Greenwich Hospital in Connecticut, Rosenberg set up a makeshift office, balancing a laptop atop a wobbly table and pulling up a nearby collapsible chair. He used a cell phone to make some sales for Paulson. Every so often Rosenberg rose to comfort his wife, before returning to his spot in the corner to make yet another trade. Dealing with labor contractions, Lisa watched it all, indulgently.

By 3 p.m., eight hours after going into labor, Lisa's doctor judged her close to giving birth and had his fill of Rosenberg and his mini-office.

"You've gotta get off the phone," the doctor said to Rosenberg. "It's time . . . the baby's coming!"

Back on Wall Street's frenzied trading floors, Cioffi wasn't the only investor buckling. A key New York–based hedge fund operated by Swiss banking giant UBS AG suffered more than $100 million in losses due to holdings of speculative second mortgages, known as second liens, made by New Century and other lenders. Two months later, UBS removed its chief executive, Peter Wuffli.

A few days later, as the ABX index dropped sharply, Rosenberg turned in his seat, peered into his boss's office behind him, and called out updates on the market. Paulson was juggling so many pieces of news while trying to run the firm that he appreciated the running commentary.

"John, it's down two points."

"Down ten points!"

"Flows are taking the market lower!"

Paulson & Co. was rolling in cash. But Paulson refused to show any excitement, determined to keep his team focused. Some afternoons, he sat in his office, picking at a tossed salad, trying to picture how bad things might get for the markets and the economy. One day, Wong came by with a question. He found Paulson lost in thought, spinning his wedding ring on his desk like a coin, over and over again. After waiting outside Paulson's office for more than ten minutes, Wong gave up and left.

Quietly, and without clueing in anyone at the firm, Paulson held off-and-on discussions about a potential sale of 10 percent or so of the firm. A number of other hedge funds had sold shares in their companies or pieces of their firms to investors. Paulson worked with a banker to examine a similar move.

In the summer of 2007, Paulson met with two executives with potential interest in buying a piece of Paulson & Co. Throughout the late-afternoon meeting in the company's conference room, Paulson seemed fidgety, as if he was waiting for an important piece of news. He talked softly and deliberately about the history of his firm and the genesis of the subprime trade. His guests couldn't figure out why Paulson seemed so unemotional, even as he spoke of the firm's accomplishments and growth. They wrote it off as an odd character trait.

Paulson's firm still seemed small to them; the air-conditioning wasn't working especially well that muggy July day and their seats were uncomfortable. But the investors were impressed by Paulson's unassuming manner and were intrigued by his subprime trade. Although he seemed nerdy and lacked the swagger of other hedge-fund managers they had met with to discuss similar deals, Paulson's grasp of the details of his firm's trades wowed them.

About an hour into the meeting, Rosenberg gently knocked on the door, interrupting the group. Entering the room, he leaned into Paulson's ear, whispering something. Paulson immediately rose, apologized, and stepped out, leaving his guests staring at an array of Snapple iced teas.

Ten minutes later, Paulson returned, appearing much more upbeat, almost jovial. A wide, Cheshire grin streaked his face. Something had happened in those few minutes away from the room; the more they watched Paulson, the more it seemed he was holding a secret that he was dying to share.

Finally, one of Paulson's guests asked if he was needed elsewhere and whether they should reschedule the meeting for a more suitable time.

Paulson finally blurted out what was on his mind: "We just got our marks for the day. We made a billion dollars today."

The investors were stunned. They had never heard of such a quick profit and didn't know what to say. In that instant, they knew they could no longer afford to buy a piece of Paulson & Co. Rising to leave a few minutes later, they shook hands and asked Paulson how much further his trade could go.

"I think they'll all go to zero," referring to the value of subprime home mortgages. "But I think I may need to get out of the positions" ahead of time, to try to ensure a profit. "That's the trick," Paulson told them.

I T WAS THIS VERY ISSUE that caused a growing rift with some of Paulson's investors, and even Pellegrini.

Most of his clients were thrilled with the sudden gains. But some were worried. Just as Paulson would look foolish if he built up huge gains only to fritter it away, many of these investors would be embarrassed if they stuck with Paulson and the profits later vanished. Investors in Paulson's other funds, which also owned some of his CDS mortgage protection, were especially on edge. They didn't have much experience with these kinds of derivatives, or those kinds of fast returns, and it was making them nervous.

Investors from Credit Suisse insisted on moving their money out of Paulson's merger fund that owned subprime protection and into another merger-investment fund without any CDS insurance, perplexing Paulson.

Another investor called Paulson & Co.: "If I could withdraw from your fund, I would. You're crazy, you should realize your gains."

Paulson patiently argued that subprime-mortgage prices were only beginning to drop.

"Take off half your gains then," the unhappy investor replied, recalling stories of other investors who squandered big gains.

"I couldn't convince them," Paulson recalls.

Some investors began to hassle his employees.

"Get out. You guys have made 60 percent; isn't that enough?" one investor badgered a staffer. "Why isn't he covering? What's he doing??"

When Tina Constantinides, a Paulson employee who dealt with investors, went to an industry conference in Florida, Tom Murray, a client of several Paulson funds, kept calling, insisting that she get back to him. Murray worked for the U.S. unit of EIM, a Geneva-based firm that invests in hedge funds and is led by Arpad Busson, a flashy international investor who had fathered two sons with supermodel Elle McPherson, his onetime girlfriend, and later became engaged to actress Uma Thurman.

"You're taking on a new type of risk," Murray told her. "How am I supposed to explain it to my investors?" Murray and his team said the investments Paulson was using were outside his area of expertise and had become too large a part of his firm's focus.

Constantinides tried to explain to Murray that the purchase of the

CDS contracts represented little risk for Paulson's funds. But after several weeks of analysis by Murray and his staff, Murray insisted on moving EIM's money out of one fund and into Paulson's merger fund, which held fewer subprime investments.

After a barrage of calls from other concerned clients, an anxious Constantinides walked into her boss's office, asking what she should tell the investors.

"The data's getting worse," Paulson said, soothingly. "Tell them to be patient."

Paulson's reassurance gave Constantinides the confidence to push back at the investors. But other employees of the hedge fund, some of whom weren't as familiar with the subprime trade, whispered that Paulson should sell more positions, in case the subprime market recovered.

Even Pellegrini, an architect of the trade, became convinced the firm was making a big mistake.

T HE YEAR HAD STARTED OFF WELL for Pellegrini. The hedge fund's huge gains in February were Pellegrini's first outright success in many years. And though the ABX soon rebounded, Pellegrini was promoted to a managing director of the hedge fund, his new stature confirmed.

As the fund added to its holdings of CDS protection, Pellegrini pored over the latest housing data into the evening, sometimes past midnight. One evening, as Wong wished him good-night, Pellegrini was so caught up in his work that he didn't even notice his colleague.

To relax, sometimes Pellegrini headed to Monticello Raceway, in Upstate New York, to drive a Ferrari around the track once or twice, before heading back home.

Pellegrini had become engaged to Henrietta Jones, a British-born executive in the retail business. That May, they were married and enjoyed a honeymoon in northern Italy at Villa del Balbianello, a historic villa overlooking Lake Como, the breathtaking location featured in Daniel Craig's rejuvenated James Bond thriller *Casino Royale*.

Pellegrini always had been superstitious, something he attributed to his Italian heritage. As the trade began to work, he became more so, try-

ing everything he could to avoid bringing bad luck upon himself and
the firm: No hats on the beds. Lots of salt thrown about the rental apartment they moved into on the Upper West Side. And never any talk
about the trade.

As a result, his wife only had a vague sense that Pellegrini was scoring
big. Sometimes she asked how it was going, but Pellegrini only smiled
kindly, without giving many details.

One day in the summer of 2007, after reading about troubles in the
subprime market, she turned to Pellegrini. "This is really good for us,
isn't it?"

"Yes," he said, still not giving her much.

Pellegrini now held the title of co-manager for Paulson's two credit
funds. But Paulson was the only one with the authority to direct a trade.
Pellegrini sometimes felt left out. He encouraged Paulson to stick with
the cheapest protection, rather than buy insurance on the ABX, which
was a bit more expensive. But Paulson usually overruled him.

"Forget it, Paolo, what's the difference? So you pay a hundred and
fifty basis points instead of a hundred," Paulson said, reminding
Pellegrini that they'd still make out well.

That's easy for John to say, he's rich already, Pellegrini thought.

They also disagreed about the need for secrecy. Laying low enabled
the fund to accumulate more positions at cheap prices, in Paulson's
view. But Pellegrini figured the cat was out of the bag, and that everyone
on Wall Street knew what they were up to. He had controlled his emotions for more than a year and it was getting harder for him to continue
doing so.

One day, Goldman Sachs economist Jan Hatzius and an analyst,
Michael Marschoun, hosted a conference call to discuss the housing
market. Pellegrini and Paulson listened in, sitting in their respective
offices.

During the call, Hatzius predicted falling home prices. Later on in
the call, Marschoun said falling home prices would lead to losses for
mortgage investments. And yet, Marschoun's outlook for mortgage
debt was surprisingly upbeat, because he was more optimistic about
home prices.

To Pellegrini, it was one more example of two-faced investment banks doing all they could to keep prices higher and to avoid putting accurate prices on the mortgage protection that firms like Paulson owned. Pellegrini was convinced that his big score would be taken away by Wall Street's establishment.

After listening to the question-and-answer session for several minutes, Pellegrini couldn't hold back any longer, asking a question of his own.

"I just want to know why Mr. Hatzius and Mr. Marschoun don't talk to each other."

Almost as soon as the words were out of Pellegrini's mouth, Paulson sent an underling racing into Pellegrini's office to disconnect his phone. A few minutes later, Paulson charged in, red in the face.

"You're being too smart for your own good, Paolo."

"He was pissed," Pellegrini recalls. "But from my perspective, it was almost like a conspiracy against us. I was saying, 'Hey, this stuff is mispriced; let's get on with it already.'"

With each piece of bad news for subprime mortgages and the housing market, Paulson directed Rosenberg to sell select CDS contracts, to lock in profit. By the summer, the firm had exited about one-third of its positions, securing hefty gains. Rumors swept Wall Street of multibillion-dollar CDO losses at Merrill and Citigroup. At Goldman Sachs, a team that included Josh Birnbaum, the trader who once had been skeptical of Paulson's heavy buying of protection, had turned bearish. Now they, too, were raking in profits.

Almost all of the selling at Paulson & Co. came from its various older hedge funds, such as Paulson's merger fund, however. He resisted selling much from his two credit funds, the ones that Pellegrini worked on.

Bear Stearns had backed off its threat to buy home loans to influence the value of all those mortgage pools that Paulson had bet against, but the threat still seemed real to Pellegrini. His experience working at a large investment bank made him deeply suspicious. All a bank had to do was buy some troubled loans and keep the losses of a pool under 5 percent, and Paulson's trades would be in trouble. Pellegrini continued to worry.

Later in the summer, Pellegrini again approached Paulson, walking into his office during a busy morning of trading.

"John, let's do some trimming," Pellegrini asked. "Let's cover some of these."

Paulson glanced up from the paperwork on his desk, looked at Pellegrini for a moment, and then went back to his work, without even responding. He had heard it all before.

A few weeks later, as Pellegrini huddled with Paulson in his office, quietly debating the market, Rosenberg turned in his seat to call out to his boss.

"John, we have a large bid to take off the index."

Pellegrini looked at Paulson, plaintively. They had received a big offer to buy a chunk of the hedge fund's CDS protection.

"John, let's do it."

Paulson didn't hesitate.

"No, I don't want to take that much off."

Rosenberg began to sense growing tension; in meetings, sometimes Paulson and Pellegrini cited different pieces of news to support their competing views.

Pellegrini had all his wealth tied in the credit funds, unlike Paulson, and he grew increasingly fearful that his chance to cash in on a fortune was about to be squandered.

Pellegrini knew Paulson could resist selling positions from the credit funds because investors were locked into the funds for two years. And Paulson already had reaped gains for himself by selling subprime positions from his other funds. But Pellegrini's wealth was tied to the credit funds. With each passing day he worried he might miss out unless they exited positions.

John's already made money from the trade, Pellegrini thought. *But I'm left with all the risk.*

IN CUPERTINO, CALIFORNIA, Dr. Michael Burry held some of the same positions that John Paulson did. As problems in the subprime market multiplied in early 2007, his mortgage protection gradually rose in value, two long years after he began buying it up.

But rather than congratulate him, many of his investors hadn't yet forgiven Burry for moving the investments into a sidepocket account several months earlier. And Burry's brokers, like Paulson's, were proving slow to mark down the value of a range of subprime mortgage–backed securities. Burry insisted to his investors that the side account, representing protection on $1.8 billion of mortgage securities, was worth much more than the $120 million value his brokers placed on it. They were having none of it. Burry's investors pulled another $50 million out of his hedge fund, placing him under more pressure.

Chafing under their criticism, and uncomfortable about locking the investors into the account, Burry reluctantly began selling some of his mortgage insurance. Maybe the sales would prove that his strategy was working, and he could win back his investors, he hoped.

In February, Burry put a small amount of the mortgage protection up for sale, testing the waters. The interest was overwhelming, enabling Burry to sell the protection for twice the price that his brokers had placed on his investments.

I knew they were screwing me! he thought.

Burry sold more pieces over the next few months, pocketing huge gains. The turn of fortune did little to reduce growing tensions within Burry's office, though. Scion's chief financial officer fell behind on the firm's 2006 annual audit. Burry was forced to tell his investors that their tax statements for 2006 would be delayed, and that they couldn't rely on the preliminary statements already sent to them. If the investors needed another reason to turn on Burry, now they had it.

The CFO soon said he was leaving the company, forcing Burry and his team to scramble to complete the audit and send the statements to investors in time for them to meet a June tax deadline. Then Burry found a discrepancy of about $1 million between the cash he had on hand and what was recorded in the firm's books. It seemed an oversight by his staff, but Burry wasn't sure.

Hoping for a respite, he took his family on a weekend getaway to a luxury resort in nearby Berkeley Hills. On the drive to the hotel, Burry's cell phone rang—it was another irate investor asking about the tax statements. He couldn't get away from it. As he put down his bags in the hotel room, still another call came through.

"How do I know there isn't a big fraud going on over there?" another investor asked.

Burry didn't know how to respond. He didn't think anything was amiss, but he didn't feel comfortable reassuring investors since the final audit wasn't yet complete. His reaction made the investors even more nervous.

Burry's team finally completed the audit, barely beating the June deadline. But it didn't prevent clients from yanking still more money from the fund. Burry lay awake at night, trying to figure out what he had done wrong and how to make things right again.

Subprime mortgages finally were falling, as he predicted, but Michael Burry was having difficulty just keeping himself, and his company, together.

12.

ONCE AGAIN, THE PHONE RANG IN ALAN ZAFRAN'S OFFICE. IT WAS late morning and the caller identification flashing on his assistant's keyboard showed a Los Angeles number. Zafran already knew who it was: Jeffrey Greene, with yet another urgent, angry call.

Months earlier, Zafran had moved from Beverly Hills to Menlo Park, in Northern California's San Mateo County, to steer his children away from the neuroses so prevalent in the Hollywood scene. Zafran still enjoyed dealing with Greene, though.

The hefty trading commissions were a big part of it, of course. But the more Zafran understood Greene's trade, the more he pulled for it to succeed. To him, Greene was a lone individual challenging an industry of cockeyed optimists and cynical charlatans, a modern-day David fighting Goliath. Zafran had come to appreciate Greene's dogged research and enjoyed helping him discover obscure housing data that might give him an edge in his trade.

But by early 2007, the calls were becoming more incessant and more heated. The pressure on Greene was building.

Greene seemed too well-off to have many real concerns. He gave his net worth on his application to Merrill Lynch for approval to buy CDS derivative contracts at $350 million, and he was a major figure in the L.A. social scene.

But at Merrill Lynch, some were not sure whether the figure they came up with for Greene's net worth was entirely accurate. He had millions of dollars of debt and an expensive lifestyle, paying for two full-time caretakers at his Malibu home and upkeep on three jets, including a Gulfstream. His real estate was valued at about $250 million, but it was rapidly falling in value and wasn't very liquid. Greene had about $100 million of other assets, but a few years of failure with his trade threatened to eat much of that up, too.

Indeed, Greene had committed to pay $14 million a year to buy CDS protection on $1 billion of subprime mortgages. And he put up about $60 million with the brokers to allow him to do the trade. Greene owned so much protection, and put so little down, that when subprime-mortgage prices rose just slightly in late 2006, he received margin calls from Merrill Lynch, forcing him to fork over several million dollars from other accounts just to keep his brokerage firm from closing out his trade.

Greene had bragged to friends and business associates about his moves and how they would pay off. His very reputation and sense of self-worth seemed tied up with the trade. But Greene's investments weren't moving, and he couldn't figure out why. He had tried to find a friend or two to join him in the trade but had failed, so Greene increasingly leaned on his two brokers.

Sometimes the calls would last hours, as Zafran patiently explained why Merrill Lynch's updated prices suggested that Greene wasn't making much money on his trade. If real estate tumbled but his trade didn't pan out, Greene would be in deep trouble.

Greene turned short, nasty, and confused when he heard the disappointing news. Picking up the call this morning, Zafran braced himself for more agita from his relentless client.

"Alan, are you aware of the kinds of loans being written?! I don't get it, why aren't these prices moving?"

Zafran tried to explain it as best he could, though he himself was a bit baffled. Housing data was getting worse and yet the Merrill Lynch traders that Zafran consulted continued to say that the insurance contracts Greene owned were not much more valuable than they were a few months earlier.

"It feels rigged! Figure it out for me, Alan!" Greene said, ending the call.

For all of Greene's concerns about his bet on the housing market, he couldn't help but eye a twenty-seven-acre estate in Beverly Hills that was up for sale. The mansion had been under construction for more than four years and was only 80 percent complete; its previous owner, a Saudi, relinquished it after becoming ensnared in a bitter divorce. The mansion had 60,000 square feet and seven acres of planted vineyard and featured a 2,000-foot-long double-wide driveway, off Coldwater Canyon.

How can I pass it up? Greene thought.

One morning in early February, Greene and his fiancée, Mei Sze Chan, showed up at a receivership hearing in a courtroom in downtown Los Angeles to bid. The odds didn't seem in their favor. Across the room stood attorneys for Anthony Pritzker, the billionaire scion of the fabulously wealthy Chicago family, and Alan Casden, a self-made real estate billionaire. Both men were listed by *Forbes* magazine as among the four hundred wealthiest people in the world.

The bidding began at $33 million. Soon it raced higher, in $500,000 increments. Greene swallowed hard and kept up with the billionaires. When Greene offered $35 million, the price proved too rich even for his wealthy rivals and they threw in the towel. Greene was thrilled—smaller properties in Beverly Hills were selling for more than $30 million. But now he would have to spend millions to complete the home and pay property taxes, adding to his financial pressures.

Hoping to finish the mansion and sell it for a profit, Greene began furnishing it in a way that might help draw attention. For the east wing, he chose two huge erotic paintings. Above the bar he hung a dark metal rendering of a dollar bill. He chose a mix of contemporary Vietnamese art and European antiques for other parts of the home. Later, Greene would hire Peruvian woodworkers to create fireplace carvings and ceiling crowns.

He christened the home Palazzo di Amore, Palace of Love. While the name sounded cheesy, Greene was convinced it would be a selling point.

"Every great home should have a great name," Greene says.

He now owned even more real estate yet was convinced that housing was set to fall.

"If [the trade] doesn't work, I'm cooked," he confided to his old friend Jeff Libert. Libert thought the expensive new home might have been a way for Greene to impress Chan. "It was very daring," Libert says. Greene had put "most of his marbles" in one trade.

Something bothered Greene about his maneuver, though. If he was buying all this subprime mortgage insurance at low prices, who was selling it to him?

"I asked a hundred people, 'Who's on the other side of these trades?'" Greene recalls. "I was sort of embarrassed to ask. I mean, I already own protection on $1 billion and only now am I asking?"

The answers weren't very illuminating.

"People kept saying 'It's CDOs looking for yield.' . . . Even after they explained, I didn't fully understand it. Don't they also want their principal back?"

Greene understood the concept of a CDO, but he couldn't get his arms around the question of why they were selling insurance on what to him were dangerous mortgages at such inexpensive prices. Was he missing something?

"I kept waiting for someone to say, 'Wait, you missed the real reason they're doing all these deals.'"

Greene's trade began to work in early 2007, and his daily calls to Zafran turned less intense.

"Finally, the market's starting to understand how bad the problem is," he told Zafran, after hearing that his bets against the ABX finally were rising in value.

When Greene read about a new government-run program called Hope Now, dedicated to helping struggling home owners stay in their homes, he panicked. He thought he'd finally found the fatal flaw in his strategy.

If the government program was a success, and more aggressive steps were taken to help borrowers, it might help to stabilize the housing market and limit losses from pools of subprime mortgages. *Should I bail out of the protection now, before it's too late?* Greene wondered.

Greene decided to call the toll-free number of Hope Now to check it out for himself. When he got through, however, he was put on hold—for more than forty minutes.

This can't be a good sign for home owners, Greene thought.

When a representative of the program finally picked up, Greene pretended he was a troubled home owner.

"Hi, I bought a condo in Canoga Park. The problem is the mortgage is $200,000 and the condo next door just sold for $160,000 and I'm really struggling to make my payments. What do you recommend?"

"There's really no point in making any more payments," the friendly voice on the other line said. "You won't get anything out of them . . . save your money and then just buy another place."

The answer floored Greene.

The government is actually telling people not to make their mortgage payments?!

If that's what the government was advocating, it was going to get real ugly for the housing market, Greene figured.

The ABX rebounded in the spring, and his positions dropped in price, giving Greene another bout of nerves. He quickly sold some of his protection and had his broker put him on a call with three senior mortgage analysts at J.P. Morgan to get their sense of the market. The analysts claimed housing prices wouldn't drop more than 24 percent, from peak to trough. Greene couldn't believe what they were saying—his own buildings seemed already down by that much. Did the guys in New York know what they were talking about? Where are they getting their numbers??

Other analysts Greene spoke with predicted that even a rush of defaults wouldn't lead to deep losses for investors in mortgage bonds, because the homes could be sold at full prices when the owners moved out. That, too, sounded unrealistic to Greene. Tenants with poor credit living in his buildings often trashed their apartments when they missed their rental payments and were evicted, taking every appliance they could manage to carry out the door.

"They usually feel ripped off," Greene told a friend. "Why would subprime borrowers be any different?"

There's going to be little for bondholders to recapture after this mess, Greene figured, making his mortgage insurance valuable.

But as the ABX kept rising in the spring, Greene's positions continued to drop further in value. He once again turned abrasive and short-tempered with Zafran. Greene became especially upset when he was told that his CDS insurance on the ABX index tracking risky mortgages still showed some gains, but similar protection on various pools of sub-prime mortgage bonds was relatively worthless. Greene had spent months picking out especially toxic pools of loans, mortgages with little equity behind them from states where housing seemed to be running into trouble. And yet his CDS protection on the loans was barely moving.

"This pool has more exposure to Florida and California, has lower FICO scores and more 'liar loans,' and yet is priced higher than the ABX," Greene told Zafran, growing more animated. "Why?!?"

On days the ABX index moved sharply, Greene sometimes couldn't even get an updated quote on the value of his CDS on various mortgage pools. And when he asked how the underlying loans in the pools were performing, his brokers often couldn't even tell him. It was like taking the biggest test of one's life and guessing at the final grade.

He hounded Zafran with more phone calls, several times a day, even on weekends. Together, they analyzed thousands of loans that Greene had wagered against, trying to get a sense for how they were doing. Greene sounded even more agitated, and their conversations were sometimes short and verging on hostile.

"Are you watching the same market I am??" Greene bellowed into the phone.

Greene couldn't figure out why he wasn't making money. Zafran couldn't understand it either, adding to Greene's frustration. As he asked his firm's traders to explain why their quotes for Greene were so bad, Zafran felt pushback from his colleagues at Merrill Lynch, who suggested that his allegiance seemed to be more in line with his client than with his employer.

To Greene, the answers that Zafran was getting from the traders just didn't add up. Housing finally was crumbling and yet his trade was a dud! At times, Greene became so angry in his calls to Zafran that his sentences ran into each other, rattled off so fast and furiously that Zafran couldn't make out what he was saying.

"Prices *have* to fall—how can you *not* understand this—call me back—bye!" Then he would hang up. One day he ended the call crying out: "Why?! Why!? WHY??!!"

A S JEFFREY LIBERT WATCHED the housing problems unfold, his own frustrations were growing as well. A handsome, salt-and-pepper-haired fifty-one-year-old real estate developer in Boston, his midsized firm controlled four thousand apartments and 1.5 million square feet of retail space throughout New England and Florida.

Libert seemed a natural candidate to profit from the real estate meltdown. He had three decades of experience in the business, starting with a handful of homes that he and Greene bought while students at Harvard. Libert had anticipated the problems with subprime mortgages and had encouraged Greene to buy CDS protection. It was Libert who had taught John Paulson years earlier that real estate investing wasn't as profitable as most thought.

Libert's father, a graduate of West Point who served under Gen. George Patton in the Battle of the Bulge, became wealthy operating a Chevrolet car dealership in Chappaqua, New York, a suburb in upper Westchester County. Libert attended upscale private schools in the area before majoring in economics at Amherst College, where he graduated in the top 3 percent of his class, and was a finalist for a Rhodes scholarship. While Greene was enjoying an extended bachelorhood on the West Coast, Libert met Mardee Brown, a Smith College graduate and the daughter of a lifetime General Electric executive, and married her.

After several years working at Boston Consulting Group, including the period with John Paulson, Libert quit the firm, unhappy with the constant travel, and went into real estate development with his brother. In 2005, Libert, worried about the local real estate market, sold one-third of his firm's holdings. He wanted to get rid of more of it, but he didn't want to have to fire his staff. Besides, his kids now worked with him and they'd have nothing to do if he sold the remainder of his properties. So Libert nervously clung to them, even as his concerns grew.

"Every doctor I knew was getting into real estate; at every upscale restaurant we went to they were speaking about real estate investing at every table," he recalls. "And you could already see higher incidence of defaults from mortgages handed out in 2006."

But Libert himself did almost nothing to prepare for a meltdown, even as it threatened his firm and the $100 million or so of wealth he had accumulated. After hearing from Greene about shorting the market, Libert called a few brokers to buy CDS contracts of his own. He was rejected by them all—Goldman Sachs, Merrill Lynch, Salomon Smith Barney. They judged Libert too small an investor to be able to buy the investments. Unlike Greene, Libert didn't push the brokers very hard, figuring it was a lost cause. Paulson agreed to let Libert into his hedge funds that were wagering against subprime mortgages, but Libert was reluctant to tie up his money, or to pay Paulson's fee of 20 percent of any gains.

"I just said screw it," Libert recalls. "Greene wasn't making money at the time and I just lost interest—how many times can I get rejected?"

After New Century's shocking news in February 2007, Libert called Greene to catch up on Greene's trade, figuring he had squandered his own chance at huge winnings.

"You must be making a fucking fortune," Libert said.

"Actually, things have moved, but not that much," Greene responded.

Greene told Libert to hurry up and figure out a way to buy his own CDS contracts before it was too late.

"You're such a wimp, Libert!"

At that point, Libert had enough. *I can't stand on the sidelines anymore.*

Libert called J.P. Morgan again, trying once more to gain approval to buy CDS contracts. This time he was transferred to John-Paul Tomassetti, the same broker in New York who was working with Greene. Over Easter weekend in 2007, Tomassetti approved Libert to buy the same CDS protection that Greene had purchased. (Tomassetti went by the nickname J.P., just as Paulson did, creating some confusion when Libert called Greene to discuss the trade. "I didn't know who he's talking about half the time when he said 'J.P. said this' or 'J.P. said that,'" Libert recalls.)

Days later, Zafran, Greene's other broker, also approved Libert to trade with Merrill Lynch. Libert spent about $500,000 to buy CDS protection on BBB-rated slices of the ABX index, just like Greene.

"It was so simple that I thought we were missing something," Libert recalls. "I figured I didn't understand the business."

Once he owned the investment, Libert discovered an odd impulse: He found himself rooting for a rash of home owners to run into problems paying their mortgages, something that would help his trade pay off. The feelings made Libert increasingly uncomfortable. He knew he had no control over whether or not home owners would make good on their mortgage payments, and yet he felt guilty. How could he root against everyday home owners?

As the investments played mind games with Libert, he tried to distract himself from the trade, vowing to check the ABX index only once a day, at the close of trading. It was as if he was trying to control an addiction.

"Greene was looking at it all day long, but I couldn't take it," Libert says. "I tried to avoid" watching the fluctuations.

As the ABX rose in the spring and Libert was dealt instant losses, he found himself pulling even harder for mortgage problems to develop. Then, as the subprime market wobbled and he made some gains, Libert felt intense shame about his feelings—while also wondering if he should have bought more protection. It was all too much.

A closet smoker, Libert began bumming cigarettes from his employees and sharing a smoke with some of them in front of their office building in Newton, outside of Boston.

"Michelle, if I was smart, I'd do more of these trades," he told one colleague on an especially stressful day. She listened sympathetically as her boss shared more of his angst. No one should own the bonds that he was wagering against, she agreed.

But when Libert's father came by the office to visit, he had a very different take.

"What do you think you're *doing*??" his father said, heatedly. "This is Wall Street you're talking about; these guys must know something."

"Dad, would you own these bonds at these prices?"

"No . . . but the guys on Wall Street know what they're doing."

Greene regularly called Libert, tweaking him for not buying more protection, making him feel even worse.

On the twenty-fifth day of each month, Libert called his brokers to check the latest "remittance" reports that provided a snapshot of how the pools of subprime mortgages were performing and the number of home owners that were delinquent on their loans that month.

For all his attempts to become a dispassionate observer of the housing market, Libert couldn't wait to get the results.

"Is it in yet? Is it in?" he would ask.

"I needed to see if defaults were escalating. I was hoping, praying, that another hundred thousand people would lose their homes."

Libert asked others for their opinions on his new investments, trying to find some reassurance that he wasn't doing anything improper. Rev. Steve Smith, a local minister and good friend, was not pleased.

"You've got to stop," Smith told him. "I can't believe you're happy about this."

"I'm *not* happy. It makes me feel creepy."

Libert's wife stepped in, trying to defend him to Smith.

"It's like being at a craps table. Jeffrey's just betting on it, he's not making the loans."

But Libert was getting excited about the signs of housing problems, the minister retorted.

A few of Libert's close friends were just as critical. Some called to take him to task, putting Libert on the defensive.

"I didn't cause it, I didn't have anything to do with the problems," he responded to one, as his wife, his moral compass, nodded.

"The friends made me feel guilty," Libert recalls. "I couldn't help myself . . . I was cheering for people to lose their homes."

Libert called his broker Zafran, to share his feelings and get some support.

"It just gives me the creeps, Alan. I'm betting on people's misery."

"I understand," Zafran responded, sympathetically.

Libert only rarely brought up his conflicted feelings with Greene, though. Greene couldn't relate to any of it.

"Libert, why are you being so uptight about it?"

"It just gives me the heebie-jeebies."

"You didn't cause it!"

"Yeah, I know. But we're cheering for it."

When it came to discussing the moral aspects of the trade, it was as if Libert and Greene spoke different languages.

"I didn't even think about it," Greene acknowledges. "If more people had been [shorting mortgages] early on, then the pricing of debt would have been higher and things wouldn't have become so crazy. The world would have been a better place had more people been shorting. We had nothing to do with what happened to home owners."

Part of Libert agreed with his friend. But he couldn't shake his qualms. It all left him a miserable ball of nerves.

M ARIO AND LETICIA MONTES were the type of home owners Libert was wagering against and the reason he was so torn about his trade.

In mid-2005, the Monteses found a home they loved, a gray stucco bungalow with a hot tub in the backyard in a middle-class neighborhood of Orange County. It cost $567,000. The only catch was they didn't have money for a down payment and couldn't afford the home unless they agreed to a mortgage with a low interest rate for the first two years, but one that would then rise, increasing their monthly payments by more than 50 percent. Their mortgage broker assured the Monteses, who earned combined salaries of $90,000, that they'd easily be able to refinance their mortgage before the rate climbed. Sitting around the kitchen table with their two teenage daughters, they decided to cut back on vacations and restaurant outings, and to take the plunge to become home owners.

By the summer of 2007, however, their home had tumbled in value and lenders finally had tightened their standards, making a refinancing impossible. They faced yearly mortgage payments of $50,000, just about their entire take-home salary.

"We have a disaster on our hands," Mario, a forty-eight-year-old warehouse manager, told a reporter. Fears of a foreclosure gripped him, he said.

"At this point," he said at the time, "we really don't have a plan."

"Bottom line, it's our little home," Leticia told a visitor. "Hopefully, we won't go down, and if we do, we're going to go down with a fight."[1]

BY THE SUMMER, the data was too overwhelming for Libert to ignore. Eight percent of a $1 billion pool of subprime home mortgage loans made in early 2007 already had defaulted—within just six months of being inked. Fifteen percent of them were in default after less than nine months. And the figures were only getting worse! Defaults didn't necessarily mean losses for the mortgage pools, but if losses in the pool reached 12 percent, or $12 million, even the AA-rated slices of the bonds would be wiped out, Libert knew.

Libert converted all his insurance on BBB-rated bonds to protection for AA-rated slices. Because they were still perceived as being largely safe, the insurance was still inexpensive, allowing Libert to get more bang for his buck. He now owned CDS insurance on $25 of toxic mortgages for each $1 he put down.

"You should really get into the AAs," Libert told Greene.

Now it was Greene's turn to feel torn. Should he follow Libert's lead and roll his own protection into insurance on those AA-rated slices? Greene arranged a phone conversation with analysts from Merrill Lynch and J.P. Morgan. They agreed that CDS contracts protecting AA-rated slices of subprime mortgages were a better bet than Greene's BBB protection.

Greene bought some protection on the AAs, but soon he became distracted. In late September, he and Mei Sze Chan married at his Beverly Hills mansion, a blowout affair that cost $1 million and was the buzz of the Los Angeles social scene. The guest list included Oliver Stone; Donald Sterling, the owner of the Los Angeles Clippers basketball team; and Robert Shapiro, O.J. Simpson's attorney. Mike Tyson was Greene's best man. Chan, wearing a gown of hand-beaded Swarovski crystals, married Greene in a French limestone gazebo.[2] After midnight, the revelers danced on a revolving dance floor in Greene's twenty-four-car garage. John Paulson didn't come, though he sent Greene a gracious card.

But Greene never stayed away from the trade for long. In the middle of the wedding, Greene pulled aside Libert with urgent news: "Your trade is at 89.72 today!"

Libert was shaken. He had bought protection on the ABX index tracking AA subprime mortgages when it was trading at 80. Now it was almost 10 points higher. He had given back half the profits from his BBB trade by shifting into the AA bonds much too early!

Then it dawned on Libert—there was no way Greene could know the price of the index in that kind of detail. Prices were never quoted to the penny. Greene was playing with Libert's head, preying on his insecurities.

He turned to his wife with a relieved smile.

"What's he talking about, 89.72??" Libert said. "I'm a schmuck; he's sticking it to me."

"He knew I just didn't have the stomach for the trade," Libert recalls.

By the end of the summer, Libert set aside his compunctions and made plans to put more money in the investments, convinced that something big was about to happen.

WITH EVERY NEW FIGURE on Greg Lippmann's computer screen in early 2007 came a single message: Your bonus is soaring!

As the ABX collapsed in February, Lippmann and his team racked up huge gains, thanks to protection they held on about $3 billion of subprime mortgages. One day early that month, they made $20 million, their best day ever. The next day, they did it again! The group followed it up with a still better day. Over one spectacular week, Lippmann's crew made $100 million of profit. Their Bloomberg terminals became best friends, the next price quote a cause for celebration, the end of the trading day a reason for sorrow.

At first, Lippmann tried to play it cool—his bonus check wouldn't be cut until the end of the year and he knew there was a lot of time for the trade to run into potential difficulties. But he couldn't help feeling relief. Walking with analyst Eugene Xu down a Manhattan street, after meeting a new hedge-fund client, Lippmann turned to his colleague with a look of astonishment.

"It's really working. Finally."

Other traders approached Lippmann, asking his advice on their own moves and where he thought the market was going. Colleagues who once snickered at Lippmann now needed his help.

"It's just starting!" he responded, urging them to get bearish. Many did, buying CDS contracts of their own. Others trimmed their holdings of mortgage-related investments, heeding Lippmann's advice.

One day, Anshu Jain, Deutsche Bank's London-based head of global markets, visited the firm's New York office. He walked over to Lippmann, greeting him with a warm smile, an acknowledgment of his huge gains and rising status at the bank. But Jain wasn't ready to congratulate Lippmann.

"Do you think you should cover here?" Jain asked. It was a pointed suggestion that Lippmann sell some positions to reap profits.

Lippmann pulled out the latest data on housing, showing Jain how the market was deteriorating.

"No, we have to hold steady," Lippmann said, according to a nearby trader. "Prices are heading lower."

Jain didn't push any further. But with every drop in the ABX, Lippmann received e-mails from superiors and risk specialists at the bank, each urging him to exit positions or at least consider trimming them. Some demanded it. Their message was clear: You better be right or you'll be blamed if the gains evaporate.

Lippmann couldn't believe it—the data was getting worse, not better. This was the time to increase the trade, not reduce it!

Didn't they get it?

As the ABX rebounded in the spring, Lippmann's mood turned sour. Nonetheless, the rally helped make mortgage protection cheaper, enabling him to generate additional commissions by teaching more hedge funds to do the trade. And home prices continued to weaken, making Lippmann even more convinced that BBB mortgage bonds were doomed.

Lippmann was less sure about top-rated bond slices, but a conversation with John Paulson persuaded him that even A-rated pieces would run into trouble. Lippmann began urging clients to buy CDS protection on those investments as well.

By then, the various hedge funds that Lippmann had educated about the subprime trade had begun making their investments with various other brokers, quickly spreading word about what Lippmann was advocating around Wall Street. He soon received a phone call from Scott Eichel, his counterpart at Bear Stearns.

"Why are you telling people that things are going to blow up?" Eichel asked him. "Why are you so sure?"

Eichel argued that the trade wouldn't work because real estate was resilient.

"Dude, when home prices fall, the subprime market is toast," Lippmann responded.

I N HIS SANTA MONICA APARTMENT, Andrew Lahde was staring at the same data that showed housing was deteriorating. February's panic brought gains to Lahde, as it did to Paulson, Greene, and Lippmann, less than three months after Lahde first bought mortgage protection and launched his hedge fund, Lahde Capital. His firm now was up to about $6 million in assets.

But Lahde was feeling more pressure, not less. The value of his positions had climbed a few hundred thousand dollars, but he hadn't sold any of them to lock in any of the gains. Instead, his expenses were piling up as he struggled to pay a few staff members. Lahde was making only a few thousand dollars a month from his tiny fund, barely enough to pay the rent. If he ran out of money, he would have to sell his CDS protection, pocket the measly few hundred thousands dollars in profit, and look for a job, once again, watching others profit from the crumbling housing market. That was the last thing he wanted to do.

Lahde had to somehow keep his trade alive and his fund going. He had to somehow find an investor who believed in him. To cut his expenses, he rarely left his apartment. For lunch, Lahde grabbed a turkey sandwich at a nearby deli. At dinnertime, he cleared paperwork from his desk table and ate tuna fish out of a can.

When the ABX index suddenly snapped back in the spring and Lahde suffered losses, it seemed like a death knell for his ambitious plan. He ignored calls from friends and family, desperate to find investors to back him. His savings were almost depleted. Dispirited, Lahde spent much of the day at the nearby beach, suntanning and ogling bikini-clad women. *Fuck it, I'm just going to hang out at the beach,* he thought.

The way Lahde figured it, he hadn't made much money. And yet, the ABX had dropped 10 percent since he started pitching his trade, making protection more expensive than it had been when he dreamed up the trade and tried to capture the interest of investors. If they didn't care about his trade then, they surely wouldn't care now that it was more expensive. He seemed out of luck.

Then Lahde caught a break. At a conference at Viceroy Hotel in Santa Monica, Lahde was introduced to Norman Cerk, a local investor who helped run a small hedge fund called Balestra Capital Partners. Cerk already had placed bearish bets against risky CDOs and the lowest slices of the ABX index for his own firm, but he wanted more. When he met Lahde, Cerk was stunned to meet someone even more worried about the financial world than he was.

"He was apocalyptic," Cerk recalls. "Here was this laid-back guy who kept saying 'The world's gonna end, you should put all your money in gold.'"

At his previous job, Lahde's histrionics turned off his boss, souring their relationship. But Cerk was impressed by Lahde's passion and conviction, and was taken by the depth of his knowledge about the housing market. Lahde recommended that Cerk buy protection on ABX tranches with high credit ratings. He even insisted that AA-rated slices would become worthless, a view that sounded radical, even to Cerk.

Lahde won him over, though, and Cerk handed him $6.5 million to invest. It was small potatoes compared with the kinds of funds Paulson and others were investing with, but it was enough for Lahde. He put the money to work as soon as the check cleared, buying more protection on ABX indexes tracking subprime mortgages. Finally, Lahde could execute the trade that he envisioned. He was sure he was months away from becoming a very rich young man.

L AHDE SEEMED TO PUT his trade on just in the nick of time. In July 2007, Standard & Poor's, the big bond-rating company, lowered its ratings on 612 classes of residential mortgage bonds made between 2005 and 2006, a total of $12 billion of debt. These were the very same investments that Paulson, Lippmann, Greene, Burry, and Lahde were betting against. S&P even warned that it was taking a look at CDOs that used subprime mortgages as their collateral, a clear threat that tens of billions of additional bonds would see their ratings slashed. S&P also dropped its ratings on $12 billion of debt issued by Lehman Brothers and Bear Stearns, bond-market powerhouses. Both firms now faced ratings that were close to "junk" level. Moody's, the other big rating company, reduced its own ratings on $5 billion of subprime debt and warned that it could reduce its grades on even more mortgages.

By the summer of 2007, it was clear that the subprime-mortgage market was in deep trouble. The ABX index tracking the riskiest home loans had tumbled to 37. On one brutal day for the mortgage market, Greg Lippmann's team scored more than $100 million in profits. Sitting on the subway on his way home, Lippmann looked stunned.

Despite the gloom in the subprime-mortgage market, Wall Street's titans seemed to breathe a sigh of relief because the rest of the economy appeared to have been spared. In late June, Blackstone Group, the leveraged-buyout kings, broke records by raising nearly $5 billion in an initial public offering that left Stephen Schwarzman, the firm's cofounder, with a stake in the company valued at almost $8 billion.

A few months earlier, Schwarzman had thrown such an extravagant sixtieth-birthday party for himself that several lanes of Park Avenue in New York City were closed in order to allow guests to come and go more easily.[3]

The message from the world's financial leaders was that the subprime mess was no reason for concern for the overall economy. Keep moving, nothing to see here, they seemed to say.

"Fundamental factors—including solid growth in incomes and relatively low mortgage rates—should ultimately support the demand for housing," Federal Reserve chairman Ben Bernanke said on June 5. "We will follow developments in the subprime market closely. However, at this point, the troubles in the subprime sector seem unlikely to seriously spill over to the broader economy or the financial system."

In Newport Beach, California, traders at Pimco, the biggest bond investors, began to buy some debt issued by big brokerage firms, convinced they were bargains. In August, Pimco's chief, Bill Gross, said, "I think the global economy is sufficiently strong and the U.S. economy probably will avoid a recession."

At AIG, Joseph Cassano, who ran a division for the insurer that until late 2005 wrote protection for billions of mortgage investments, said on an investor conference call: "It is hard for us, without being flippant, to even see a scenario within any kind of realm of reason that would see us losing $1 on any of those transactions."

Even the ABX index tracking risky BBB-rated subprime mortgage bonds popped up a bit, topping 40. The index following AA-rated loans surged past 95. And in early October, the Dow Jones Industrial Average hit a record 14,164, amid growing confidence that the worst was over.

While others rejoiced that the good times were back, John Paulson sat on a secret few were privy to. The subprime-mortgage domino had indeed been toppled. But many more were set to fall.

13.

JOHN PAULSON LEFT WORK EARLY AND WALKED TO A NEARBY SUBWAY STA-
tion. It was a slow Friday in early August. Manhattan was steam-
ing, and Paulson was looking forward to a relaxed weekend with
his family in the Hamptons. But first there was someone he needed to
meet.

Paulson hopped on a No. 7 train heading toward the borough of
Queens, one of thousands getting a jump on the weekend. Two stops
later, at Hunters Point Avenue, Paulson got off and transferred to the
4:06 p.m. "Cannonball Express," a Long Island Railroad train heading
east. Paulson was a regular most Fridays in the summer and usually
reached his home in Southampton less than two hours later. A car and
driver, or even a helicopter, couldn't get him there nearly as fast, he told
friends, explaining why he still took the train.

Sliding into a seat already saved for him in a front car, Paulson
greeted his friend Jeff Tarrant. Soon, throngs of passengers crowded in,
some carrying tall beers in the aisles.

Opening a cold bottle of water, Paulson seemed to relax as the train
pulled away from New York, as if a load had lifted from his shoulders.
Paulson always loosened up on the weekly ride, showing a glimpse of
his former self. A few weeks earlier, Paulson noticed his college mate
Bruce Goodman and his son, John, on the train and invited them to sit
with him.

"I want you to hear what I did," Paulson said, more enthusiastic than
boastful. He spent more than an hour patiently explaining details of his

bet against subprime mortgages, as John Goodman, an economics student who once spent a summer at Paulson & Co., listened eagerly.

On this August Friday, though, the financial markets seemed increasingly fragile, and Paulson and Tarrant met to trade intelligence and to answer a billion-dollar riddle, one that threatened the sunny day with thick, dark clouds: If Paulson was sitting on a stunning $10 billion of gains that year, who was facing dramatic losses? Which firms were hiding deep problems, and what would the consequences be?

Paulson's tie was loose and he looked tired, if relaxed. It was the cost of making more than $100 million during that week alone. Normally, Tarrant, well dressed in a crisp blue blazer, his silver hair perfectly coifed, looked as if he had stepped out of an issue of GQ magazine. But this afternoon Tarrant seemed frazzled. His firm, Protégé Partners, had invested in a number of hedge funds and other kinds of financial firms; Tarrant worried there could be more shoes to drop on the economy and the market, potentially crushing his company. He needed to know if he had placed money with firms that were on the other side of Paulson's trades.

"Who's holding the bag on all this stuff?" Tarrant asked Paulson.

Tarrant had consulted with a round of experts who told him that European insurance companies had sold the bulk of the CDS contracts to investors like Paulson. Many of these companies didn't need to own up to any losses, at least immediately, thanks to various accounting conventions, so the problems likely would be swept under the rug and wouldn't cause too much damage, they assured Tarrant.

He didn't buy it. Many of his clients were European insurers and they promised Tarrant that they hadn't touched the insurance on subprime debt.

"Who owns this stuff?!" he again asked Paulson, before rattling off a series of his other worries about the financial system.

Paulson seemed oddly serene as Tarrant continued with his hand-wringing.

That's when Paulson let his friend in on a secret. A few months earlier, he had reflected on how easy it was for him to buy billions of dollars of protection on all those toxic mortgages. All day long, his trader, Brad Rosenberg, heard the same answer when he asked to purchase buckets- ful of CDS protection: "You're done"—trader lingo for a completed trade. No hassle, no problem, the insurance was theirs for the taking.

Paulson began to wonder, if his fund found it so easy to buy billions of dollars of protection, who was selling it all to them? And what would happen to them as housing came crashing down?

Back in July, Paulson popped his head into Andrew Hoine's office and asked his research director to swing by for a chat. Hoine once had spe- cialized in brokerage stocks as a young analyst. So Paulson put him on the case, asking Hoine the same question that was now puzzling Tarrant.

"If we're making all this money, who's on the other side?" Paulson wanted to know. Maybe there was a chance to pull off another big trade by wagering against some of these apparent losers, Paulson thought. Even if it was half as alluring as betting against subprime mortgages, it could be a coup.

Hoine spent days pestering the salesmen selling Paulson all that pro- tection. Was there a big, bullish investor on the other side of the trades? Was it a group of hedge funds or some other investor?

The salesmen weren't allowed to give Hoine much intelligence, in keeping with custom in the marketplace, where trades are supposed to take place in anonymity. But after asking enough questions, Hoine began to surmise the answer: Banks were selling subprime protection to investors like Paulson and often keeping the positions for themselves. The banks then fed the positions to CDOs and other products and kept slices of the CDOs on their balance sheets, like retailers holding on to the merchandise for their own families.

"They wouldn't say the specific banks, but we got ideas," Hoine says. "You could tell from traders that Merrill and some others couldn't sell it all."

It all made sense to Paulson. Much like Greene on the West Coast, Paulson has been struck by how far the ABX index had fallen for much of the year, even though prices of most CDOs and other mortgage pools made up of subprime mortgages were barely budging. The CDOs and other pools didn't trade as frequently as the ABX, so there was a lag in their pricing, Paulson understood. But he became concerned that banks were overstating the value of the CDO slices they quoted, to avoid owning up to big losses of pieces that they themselves owned. Paulson had an associate join a group of hedge funds to write a pointed letter to the Securities and Exchange Commission. Now they were asking questions of the banks.

Even if the inquiries didn't lead anywhere, Paulson knew that as long as the ABX kept tumbling and home owners continued to have difficulties meeting their monthly mortgage payments, all the pools of dangerous mortgages, and the CDOs built from them, were bound to eventually fall in price, too. Then, the banks and others holding these investments would have to record deep losses because they held so much of it themselves. It was just a matter of time before the pain began.

It was no secret that banks and investment banks like Merrill Lynch, Morgan Stanley, Countrywide, and Bank of America had pushed into subprime lending. They hadn't acknowledged any huge losses just yet, though, reassuring some investors. But as the ratings companies lowered their grades on various pools of subprime home loans, it would have to happen, Paulson told Hoine.

Hoine and another analyst at the fund took a guess at how exposed various banks were to CDOs, and to every kind of home loan— subprime, "Alt-A," "jumbo," and "Prime-rate." They added up all the potential losses and compared them to the capital of the banks, instantly identifying which institutions likely would run into problems. Then they figured out how many of the banks' assets could be difficult to price or sell, called Level One and Level Two assets, adding more demerits to certain banks.

Paulson kept shaking his head as he read the latest figures on how much money investment banks had borrowed to run their businesses. It made him more certain of trouble ahead. Hedge funds like his could never get away with all that leverage, he said.

"This could be the next wave!" Paulson exclaimed to Hoine as he showed him a spreadsheet of all the debt problems.

They also realized that those selling the CDS contracts didn't have to set aside much money to cover payments they might have to make. An investor selling Paulson CDS insurance on even $1 billion of subprime bonds didn't have to have nearly as much money ready to pay for it.

When Rosenberg told Paulson how inexpensive it was to buy CDS protection on a range of financial companies, it reminded Paulson of his subprime trade—very little downside and tons of upside.

So the Paulson team began accumulating protection on all kinds of companies. CDS contracts to insure $100 million of Bear Stearns debt cost just $200,000? We'll take it! Lehman protection costs $400,000? We'll take that, too, please. UBS, Credit Suisse, and all kinds of other big financial players? Most definitely. They could have it all for well under 0.50 percent of any amount they wished to insure. It was as if Paulson's team was shopping at a dollar store, but finding the choicest goods from Tiffany down each row.

"Look at these spreads!" Paulson said to Rosenberg after getting an update on the latest pricing. "You don't need a smoking gun" proving that a bank was in trouble—the insurance was so cheap, it was worth holding just on the off-chance trouble developed.

As Paulson recounted it all to Tarrant on the train out to Long Island, his friend turned anxious. He recently had met a senior banker who hinted at "systemic" problems if the housing market turned still lower. Now he had confirmation of his worst fears.

"Oh my God, these guys really have retained it all," Tarrant said.

Paulson moved closer to Tarrant's seat, trying to keep their conversation private.

"It's even beyond that, Jeff," Paulson said quietly. Even if it turned out that the banks had somehow sold off much of the mortgage protection to clients, the losses likely would run so deep that the clients wouldn't be able to handle them, leaving the banks on the hook.

"They're stuck," Paulson said, referring to the big banks, which seemed in trouble either way.

In one sitting, Paulson had described why the entire financial system was in jeopardy. And yet, Paulson seemed calm, even upbeat. Tarrant couldn't figure out why.

"What are you going to do?" Tarrant asked.

Paulson confided that his firm had purchased CDS protection on all the investment banks his firm traded with. That way, even if they went under and couldn't pay him his winnings, he'd profit on the way down.

"How can these smart guys get into these positions?" Paulson asked with a shrug of his shoulders and a little smirk, as if he had it all figured out. Tarrant was left shaken, unable to muster much of an answer.

When they got off the train, Paulson and Tarrant were met by their wives and whisked away to their respective estates.

But Tarrant couldn't shake a morose feeling.

Over a martini that night, he described Paulson's doomsday scenario to his wife. That night, Tarrant, normally a deep sleeper, tossed and turned, waking her. Tarrant had figured that investing with Paulson was like a security blanket, one that could protect him and his firm in case housing and the economy went south. But the conversation he had with Paulson on the train left Tarrant rattled. He realized he was going to need much more protection for the coming storm.

BACK IN NEW YORK, Paulson received another tip that bigger problems were brewing. In September, a nanny for Paulson's two young daughters quit and moved out. Bills began to come for the woman, an immigrant from Eastern Europe. It turned out that she had given Paulson's address to a string of credit-card companies, cellular-phone providers, department stores, and others, and she never paid any of the bills.

Paulson couldn't track down the woman, so he began to trace her billing history, trying to get the creditors off her back and halt the sometimes threatening letters coming to his home. It turned out that the nanny had a pattern of ordering cell-phone service, ignoring the subsequent bills, and then simply moving on to the next provider when they cut off her service. Sprint to T-Mobile to AT&T and then to Verizon, thousands of dollars in unpaid bills left in her wake. She sometimes defaulted on her account and found new providers eager to win her business. She also had ignored her dozens of credit cards and store cards.

"I can't believe this," Paulson said to Jenny, a touch bewildered. "It's out of control what's going on."

Each company Paulson called seemed more bureaucratic than the next. He couldn't get to the bottom of how much his former nanny owed, or how to stop the bills from coming.

When Paulson got to his office, he shared the story of his nanny, ranting about the endless chain of bills.

"Can you believe she doesn't pay her bills and she's still getting new credit-card promotions left and right?" Paulson asked Andrew Hoine.

Paulson looked befuddled, as if he had just gained a glimpse of how the other half lived, much like President George H. W. Bush when he encountered a supermarket scanner during his presidency.

Hoine wasn't surprised. A good friend who made automobile loans to low-rated borrowers in Florida told him that a cook at a local Applebee's restaurant recently obtained a loan to buy a new Bentley, agreeing to pay sky-high rates. And there was heated competition among lenders to make the loan, despite its low probability of being paid in full.

Paulson now was even more convinced that the nation's debt problems weren't confined to subprime home mortgages. He told his team to begin shorting shares of banks with significant exposure to the credit-card business, as well, and those making commercial real estate, construction, and almost other kind of risky loans.

Gary Shilling, the downbeat septuagenarian economist from New Jersey, kept telling Paulson's team that subprime mortgage problems would infect the entire housing market. So Paulson's hedge fund shorted shares of Fannie Mae and Freddie Mac, the big mortgage lenders, as well.

At the time, others were becoming more upbeat about the future of the economy. At a panel discussion at an industry conference, Jim Wong, Paulson's head of investor relations, endured a series of presentations about the big returns that hedge funds were making buying "leveraged loans," or those made to companies dealing with heavy debt from recent takeovers. Asked his opinion, Wong said his firm viewed these loans as too risky.

After the discussion, an investor pulled aside Wong, saying, "Paulson's gonna miss the boat on leveraged loans . . . he doesn't understand these securities are safe."

Back at the office, Wong relayed the conversation to Paulson. He appeared more amused than angry at the insult. "Go tell him that I don't want to be on that boat," Paulson replied with a grin.

B Y THE FALL OF 2007, the dominoes were beginning to topple. As more borrowers ran into problems paying their home mortgages, ratings firms scrambled to lower their ratings on all kinds of mortgage debt. It turns out that the debt was risky after all, they acknowledged. In October, Moody's downgraded the ratings on $33 billion worth of mortgage-backed securities. By mid-December, ratings had been dropped on $153 billion of CDO slices. Because banks and investment banks around the globe, such as Citgroup, UBS, Merrill Lynch, and Morgan Stanley, owned many of the slices of CDOs made up of toxic mortgages, they were forced to write down more than $70 billion in three short, painful months.

Blame was soon apportioned. Chuck Prince, Citigroup's chief executive—who once said his bankers would dance until the music stopped—was ousted. So, too, was Stanley O'Neal, Merrill Lynch's CEO, who was paid $46 million just a year earlier and lauded for pushing Merrill to hold $40 billion of CDO slices, up from $1 billion two years earlier. Shares of many major financial companies were cut in half in a matter of weeks.

(O'Neal left with $161 million in his pocket, on top of $70 million that he took home during his four-year tenure; Prince was given $110 million, an office, an assistant, a car, and a driver.)

Other losses soon sparked concern about companies like Ambac that insured bonds for investors, adding to the market's angst.

Pellegrini had spent countless hours worrying about what could upend the firm's trades and making sure its winnings were secure. About $10 billion of profits was waiting for them at various firms, the sum of the daily exchange of cash from those who sold the hedge fund protection. Now, Pellegrini had it placed in institutional Treasury-bond funds to which the hedge fund had easy access, rather than allow it to sit within reach of investment banks under increasing pressure. The profits they had accumulated so far seemed safe.

But some of Paulson's team had concerns about how they were going to exit their remaining investments without pushing down the price. The debt markets they focused on had limited trading, and it wasn't clear how they would get out of the trades. Selling so much mortgage protection might push down prices dramatically, slicing their gains. They had sold a number of their more liquid positions, but who would buy the rest of it, especially the mortgage protection that traded so infrequently?

It was time for Paulson to test the waters. He walked out of his office to the desk of Brad Rosenberg and asked the trader to begin circulating BWIC lists, or bids wanted in competition. Various ABX indexes had crashed below 50. Investors' perception of risk seemed at panic levels. Paulson wanted to see what kind of demand he might find for his CDS insurance.

Rosenberg made a round of calls and walked into Paulson's office with news he wanted to hear: Banks and investors were clamoring for their insurance, to protect their holdings of mortgage securities. Over the next few weeks, Paulson sold about 40 percent of his CDS insurance. The rest proved harder to get rid of, frustrating Rosenberg at times.

Paulson got some help from a surprising place, however. Among the traders most eager to buy Paulson's CDS insurance were some at Bear Stearns, of all places, the firm he squabbled with and was among the most critical of his original thesis. Scott Eichel and other senior traders at Bear Stearns, who once scoffed at Paulson and Lippmann, realized the severity of the real estate problems. It was late in the game, but the traders now called the Paulson team, desperate to buy their positions.

Eichel's group eventually made about $2 billion of profits owning protection that Paulson had discarded. It was a valiant effort to save their firm.

Tension was building elsewhere within Bear Stearns, as executives argued about how to right their sinking ship. The investment bank held too many risky mortgages, and clients, including major hedge funds, were losing faith. Some discussed pulling their money from the firm. Within the executive suites, some argued for urgent action.

"Cut the positions, and we'll live to play another day," argued Wendy de Monchaux, a senior trader.

"We've got to cut!" agreed Alan "Ace" Greenberg, the firm's former CEO and fifty-nine-year veteran.

But the firm's chief, Alan Schwartz, urged caution. Many of the markets for mortgage debt had become difficult to trade in. Unloading tens of billions of dollars' worth of mortgages and related bonds at fire-sale prices would create devastating losses, he argued.

"Stand calm . . . we've got it under control," he told some at the firm.

WHILE IT WAS MONEY that drove John Paulson, he also wished to be recognized as one of the investment wizards, an objective that long eluded him over the years as he toiled in obscurity.

In the fall of 2007, that all began to change. One day he got a phone call from George Soros, the man renowned for his own famous trade, a 1992 bet against the British pound, one that earned $1 billion for his Quantum hedge fund. The figure paled in comparison to the $12 billion or so of gains that Paulson had accumulated at that point. But Paulson didn't have the heart to bring that up when Soros invited him to lunch at his office, at Seventh Avenue and 57th Street.

Although Soros's nephew, Peter, was a longtime friend of Paulson's and an investor in his funds, Soros had heard about Paulson's coup through his contacts on Wall Street. Soros, quasi-retired at the time, was itching to get back in the game. He turned to Paulson for help.

Soros was painfully aware that the investing game had dramatically changed in recent years; he was like a ballplayer attempting a comeback and realizing that the rules had been altered. Stocks and other investments listed in the daily newspaper and running across the bottom of business-television screens were no longer as crucial to making the big money. Instead, credit-default swaps, instruments that didn't even exist a few years earlier, were where the real action was. After complimenting Paulson on his coup, Soros asked for a tutorial.

Over grilled halibut and vegetables, Paulson described the ABX indexes, how CDS was traded, and some of his moves. At first, Soros seemed preoccupied, even perturbed. It turns out the fish wasn't up to his standards and he complained about it to his assistant.

But Soros enjoyed the patient and thorough lesson and was struck by Paulson's understated manner. Weeks later, Soros became more engaged at his firm, and in the last three months of the year, he racked up several billion dollars of profits of his own.

During the lunch, when Paulson argued that banks were in trouble and shared that he was betting against some of them, however, Soros thought he was a bit too downbeat. "I thought the risk-reward was better in other trades," Soros recalls.

Even in Paulson's moment of triumph, skeptics thought they knew better.

JEFFREY LIBERT bought some protection on subprime mortgages rated BBB− in early 2007, and then converted it to insurance on even more AA-rated loans in August.

He remained torn about whether to add more or whether to give in to his misgivings and just get rid of the investments. He watched the market closely, trying to decide what to do. The ABX index tracking top-rated loans was at 90, implying that few thought they would run into any trouble. But these were dangerous mortgages made to home buyers with scuffed or limited credit. There's no way they were genuine AAA bonds, Libert concluded.

Libert was set to spend $1 million to buy CDS contracts on $10 million of these loans. But he didn't have an opportunity to speak with his broker before leaving with his wife to spend a week at their home in Provincetown, the picturesque town at the tip of Cape Cod. Libert was recovering from back surgery and hadn't worked for several months as he tried to deal with the pain. He figured he'd just call his broker and make the trades a few days later.

On their first day in Provincetown, Libert received a call from his broker in New York. Tomassetti sounded unusually stressed as he filled in Libert on startling losses announced by Citigroup and Merrill Lynch.

Tomassetti told Libert that the ABX indexes were reacting dramatically to all the news, as investors and banks scrambled to buy their own insurance on toxic mortgages.

"Jeffrey, they're really moving."

It was time to do the buying he planned, Libert decided, sure that big profits awaited.

"Okay, get me in at ninety."

"We can't, we're way past that."

"What?! You mean we're at eighty??"

"No—it's seventy."

"What? In one day?!"

Libert was in a panic. He was finally prepared to toss his moral qualms into the nearby Atlantic Ocean, but now it was too late. The sharp drop in the index meant that the CDS insurance he already owned was worth millions of dollars. He was miserable, though, thinking about the gains he had squandered by dithering.

The AAA-rated mortgage loans that Libert wanted to bet against traded at sixty cents by the end of that month. Libert would have made close to $10 million more had he picked up the phone and pulled the trigger on his trade.

"The truth is, when Greene thinks he's right, he puts the wad down," Libert says. "When I think I'm right, I'm not as sure."

B Y OCTOBER, Jeffrey Greene's own CDS protection had climbed in value by as much as $300 million. If he cashed out, Greene knew he could live as extravagantly as he wished the rest of his life and never have to think twice.

But unlike his former friend John Paulson, Greene couldn't bear to let go of his mortgage protection, convinced that deeper troubles for housing were ahead. Every day in the fall, Greene received a summary of his account. And every day, his positions climbed in value by

millions of dollars. This was what Greene spent almost two years waiting for. He wasn't going to close his glorious trade now.

Months earlier, Greene had peppered Zafran with calls, trying to understand why his trade wasn't working. Now it was Zafran's turn to pursue Greene. He called at least once a week, urging his client to do some
selling.

"Jeff, you really should take some chips off the table. Don't be foolish,
just take a hundred million out," Zafran advised his client. "God forbid,
the government gives one hundred percent mortgage relief to everyone," then the CDS insurance will be worthless.

"No way," Greene responded. "They're going down further, they're
fundamentally bad."

Later in the fall, though, friends helped convince Greene to take some
profits. He was up twentyfold and even fortyfold in some of his investments. Why not take some off the table?

Greene called Zafran, ready to do some selling. Zafran rang various
traders within Merrill Lynch to get a price at which they could find a
buyer for Greene's protection. The CDS insurance he had bought on
various slices of the ABX index was a cinch to sell, so Greene did some
of that. But he owned protection against specific pools of ugly mortgages, and they were such unique investments that it was hard to get
prices for the protection, let alone find someone to buy it. Sometimes it
took Zafran days to get back to Greene with a quote; other times it took
several weeks.

Greene turned livid, unable to comprehend the delay. "You've got to
be kidding me," he barked at Zafran. "What kind of amateurish operation does Merrill run?"

The pricing issues were part of the reason why Merrill and other
firms had been so reluctant to sell these instruments to individuals—
they might be hard to exit if no buyers emerged. Zafran didn't want to
mention that and set Greene off again, though. "I told you so" likely
would make him even angrier, Zafran figured.

Sometimes, Zafran came back with quotes on only three of the eighteen pools of mortgages that Greene was betting against—and the three

were the best-performing pools, not the ones that Greene figured to make the most from.

Greene was sick and tired of Merrill's traders and their quotes. And he wasn't sure whether Zafran's true interests lay with his firm or with Greene. For their part, Merrill's traders had had enough of Greene— over and over again they had to round up quotes for his tricky investments, but he never did any trading. Now he said he wanted to sell, but how could they be sure?

Greene tried pushing his broker to get better prices: "Alan, you're a big guy at Merrill; get it done."

Zafran understood Greene's nervousness. If he couldn't sell the positions, his hard work might be for naught.

Finally, Greene gave up, exasperated. He told Zafran that he was just going to hold on to his investments and not try to sell any more of them, at least for now.

"I would have closed the positions at fifty cents on the dollar but I couldn't even get a bid," Greene recalls.

THROUGHOUT THE FALL OF 2007, Greg Lippmann scored huge gains. A growing number of Deutsche Bank executives hinted that he should do some selling but Lippmann fought to hang on to his investments.

They put even more pressure on Lippmann after a Rose Garden speech by George Bush on August 31, when the president announced measures to help some borrowers and suggested more might be in the offing.

Meeting with Lippmann and a half dozen senior executives in a conference room in Deutsche Bank's New York office, Rajeev Misra was clear with his orders: The subprime trade has worked, we've made money, let's move on.

"It's been a great race," but it's coming to an end, Misra said. He didn't believe the housing troubles were over, but it was time to move on to another trade, he repeated.

Lippmann wouldn't let it go, though, like a dog clinging to a bone.

"Why?" Lippmann asked, looking straight at Misra. The senior banker backed off.

In the subsequent weeks, most of Deutsche's traders who had purchased CDS protection exited many of their trades. Misra himself was forced to cut short many of the positions he held after his own superiors urged caution. Lippmann cashed in some chips. But he convinced his bosses that the market was getting worse. Once again, they let him hold on to most of his positions, grudgingly.

The sudden panic in the fall of 2007 created a peculiar scene at Deutsche Bank. In one corner, Lippmann and his team of twenty-five traders racked up large gains, almost on a daily basis. But many of the rest of the hundred or so traders in Deutsche's large trading room looked glum, sometimes because they were holding the very same investments that Lippmann bet against. It was as if they existed in a Bizarro World of finance—everything that went wrong for these traders went right for Lippmann and his crew.

Lippmann had waited for this moment for two years. Now that it was here, he was going to enjoy his vindication to the utmost.

"The market is tanking!" he yelled across the trading floor one day, in a teasing tone. "Ha, ha, ha, ha."

After seeing Lippmann carrying on, a salesman warned him: "Be careful what you wish for."

Lippmann laughed him off. But by the end of 2007, Deutsche had acknowledged making some of the same mistakes that the other investment banks had made. It couldn't sell all the CDO deals that it had created to help Paulson short more securities. Like a game of hot potato, the big bank found itself stuck with too many CDO slices.

When Lippmann sat down at year's end with his bosses, including Rajeev Misra and Richard Dalbear, they were complimentary and appreciative. Then they gave Lippmann the figure he had been waiting to hear all year: his bonus. He had taught dozens of hedge funds how to score billions of dollars of profit in a single year. And he directed a team that made close to $2 billion in profits.

Lippmann's reward was more than he ever expected to make in a lifetime, let along in a single year: $50 million, much of it in Deutsche Bank shares. It was an astonishing figure, even for a Wall Street trader.

But Lippmann couldn't help feel slighted. If not for him, the bank would have suffered like many other of the biggest financial players.

"This is not fair," Lippmann told his superiors, his voice rising. "It's too low!"

They ignored his tantrum. Lippmann threw a fit every year, then he settled down and nothing much changed.

Lippmann was upset enough that he quietly interviewed for jobs with a number of hedge funds and other firms, to see if he could do better. Word got back to Misra.

"If he doesn't get paid, he's gonna come work for us," one hedge-fund manager told Misra.

"Fine," Misra responded, nonplussed. "We paid him well."

In the end, Lippmann stayed at Deutsche Bank, partly out of loyalty and also because he would have been forced to forgo all of the shares had he bolted.

BY AUGUST OF 2007, Michael Burry's hedge fund was up 60 percent in the year, making it one of the best performers in the world. The subprime housing market had crumbled, just as Burry predicted.

His returns were so impressive that his staff hesitated to tell clients, just in case there was another snafu in the accounting department, as they had had earlier in the year.

"Please check that again," Steve Druskin, Burry's general counsel, said to staff members going over the results. "We can't afford a mistake right now."

Burry couldn't enjoy his belated success, however, still weary from the battles with his investors and too sensitive to ignore their unhappiness. Most nights, Burry came home glum, frustrating his wife.

"Has Joel called to apologize to you?" she asked him one evening in August. She was referring to Joel Greenblatt, Burry's original investor.

Burry shook his head, looking even sadder. "Look how far you've come! Try to enjoy it," his wife said. All Burry could do was shrug. She urged him to splurge on a present for himself, but he couldn't think of anything he wanted.

Burry flew to New York to apologize to Greenblatt for the audit snafu, reestablishing more cordial relations with him. By then, though, Burry had had enough of the headache of the side account that antagonized so many of his investors. He shifted the remaining CDS investments from the account back to his main fund, just as the credit crisis erupted in full sight. Over the next few months he successfully exited the positions, slowly selling the mortgage insurance.

He finished 2007 with a gain of over 150 percent. Scion itself pocketed about $700 million in the year. Burry's subprime trades had quadrupled in value, scorings gains of about $500 million, over two years. He personally made about $70 million.

He wasn't done, though.

"I patiently await a deepening of the U.S. recession and the string of bankruptcies that are sure to follow," he wrote his investors in early 2008. "For the record, I do not smile fiendishly as I do so. If you know me, you know I neither smile fiendishly nor easily."

Maybe he still had a chance to pull off his historic trade.

PAOLO PELLEGRINI remained reluctant to tell his wife, Henrietta Jones, much about how the firm's trade was doing, still unwilling to risk jinxing it. But as the problems of the housing market became as clear as the front page of her morning New York Times, Henrietta couldn't resist bringing up the matter with her husband.

One day in September, she turned to Pellegrini, asking, "We don't really need me to work, do we?" She enjoyed her position running a division for retailer Donna Karan and wasn't demanding to quit, but her paycheck had become a drop in the family's bucket and she had a young daughter she enjoyed spending time with. If Pellegrini's bonus at the end of the year was likely to be sizable, she might like the chance to spend more time at home.

Pellegrini couldn't give her a sense of how much he was going to make. He didn't know what kind of bonus check Paulson might give him. But he agreed that Jones probably didn't need to work. She soon quit her job.

In late November, Paulson & Co. held a dinner for five hundred or so thankful investors at Manhattan's Metropolitan Club. The two credit funds were up an average of 440 percent that year, even as the stock market rose 3.5 percent, such a stunning figure that some investors at the dinner gushed their appreciation when they grabbed a few minutes with Paulson and Pellegrini. Others chatted about how big the firm had become—it now managed a shocking $28 billion, making it one of the largest hedge funds on the planet, all from investors who were far under the radar screen just a year earlier.

The mood was jovial as a cocktail reception was followed by a three-course dinner featuring boneless duck confit over celery root and black truffles, and roast rack of lamb.

Paulson gave a downbeat presentation about the economy, warning that a recession was likely. He provided details about how he and his team were shifting to wager against financial companies while trimming their protection against subprime mortgages.

Paulson named Bear Stearns, Merrill Lynch, Citigroup, and bond insurer Ambac Financial group and credit-ratings company Moody's Corp. as those in hot water, a suggestion to his investors that the firm was betting against those companies.

It was still "not too late" to bet against those firms, Paulson said.

Pellegrini proudly did his part at the event, starting off the evening's wine tasting by explaining that all the evening's selections were from his native Italy. It was a tip of the cap from Paulson to Pellegrini. The duck appetizer was accompanied by a $200 bottle of Tenuta San Guido 1999 Sassicaia.

But Pellegrini soon began to chafe. He had been an architect of the subprime trade, working elbow-to-elbow with Paulson to craft moves that now were reaping billions of dollars. Pellegrini had begun to gain his own recognition on Wall Street and sometimes was asked to speak on various economic topics.

Paulson & Co. had bet against about $5 billion of CDOs and made more than $4 billion from these trades—including $500 million from a single transaction—according to the firm's investors and an employee of the firm. One of the biggest losers, however, wasn't any investor on the other side. It was the very bank that worked with Paulson on many of the deals: Deutsche Bank. The big bank had failed to sell all of the CDO deals it constructed at Paulson's behest and was stuck with chunks of toxic mortgages, suffering about $500 million of losses from these customized transactions, according to a senior executive of the German bank.

These were some of Paulson & Co.'s largest scores. And they were moves that Pellegrini had masterminded.

As 2007 drew to a close and the firm's focus shifted away from sub-prime mortgages, Pellegrini felt left out, however. He was just as convinced as his colleagues that the banks were in trouble—he knew where all the bad mortgage loans were buried. And yet Hoine, not Pellegrini, was given the mandate of helping Paulson quarterback the new trade. Pellegrini couldn't even make the final decisions about which subprime-mortgage protection to sell.

"John never got to the point where he would trust me," Pellegrini recalls. "He never gave me trading authority."

Paulson continued to tease Pellegrini about how methodical he was. When Paulson moved another analyst to work under Hoine's wing, to focus on the financial companies and their debt, Pellegrini was hurt. He viewed the decision as an attempt by Paulson to preserve his control of the firm, handing power to Hoine because he was younger and represented the next generation.

"I wanted an analyst to work with me to short the equities but he gave it to Andrew; John didn't want to give me that," Pellegrini says. "So I became disengaged."

Pellegrini still helped manage the two big credit hedge funds, though, and they were a whopping $9 billion in size. Late in the year, Pellegrini came to Paulson with an idea: Let's give back half the money in the fund and extend the fund's "lockup" for another few years. That way, the firm could cash in some of its gains while ensuring that investors wouldn't pull all the money out when the existing lockup ended in 2009.

Pellegrini already was hearing complaints from European investors who were desperate for cash amid the market's downturn and unhappy they couldn't pull any of their huge gains from the hedge funds, due to the lockup agreement. Other investors grumbled that the Paulson credit funds had pocketed some cash from various sales of investments but they were not doing anything with the money. Why not give some money back and then raise money anew in 2008? Pellegrini argued to Paulson.

Paulson seemed taken aback. Maybe it was a sign that Pellegrini didn't believe in the remaining positions. Or he was just looking to make sure he had a key role at the firm for an extended period, while he helped run those funds.

"When I hear you saying these things, it makes me question what you've accomplished in the last two years," Paulson responded, tersely.

Paulson's comment "made me feel I was no longer special," Pellegrini recalls.

O N THE FRIDAY BEFORE CHRISTMAS, Paulson called an emergency meeting in the firm's reception area. Standing in front of the group, with Pellegrini and Rosenberg nearby, Paulson opened a case of French champagne sent over by an investment bank as a thank-you for all the trading commissions of the previous year.

Paulson passed around bottles of the bubbly, poured a glass for himself, and raised it to his team. He beamed; some of his staff never had seen their boss look so happy. Paulson then toasted his employees, singling out the firm's back-office staff and some other areas away from the limelight.

"I just want to thank everyone," Paulson said, looking around the room, meeting the eyes of both senior and junior executives. "It was the best year ever."

Applause rocked the office. Then the team quickly got back to work, to try to make some more money.

A few days later, Pellegrini took his wife on vacation in Anguilla. Stopping at an automated-teller machine in the hotel lobby on New Year's Eve to withdraw some cash, she checked the balance of their checking account.

She was immediately taken aback. On the screen before her was a figure she had never seen before, at least not on an ATM. It's not clear how many others ever had, either: $45 million, newly deposited in their joint account. It was Pellegrini's bonus for the year, including some deferred compensation. He was still special to John Paulson, after all.

In truth, Pellegrini had withheld more from his bonus than he needed in order to pay the year's taxes, so the figure in the bank account that day was skimpier than it could have been. Paulson paid him about $175 million for his work in 2007. Pellegrini would never again have to worry about finding a career, keeping a job, or stretching his savings.

"Wow," his wife said quietly, still staring at the ATM.

Then they left, arm in arm, to meet a chartered boat to take them to nearby St. Barts.

Paulson did quite well for himself as well. His hedge fund got to keep 20 percent of the $15 billion or so of gains of all his funds. He also was a big investor in the credit funds. His personal tally for 2007: nearly $4 billion. It was the largest one-year payout in the history of the financial markets.

ON FEBRUARY 20, 2008, PAULSON RECEIVED AN INVITATION FROM Samuel Molinaro, Jr., the chief operating and financial officer at Bear Stearns, inviting him to a lunch at the investment bank's executive dining room. A rash of hedge-fund clients had pulled money out of Bear Stearns and shifted accounts to rival brokers, worried about the firm's health. The moves left Bear in a weak position and fed rumors that the storied firm might not survive. If Molinaro could bring the hedge funds back into the fold it would be a shot in the arm for Bear Stearns and could help right his tottering ship.

Paulson & Co. was an especially attractive catch for Molinaro. It now was among the world's largest funds, and Paulson had remained a loyal customer of his former employer, despite the speculation about Bear Stearns' future. But Paulson also had moved cash elsewhere, concerned about the health of the investment bank. If Molinaro could get Paulson back in Bear Stearns' corner again, it would be an instant boon and likely would reassure others who were mulling over whether to return as clients.

After a lunch of salad, grilled chicken, and chilled string beans, Molinaro rose to address the select group of twenty or so hedge-fund bigwigs, all facing one another around a circular dining-room table. For twenty minutes, Molinaro outlined how Bear had improved its financial position, why its business was healthy, and how much cash the firm held. The press had it out for Bear Stearns, Molinaro emphasized. There really was nothing terribly wrong with the firm.

Then another Bear executive gave a speech, saying that he couldn't share many details, but business definitely was picking up. He appealed to the group to bring back the cash, reminding them of the long-term relationships many had with Bear and how the investment bank had helped many of their firms in times of need. Listening to it all, some of the hedgies began to feel pangs of guilt, remembering times they indeed had been aided by various Bear Stearns executives.

For another twenty minutes, Molinaro easily handled softball questions from the group. It seemed he was winning them over and a crucial victory was within sight. Maybe Bear Stearns could save itself after all.

Then John Paulson raised a hand. The executives turned to watch him, eager to hear what he might say.

"Sam, do you know what your Level Two and Level Three assets are on your balance sheet?" Paulson asked, referring to investments that could be hard to price, sometimes because they are risky.

"Not off the top of my head."

"Do you have an idea?"

"I'd rather not guess, John. Let me give you the right number when I get back to my desk."

"Well, I'll tell you what the number is. It's $220 billion. So what I'm seeing is that if you have $14 billion of equity and $220 billion of Level Two and Level Three assets, a small movement in the assets can wipe out your equity completely."

Molinaro didn't realize it, but Paulson had spent weeks reworking his firm's holdings, dropping dozens of stocks and bulking up its bets against a range of financial giants, from Lehman Brothers and Washington Mutual to Wachovia and Fannie Mae. He had deep concerns about Bear Stearns, too. Investors had poured $6 billion into his firm in the previous year, and Paulson had put a good chunk of it to work wagering against banks and investment banks with flimsy balance sheets. He had done his homework.

Molinaro suddenly looked uncomfortable. He either didn't have a good response for Paulson, was wary of publicly squabbling with a good client with a growing reputation, or didn't want to give a faulty figure.

"I'll have to check the number, but you may not be accounting for the fact that some of the assets are hedges." In other words, Paulson might not be getting a true view of the firm's risk, Molinaro argued.

His response was for naught. Paulson had pushed open the floodgates. Two other hedge-fund managers quickly followed Paulson with their own questions, adopting much harsher tones.

"How can you not know the number, Sam?!"

"Paulson's right, you guys are in trouble!"

Paulson watched quietly as the two investors bullied Molinaro for several more minutes. The grilling got so harsh that some of the investors began to feel sorry for Molinaro. So many doubts had been raised about Bear Stearns' health, though, that the accounts never would return to the investment bank.

As the meeting broke up, one hedge-fund executive said to a friend, "Shit, Bear's *really* in trouble." Chatter about the meeting began to circulate as soon as the executives returned to their firms.

It was a dagger in the staggering investment bank's heart. Soon a rash of hedge funds pulled money out of Bear Stearns, including a $5 billion shift by hedge fund Renaissance Technologies.

Tempers flared within Bear Stearns as the investment bank's shares plunged and its cash dwindled. The firm's CEO, Alan Schwartz, tried to calm various executives. During one meeting, though, Michael Minikes, a sixty-five-year-old veteran, abruptly cut off his boss.

"Do you have any idea what is going on?" Minikes asked. "Our cash is flying out the door. Our clients are leaving us."

A month later, Bear Stearns had to be rescued in an emergency sale to J.P. Morgan coordinated by the Federal Reserve and the Treasury Department at a price of just $2 per share, a figure later increased to $10 per share.

After the original sale was struck, Alan Schwartz wearily made his way to the company gym for an early-morning workout. Dressed in his business suit, he trudged into the locker room. There, Alan Mintz, a forty-six-year-old trader at the firm, in sweaty gym clothes, made a beeline for his boss.

"How could this happen to fourteen thousand employees?" Mintz demanded, getting in Schwartz's face. "Look in my eyes, and tell me how this happened!"[1]

On the Sunday that Bear Stearns fought for its life, and while others on Wall Street were glued to their computers, worrying about the impact, Paulson watched his two daughters frolic in his home's indoor pool. Months earlier, he had shifted almost all his firm's cash from a Bear Stearns account to a money-market account at Fidelity Investments secured by U.S. Treasury bonds, just in case the investment bank's health deteriorated.

It was the beginning of a year of historic troubles for leading financial companies around the globe, as the firms finally acknowledged they were sitting on deep losses due to real estate-related holdings and hadn't adequately prepared for a downturn.

Executives at Lehman Brothers were among those most confident they could weather the storm. Richard Fuld, Lehman's CEO, had turned down a lucrative investment from the Korea Development Bank. Fuld and his bankers also had spoken with Bank of America, MetLife, HSBC Holdings, and others, but no deal materialized. Fuld had been through crises before, and this one seemed to be just another that he and his team would maneuver around. He blamed growing weakness in the company's shares on short sellers, many of whom were hedge funds buying CDS protection on Lehman's debt. His complaints didn't sit well with these funds, though, many of whom were Lehman's own clients and were nervous enough about the health of the firm.

On September 9, after talks with the Korean investors finally fell through, Lehman's shares dropped in half, the largest one-day plunge on record. Worries about Lehman's $33 billion of commercial real estate holdings swept Wall Street. Lehman executives calculated that the firm needed at least $3 billion in fresh capital. A day later, though, they assured investors on a conference call that the firm needed no new capital. Wall Street rivals who viewed Lehman's huge real estate portfolio said it was overvalued by more than $10 billion, but Lehman executives insisted that it was valued properly.[2]

J.P. Morgan didn't like what it was seeing. The big bank played middleman between its clients and Lehman in various trades and was privy to more details of Lehman's operations than most investors. A week earlier, J.P. Morgan had asked Lehman for $5 billion in additional collateral—easy-to-sell securities to cover money lent by J.P. Morgan's clients to Lehman. Steven Black, co-CEO of J.P. Morgan's investment bank, phoned Fuld, saying that in order to protect itself and its clients, J.P. Morgan needed $5 billion in additional collateral—in addition to the $5 billion J.P. Morgan demanded five days earlier, which had yet to be paid.

Lehman sent some of the money, but held off J.P. Morgan on the rest as it tried to reassure clients.

"Our balance sheet is better than ever," Christian Lawless, a senior vice president in Lehman's European mortgage operation, told investors seeking to pull out assets.

But so many hedge funds pulled money from their accounts at Lehman that the firm couldn't properly process the requests, as panic grew within the firm.

Lehman tried to entice rivals to buy the firm or certain assets. But two Wall Street executives who reviewed Lehman's real estate documents passed, saying that Lehman had placed a valuation on its real estate holdings that was 35 percent higher than it should be. Treasury Secretary Henry Paulson insisted the government wouldn't lend financing for a purchase.

Lehman was so weakened that the 158-year-old Wall Street firm turned to the Federal Reserve and Treasury Department. Like other investment firms, Lehman had spent years enjoying outsized profits and enormous wealth from a raging real estate market. Now that housing was on its knees, however, Lehman went to the government, hat in hand.

Late one evening, standing in front of about fifteen silent members of Lehman's executive committee, Tom Russo, Richard Fuld's legal counsel, tried reaching Timothy Geithner, the head of the New York Fed. Russo tried Geithner in his office and on his cell phone. Nothing. He paged him, buzzed him. Still no answer.

The Lehman executives had one last chance: George Walker IV, a top investment banker at the firm who also happened to be a cousin of the

president of the United States, George W. Bush. Walker was scared and
looked pale. His shirt was soaked with sweat at the thought of calling
the White House. His colleagues told him they had no other choice.

"I'm on my hands and knees," one colleague, Mike Gelband, told
Walker. "We are looking at an unmitigated disaster on a global scale,
George."

Walker paced the room and looked over at Fuld, who was on the
phone with the Securities and Exchange Commission. Then he went to
the firm's library and placed the call. He was put on hold for minutes
that seemed like hours, and then the operator came back on the line.

"I'm sorry, Mr. Walker. The president is not able to take your call at
this time."[3]

The government's decision not to bail Lehman out led to a bankruptcy six times larger than any other Chapter 11 case in U.S. history. It
also set off a near panic among investors and lenders worldwide that
September, one that forced the United States to push through a historic
rescue plan for the financial system. The government and Federal
Reserve stepped in to rescue Fannie Mae and Freddie Mac, guaranteeing
over $300 billion of debt. It also helped force struggling Merrill Lynch
into the arms of larger Bank of America, a step taken to try to avert still
more fear among investors.

The moves worked only partially. The stock market continued to
plunge, tumbling more than 60 percent between the fall of 2007 and
early 2009, the worst bear market since the Great Depression and one
that coincided with the worst recession since World War II.

The troubles sent the value of all the protection that John Paulson
had purchased soaring in value, enabling Paulson & Co. to tack on another $5 billion in profits in 2008. The firm made hundreds of millions
of dollars when its CDS contracts on Lehman Brothers paid off in the
fall, as the investment bank was forced to seek bankruptcy.

The hedge fund also made $1 billion by shorting British banks such as
Royal Bank of Scotland, Barclays, Lloyds Banking Group, and HBOS, all
of which had high exposure to British mortgages. Later, when regula-
tory changes forced Paulson to reveal these positions, he became something of a public enemy in corners of the United Kingdom.

"So I'm eating my cornflakes and I read that John Paulson, the New York hedge fund king, has made £270 million betting that the Royal Bank of Scotland share price would fall over the last four months," Chris Blackhurst wrote in London's *Evening Standard* in February 2009. "Prison isn't good enough for the short-selling fiend! He should be paraded down Fifth Avenue, naked, and then tied to a lamp-post so we can all take out our anger and despair on the grasping monster!"

Paulson was uncomfortable shorting these stocks—not so much because of any guilt about profiting from falling shares but because there was more downside to wagering against stocks, which can soar an unlimited amount, than in owning them. That's why he didn't place nearly as big a bet against financial companies as he did against subprime mortgages. Paulson still scored impressive gains of 30 percent or so for most of his funds in 2008, even as the overall market tumbled 38 percent and some larger hedge-fund rivals threw in the towel and closed down, but Paulson couldn't match 2007's gains of 590 percent and 350 percent for his two credit funds.

For those on the other side of Paulson's trades, and the executives running financial firms that collapsed so suddenly, 2008 was about recrimination. One Thursday morning in June 2008, the two executives who ran Bear Stearns' hedge funds that made wrong-way bets on CDOs and other mortgage investments, Ralph Cioffi and Matthew Tannin, were hauled into a Brooklyn jail cell, to be arraigned for allegedly misleading their investors about the health of their failed funds. Their upbeat comments to the investors were at odds with the caution they shared with each other as well as their own actions, prosecutors alleged. Shackled and in shock at the turn of their fortune, Cioffi asked Tannin: "How did we end up in this spot?"[4]

I N THE SPRING OF 2008, Paulson and Pellegrini visited Harvard University, their alma mater. Pellegrini was excited about the trip and looked forward to explaining to the students how the firm had anticipated the credit crisis.

But when they got there and the class settled into their seats, Paulson approached the dais and addressed the group by himself, while Pellegrini watched from the back of the room. Later, Pellegrini helped his boss answer some questions from students, but it stung Pellegrini that he wasn't invited to address the class. Paulson's shadow never seemed so huge.

"It was humiliating to me," Pellegrini recalls.

Pellegrini spent most of the year working with Rosenberg to sell the last of the firm's subprime insurance. Others, like Jeffrey Greene, ran into problems finding investors willing to buy the investments at prices that seemed reasonable.

But Pellegrini and Rosenberg played a waiting game—when markets were buoyant and optimism reigned, they held back; when a securities firm, bank, or hedge fund imploded, they swooped in to offer their CDS protection, usually finding a huge appetite.

By July 2008, as subprime-related investments fell to pennies on the dollar, they had exited almost every trade, cashing in the remaining chips of the remarkable trade. The two Paulson credit hedge funds invested a total of $1.2 billion of cash and racked up nearly $10 billion of gains, all in two remarkable years. Paulson's other funds enjoyed about $10 billion of their own gains, all from obscure protection on mortgages most experts said would never get into trouble.

Pellegrini spent the rest of the year hiring specialists to refine the firm's valuation methods for mortgages, preparing for the time when it looked safe to buy them. Over several months, Paulson sometimes pushed Pellegrini to look for cheap mortgage investments, but Pellegrini remained skeptical, and the hedge fund held off doing much buying until the fall of 2008.

By then, Pellegrini had one foot out the door.

JEFFREY GREENE began 2008 with a burst of confidence. He already had cashed in nearly $100 million of his investments and had decided to stop fighting his brokers with their unreliable quotes. He'd simply hold on to the rest of his CDS mortgage insurance, which he figured was worth $200 million or so. If all those home mortgages ran into problems, as he knew they would, the insurance would pay him in a big way. He didn't *have* to sell his holdings.

His friend in Boston, Jeffrey Libert, was panicking. He wanted to sell his own investments but also was hoping to keep them until the summer, so he would hold them for a year and could pay a lower tax rate, something Greene also was doing.

"Chill out," Greene told his friend.

Libert eventually cashed out, settling for profits of about $5 million from his trade. It was a big score but it came with regular ribbing from his friend for not being "gutsy" enough to do the trade in a bigger way.

"I should have done more, I'm kicking myself," Libert says. "But it just wasn't for me."

In the fall of 2008, when Lehman Brothers collapsed and Merrill Lynch ran into deep problems, it was Greene's turn to sweat. He hadn't paid enough attention to the health of his broker. Now he realized that if Merrill Lynch went under, he might not be able to gain access to his positions. He'd be just another desperate creditor lining up at bankruptcy court to lodge a claim.

"I'm thinking, 'If Merrill goes out of business I'm out $200 million!'" Greene recalls.

By then, Zafran, his Merrill Lynch broker, had left to start his own firm. Greene picked up the phone to call J.P. Morgan, hoping the bank, in a safer position, would engineer a transfer of his positions from Merrill Lynch and help him sell it all. On hold, Greene waited nervously as his broker asked a few traders if they could help.

"Sorry, we're not willing to go to market with any Merrill Lynch counterparty risk," the J.P. Morgan contact told him. They wouldn't help wind down any trades with Merrill Lynch on the other side.

Greene's stress level soared. "I wanted out right away but now I only have Merrill to help me, of all places."

Greene called up his new Merrill Lynch broker and decided to play it cool, trying to hide the fear building inside.

"Hey, it's Jeffrey Greene," he said, very casually, as if he was bored and looking for something to occupy his time. "I wouldn't mind winding down some of those positions; do you mind getting me a bid or two?"

"Well, it could take us a day or two," the broker responded.

"Oh, that's fine, thanks."

Greene got off the phone, beating himself up for waiting so long to sell.

What an idiot I am!

"I'm thinking if they give me fifty cents [on the dollar], I'm going to have to take it," Greene recalls.

When the broker called back, he had an offer for Greene: "We'll pay you $156 million" for the position.

Greene couldn't believe it—they were willing to buy his positions at eighty-seven cents on the dollar. He had been willing to sell them for just fifty cents. Maybe his bluff was working.

He decided to push it a bit further.

"Well, let me see. I'll think about it."

He hung up. Merrill soon called with a new offer: ninety-three cents on the dollar.

"Do it," Greene responded.

Greene didn't realize it at the time, but John Thain, Merrill's new chief, had just issued an order to his troops to get rid of any exposure to toxic mortgages, no matter the cost. Merrill Lynch was eager to get out of their trades with Greene, at any price.

Dragging his feet worked to Greene's benefit. "I was totally lucky at the end," he acknowledges.

After Greene hung up, though, he realized he had another issue to worry about: If Merrill Lynch went under before his trade was complete, Greene's profits would be in danger.

He rang the Merrill Lynch broker, once again.

"Um ... when does this trade settle?"

Not taking any chances, Greene had his trade transferred to Credit Suisse, a more stable Swiss bank, to ensure that it went through.

By 2009, Greene was down to just $100 million in CDS protection, a valuable memento of a trade that netted him about $500 million in profit, one of the largest gains by an individual investor in Wall Street history.

"The trade worked better for amateurs than professionals," Greene says, noting that those not a part of the business could more clearly see the looming problems, as well as dismiss potential obstacles to the trade. "There were so many things that could go wrong."

DESPITE GREG LIPPMANN'S SUCCESS, his superiors seemed as skeptical as ever as 2008 began. As the ABX fell further, Anshu Jain, one of the bank's top executives, e-mailed Lippmann, pushing him to sell some of his positions.

"No, it's going to zero," Lippmann shot back, according to an executive who saw the e-mail. Lippmann also began warning some on Deutsche's trading floor that the housing troubles would infect other areas of the economy.

Watching a commentator on CNBC judge the stock market's weakness as temporary, Lippmann quickly yelled out: "In your dreams!"

Sometimes, Lippmann was so openly joyful, shouting and screaming with so much pleasure, that it rubbed some other traders the wrong way, especially those losing money.

On one particularly bad day for the market, Lippmann called over a salesman, pointing to a spreadsheet on his computer.

"Look, I'm up $400,000!"

Flashing a big smile, Lippmann explained that in his personal account he had bet against an exchange-traded fund that tracked financial companies, like banks and brokerage firms. The worse things got for Deutsche's brethren, the more his account rose in value.

"That's wonderful for you," the salesman said to him, sarcasm dripping, as he shook his head.

At one point, his boss, Misra, sat Lippmann down to tell him not to be so obnoxious about his winnings.

Lippmann's cockiness masked a growing unease as he watched a figure in the corner of his computer screen: the tumbling shares of Deutsche Bank as its own problems multiplied. Lippmann's team was a relatively small part of a global bank; he could see the profits and losses of some others and it was an ugly picture. By the middle of the year, the bank had taken $11 billion of write-downs, dwarfing Lippmann's gains. His bets against financial shares—approved by the bank—were a futile attempt to limit the damage from the loads of Deutsche shares in the account. On the day his personal account rose $400,000, his Deutsche shares fell about $800,000.

Lippmann was almost right in his prediction to his bosses—the ABX index tracking the riskiest subprime mortgages eventually fell to two cents. His group would make several hundred million dollars more in 2008. In the fall, Lippmann even began recommending select subprime bonds that he thought had become attractive, bonds that began to rise in early 2009.

For all Lippmann's success, Deutsche was dealing with so many problems by late 2008 that it could pay him only a few million dollars as a bonus, another disappointment for him. Adding salt to his wounds, his Deutsche shares had dropped more than 70 percent over the previous twelve months.

I N SEPTEMBER 2007, Andrew Lahde pressed his bets, raising a larger fund from newly interested investors to buy protection against commercial mortgages and another fund to wager against banks, brokerage firms, and other companies that he was sure would fall.

"Our entire banking system is a complete disaster," he wrote in late 2007. "In my opinion, nearly every major bank would be insolvent if they marked their assets to market."

By the end of the year, Lahde owned protection on $1 billion of subprime debt in three hedge funds and managed $100 million. But as he became increasingly worried about the fragility of the financial system, he began doing some selling.

In March, exhausted from a grueling year, he invited two young women to Miami, trying to relax. He rented a penthouse suite at the Ritz-Carlton for the women and another room nearby to ensure that he'd get some rest during the day as the women shopped. Lahde couldn't seem to relax, however. He still held hundreds of millions of dollars of protection and increasingly was convinced that he needed to cash in his big trade before it was too late. Two weeks later, bringing a young woman with him, he left for St. Thomas to research the tax benefits of moving to the island. The hotel was so crowded, in part due to a visit to the island by a group including President Barack Obama, that Lahde was unable to book an extra room and, frustrated, he was forced to share his suite with his traveling partner.

For days, Lahde avoided calling his office, trying unsuccessfully to catch up on his rest. One afternoon, napping in bed, he reached for his BlackBerry and saw a text message with the subject line "Bear Stearns is 700 over." Lahde sat straight up and reached for his nearby cell phone to dial his office.

"Dude, is Bear really at seven hundred?!" he asked Rich Eckert, his chief financial officer.

Credit-default swap contracts protecting the debt of Bear Stearns indeed were trading at 7 percentage points above the rate that top-rated banks lent to each other. Lahde instantly understood that the market had turned desperately worried about the health of his brokerage firm, which still owed him millions of dollars of profits from his remaining positions.

Lahde long had expected banks to collapse under the weight of all their toxic mortgages. Now it was happening, but like a gambler sitting on huge piles of chips from a casino on its last legs, Lahde fretted he might not be able to cash in his winnings.

"Shut it down tomorrow," he told Eckert, a tinge of fear in his voice.

As calmly and deliberately as he could, Lahde gave his associate detailed instructions about how to sell the firm's entire positions. Do it slowly and before anyone can figure out what we're doing, Lahde said. That way, traders couldn't take advantage of his sudden desperation to sell and push prices lower.

Eckert managed to exit all of the commercial fund's positions just days before Bear Stearns was forced to sell itself to J.P. Morgan. By September, Lahde had closed his credit fund, and in October he shuttered his entire firm, unwilling to trade with any brokers or banks, many of which he feared were close to collapse. These funds weren't nearly as successful as the one that bet against subprime mortgages, leaving some investors grumbling and giving Lahde one more reason to think about quitting the business.

Investing in mortgage protection in the eleventh hour of the housing craze, in late 2006, Lahde's residential-mortgage fund gained 1,000 percent, or about $75 million, over just fifteen months, one of the best runs in history. Lahde himself pocketed more than $10 million from his trade and more than $100 million for his clients.

As SUBPRIME MORTGAGES continued to plummet throughout 2008, John Devaney suffered so many losses that he had to take drastic measures. Just a year earlier, he had mocked those nervous about sobering news from New Century.

"In a funny way I want to thank the market for dealing me a direct hit," he told the *New York Times* in February, adding that he was buying still more bonds, taking advantage of the lower prices. "I don't think there is anything fundamentally wrong. . . . Most of the stuff I have has limited downside."

By the summer of 2008, however, Devaney was desperate for cash. First he sold his Renoir painting for $13.5 million, and then his helicopter, his Gulfstream plane, and even his mansion in Key Biscayne. Then came his 145-foot yacht. It wasn't enough, though. In late June, just before his thirty-eighth birthday, Deutsche Bank called in a loan, demanding that Devaney repay $90 million the next day. When he couldn't, the bank seized his fund's remaining assets.

In July, Devaney shuttered his fund, telling his investors that he had lost all their money.

"I'm devastated, I'm totally devastated," Devaney told the *New York Times,* saying that he personally had lost more than $150 million. He also suffered $50 million of trading losses at his brokerage firm, United Capital Markets Holding, which remained in business.

MICHAEL BURRY began 2008 worried about the economy and determined to cement his own legendary trade. His concerns soon were borne out.

But Burry's investors continued to bolt, pulling more than $100 million from his fund early in the year, convinced that he couldn't replicate his huge gains of the previous year. Their withdrawals forced him to do some more selling of prized investments.

Burry ended up losing money in 2008, getting back into the market several months too early, though he beat the overall market. Few new clients emerged and his existing investors continued to grumble.

After a front-page story in *The Wall Street Journal* described John Paulson's winnings from his subprime trade, Burry shot off an e-mail to the reporter that was as bitter as it was factual: "Well, I was first. If anyone can be shown to be one that really did his own work and created this strategy from scratch, it'd be me. . . . A physician with no true education in anything Wall Street. Completely self-taught, working by myself."

Late in 2008, clients entrusted just $450 million with Burry, down from $650 million when he first discovered the mortgage protection in 2005. At the end of the year, Rob Lusardi, an executive at White Mountains Insurance Group, one of Burry's original investors, said, "To us here at White Mountain, you're a zero." (Lusardi says he didn't call Burry a "zero"; rather, his company had "zero" interest in investing with Burry.)

"I'm running less money than I gained last year, less than I managed even in 2003," Burry said to his wife. "No one cares." *Why am I doing this?* Burry thought.

By late 2008, Burry had had enough. He was thirty-seven, had millions in the bank, and was worn out. He came to the office one morning to tell his employees he was closing down his firm. Just before Burry went into a meeting with the staff, he heard a hard pounding on the door. It was his wife, Anh-Thi.

"Don't do it, don't do it," she pleaded with her husband, convinced he would regret the move.

"I've made my decision," he said somberly.

Burry then told his investors he was going to shutter his firm in early 2009 and spend more time with his family. He might go back to medicine or even get a Ph.D. in astronomy, he told one. Few of his clients protested his decision.

For Burry, the subprime trade brought wealth, but it also gave him reason to ponder what could have been. If his investors had backed his idea for a housing-dedicated fund, or if they didn't force him to sell so much mortgage protection before cracks began to show in the housing façade, Michael Burry might have joined John Paulson as a Wall Street legend.

"It was a successful trade; it just wasn't what it could have been. I didn't realize my full potential," Burry says.

As his voice seemed to catch, and his eyes filled with tears, Burry explained that he was worried about friends who were losing their jobs and how many would suffer from the economic downturn.

"I thought this was my Soros trade."

F OR MOST OF 2008, John Paulson tried to keep a low profile. He told a reporter that he was reluctant to celebrate while housing troubles were causing pain for others. On rainy days, when it was hard to find a cab home, he still hopped on the local bus heading uptown to his East Side town house. The locals didn't seem to realize they had a billionaire in their midst, and Paulson liked it that way.

As for big charitable gifts, Paulson mostly held back. Paulson told some associates that he planned to do more, but gave few details. Naming a building or institution after himself wasn't his style. Still, friends and associates said Paulson never shared any ambitions about tackling big charitable projects.

The best use of his time is to make still more money, Paulson says, so that there might be more wealth to give away someday down the line, a stance that investor Warren Buffett adopted until his later years.

"It takes a lot of time to contribute intelligently," Paulson says. "My greatest advantage now is managing money; there's a time for that and a time for this."

Paulson got to know a bit of the discomfort the rest of the country was feeling. Early in 2008, he traded up in Southampton, spending $41.3 million for a 10.4-acre lakefront estate known as Old Trees, a 1911 Georgian mansion with two guesthouses, a pool, staff quarters, and a vast expanse on Lake Agawam.

But when Paulson tried to sell his 6,800-square-foot "cottage" nearby, it sat for more than a year. He slashed the price from $19.5 million to $13.9 million but still found no takers. Finally, in the summer of 2009, he sold it for $10 million, well below the $12.75 million price he had paid for the home in 2006. Few seemed to feel very sorry for Paulson.

In November 2008, more than one hundred of Paulson & Co.'s investors converged on Manhattan's Metropolitan Club, facing Central Park, for the fund's annual dinner. A year earlier, Pellegrini had picked and introduced the wines. This year, Paulson hired a sommelier to present the French wines, including $500 bottles of Château Haut-Brion, Château Margaux, and Château Rothschild.

The dinner, which took place in the teeth of a developing recession and the worst financial crisis since the 1930s, seemed a bit over the top: jumbo crabmeat and avocado; Colorado rack of lamb with tarragon jus; and Parmesan polenta cake, eaten by candlelight. But Paulson seemed determined to enjoy his success, saying that he didn't feel any shame celebrating the firm's accomplishments.

Paulson's choice of a speaker for the agenda also suggested something of a tin ear: former Federal Reserve chairman Alan Greenspan, a new consultant to the Paulson team. While others leveled blame at Greenspan for keeping interest rates low enough to pump air into the housing bubble, Paulson defended his recent hire, calling the critics Monday-morning quarterbacks and telling colleagues he was proud to call on Greenspan for his views.

At the event, Paulson spoke a bit about developing opportunities, even in troubled mortgages, though he said it was premature to do much buying. What Paulson didn't share was that he was in the early stage of planning a new trade, one that would be just as unorthodox and controversial as his subprime trade and would be implemented in early 2009.

Paulson also didn't speak about a surprise subpoena he had received a month earlier from the House of Representative's powerful House Committee on Oversight. The day he received it, Paulson seemed nervous as he walked into Michael Waldorf's office, asking the attorney for his advice. There was an ongoing backlash against well-paid executives in the financial world and against those firms taking too much risk in the markets; the committee had asked for a range of sensitive information about how Paulson's hedge fund was being run.

"Why do they want to hear from me, I didn't do anything wrong?" he asked Waldorf with some annoyance. Paulson was especially concerned that details of his pay would be released publicly.

When the committee met on November 13, Paulson sat in a row of luminaries of the hedge-fund world: George Soros, Jim Simons, Kenneth Griffin, and Philip Falcone. For years, Paulson aspired to be viewed as one of the top investors. Now he would have to deal with the consequences.

As the hearings got under way, Soros expounded on global markets while Griffin showed a feisty side, pushing back against a congressman who challenged some of his initiatives. When it was his turn, Paulson was so soft-spoken that he repeatedly was asked to speak up. He adjusted the microphone and moved it closer, but it didn't seem to have much effect. One congressman asked if the mic was even working. When another incorrectly minimized his track record, Paulson remained silent.

But when the question-and-answer period began, the congressmen warmed to Paulson, who gave his own views on how to improve the banking crisis.

"I'm thinking we've probably got the wrong Paulson handing out the TARP money here," said Massachusetts Democrat John Tierney, a dig at the treasury secretary at the time, Henry Paulson.

Referring to Paulson's huge gains in 2007 and 2008, Simons said, "I didn't have that kind of wisdom."

As he left the hearing, Paulson looked relieved.

"It went pretty well today," he told Waldorf at Washington's Union Station. "I felt good."

Paulson then said good-bye and boarded a late-afternoon Amtrak train to head home.

epilogue

There is no intoxicant more dangerous than cheap money and excessive credit.
—Benjamin M. Anderson, economist, 1929

GREG LIPPMANN'S SUCCESS BROUGHT WIDESPREAD RECOGNITION on Wall Street. Salesmen at Deutsche Bank took to introducing their star trader to potential clients, trying to impress them. Lippman usually didn't let them down.

"If it wasn't for me, Deutsche Bank would be UBS," he told one prospective client in early 2009, as a salesman looked on, beaming with pride. "I made more than one billion dollars for Deutsche in 2007 and another billion in 2008."

But as it became clear how much damage Wall Street had inflicted on the broader economy, a backlash developed against those like Lippmann who created the derivative products at the heart of the collapse. He had helped introduce "synthetic" mortgages that acted like subprime mortgages, enabling more banks and investors to own this toxic product.

Lippmann's clients made more than $25 billion by betting against these investments. Phil Falcone, who had adopted Lippmann's trade after a pitch that lasted less than an hour, racked up several billion dollars for his firm.

But for every hedge fund that Lippmann convinced to short these risky mortgage securities, an investor or bank was found to take the other side, usually leading to losses. And Deutsche Bank sold subprime mortgage products to various investors, even as Lippmann and his team were shorting them, angering some. The moves led to an investigation in late 2008 by the New York Attorney General's office, even though the buyers all were sophisticated investors who should have known better and never were forced to open their wallets.

Scathing letters were sent to reporters blaming Lippmann for wagering against risky mortgage debt even as his firm was creating more of it. One Web site posted Lippmann's picture, saying that Lippmann was "a 'Number 1 Asshole' in creating the 'Financial Engineering' behind the debacle." As the financial problems grew in early 2009, Lippmann assumed a lower profile, refusing to talk with reporters, worried that he was being painted a scapegoat. Rather than defend himself publicly, Lippmann griped to friends that all he did was help create a product and show hedge funds how to use it to profit from a crisis he saw coming.

"I didn't create the mortgages, I was just the guy who said the emperor has no clothes," Lippmann told one friend.

Others won more acclaim. On the West Coast, word got out about Jeffrey Greene's success, and the more than $500 million that he pocketed from his trade. That was partly because he hired a public-relations pro to spread the news, resulting in glowing features on *Nightline* and CNBC.

Soon, Greene fielded phone calls from longtime friends and acquaintances asking for financial advice. For the first time, they paid full attention to Greene's answers. Mike Tyson and a few others heeded Greene's caution and held off on various real estate purchases. In early 2009, Greene helped check out an upscale home that a friend, film director Oliver Stone, was considering purchasing. It didn't take long for Greene to weigh in with his decision.

"Don't buy it, Oliver," Greene told Stone. "We're still in the early stages" of a housing meltdown.

As Greene spoke, he noticed Stone had pulled out a pen and was writing down what Greene was saying. It was as if Greene had suddenly been transformed into the E.F. Hutton of the Hollywood set, his every utterance worthy of rapt attention.

"Now, when I say things off the cuff, people listen," says Greene with some amazement. "It's scary."

He doesn't have as much time to check out real estate, though. Greene and his wife now spend most of their time on their yacht or in a new home in Miami, as they await the birth of their first child. Sometimes, though, they fly a newly purchased G5 plane to visit their California houses, keeping tabs on real estate in the area.

Others who discovered the greatest trade in history found themselves largely ignored. In Southern California, Andrew Lahde turned increasingly bitter about the nation's troubles, ranting to friends about the heavy contributions made by oil and financial companies to political candidates and blaming Congress for failing to curb predatory lending despite plenty of warnings. After he failed to get some journalists to focus on Congress's culpability, Lahde complained that the nation seemed to care less about fixing the political system than it did "about Britney Spears's vagina."

In late 2008, he threw himself into the writings of his longtime hero Timothy Leary, the 1960s counterculture icon and advocate of psychedelic-drug research. He began to warm to the idea of dropping out, as Leary advised, saying it was "baffling" that Paulson was still so focused on investing. Lahde found a distant island and leased a beachfront home. He snorkels most days while searching for a suitable young female partner to join him on his adventure.

After Lahde closed his firm and arranged to mail the last checks to his investors, there was only one thing left to do: stick it to everyone who had ever pissed him off. Lahde sent an open letter to his clients that quickly circulated throughout the investing world, a Jerry Maguire–like mission statement for the Wall Street set, the kind of farewell that more than a few traders said they wished they'd had the gumption to issue:

October 27, 2008

Today I write not to gloat. Given the pain that nearly everyone is experiencing, that would be entirely inappropriate. Nor am I writing to make further predictions, as most of my forecasts in previous letters have unfolded or are in the process of unfolding. Instead, I am writing to say good-bye.

. . . I was in this game for the money. The low-hanging fruit, i.e., idiots whose parents paid for prep school, Yale, and then the Harvard MBA, was there for the taking. These people who were (often) truly not worthy of the education they received (or supposedly received) rose to the top of companies such as AIG, Bear Stearns, and Lehman Brothers and all levels of our government. All of this behavior supporting the Aristocracy only ended up making it easier for me to find people stupid enough to take the other side of my trades. God bless America.

There are far too many people for me to sincerely thank for my success. However, I do not want to sound like a Hollywood actor accepting an award. The money was reward enough. . . .

I will no longer manage money for other people or institutions. I have enough of my own wealth to manage. Some people, who think they have arrived at a reasonable estimate of my net worth, might be surprised that I would call it quits with such a small war chest. That is fine; I am content with my rewards. Moreover, I will let others try to amass nine, ten, or eleven-figure net worths. Meanwhile, their lives suck. Appointments back to back, booked solid for the next three months, they look forward to their two-week vacation in January during which they will likely be glued to their BlackBerries or other such devices. What is the point? They will all be forgotten in fifty years anyway. Steve Ballmer, Steven Cohen, and Larry Ellison will all be forgotten. I do not understand the legacy thing. Nearly everyone will be forgotten. Give up on leaving your mark. Throw the BlackBerry away and enjoy life.

So this is it. With all due respect, I am dropping out. . . . I truly do not have a strong opinion about any market right now, other than to say that things will continue to get worse for some time, probably years. I am content sitting on the sidelines and waiting. After all, sitting and waiting is how we made money from the subprime debacle. . . .

On the issue of the U.S. Government, I would like to make a modest proposal. First, I point out the obvious flaws, whereby legislation was repeatedly brought forth to Congress over the past eight years, which *would have reined in the predatory lending practices of now mostly defunct institutions. These institutions regularly filled the coffers of both parties in return for voting down all of this legislation designed to protect the common citizen. This is an outrage, yet no one seems to know or care about it. Since Thomas Jefferson and Adam Smith passed, I would argue that there has been a dearth of worthy philosophers in this country, at least ones focused on improving government. Capitalism worked for two hundred years, but times change, and systems become corrupt. George Soros, a man of staggering wealth, has stated that he would like to be remembered as a philosopher. My suggestion is that this great man start and sponsor a forum for great minds to come together to create a new system of government that truly represents the common man's interest, while at the same time creating rewards great enough to attract the best and brightest minds to serve in government roles without having to rely on corruption to further their interests or lifestyles. . . . I believe there is an answer, but for now the system is clearly broken. . . .*

Lastly, while I still have an audience, I would like to bring attention to an alternative food and energy source . . . hemp. . . . At a time when rhetoric is flying about becoming more self-sufficient in terms of energy, why is it illegal to grow this plant in this country? Ah, the female. The evil female plant—marijuana. It gets you high, it makes you laugh, it does not produce a hangover. . . . My only conclusion as to why it is illegal, is that Corporate America, which owns Congress, would rather sell you Paxil, Zoloft, Xanax, and other addictive drugs, than allow you to grow a plant in your home without some of the profits going into their coffers. This policy is ludicrous. . . . With that I say good-bye and good luck.

All the best,
Andrew Lahde

L IKE LAHDE, Paolo Pellegrini figured that his success would give him a voice in the financial world. As the markets melted in late 2008, Pellegrini developed ways to potentially stabilize the housing market.

He reached out to a leading congressman, hoping he might embrace the ideas. The meeting was rescheduled a few times, but Pellegrini finally scored an appointment. A driving snowstorm delayed him by about ten minutes, but Pellegrini arrived at the office brimming with confidence.

He wasn't greeted with much enthusiasm, however.

"You're late," the congressman said when Pellegrini made it to his office. "Don't you know I'm going to have dinner with my wife?"

Pellegrini watched as his host walked past him and right out the door.

Later, Pellegrini wrote an elaborate opinion piece arguing for auctions of distressed home mortgages and subsidized funding for buyers. Pellegrini hired Rubenstein & Co., a high-powered public relations firm, to shop his editorial to newspapers, including *The Wall Street Journal*. But Pellegrini received rejection after rejection. The only outlet willing to publish the piece was a blog site run by the *New York Times*. The piece was largely ignored on Wall Street and in Washington.

Pellegrini wasn't making much more progress within Paulson & Co. Andrew Hoine and others on the research team were helping John Paulson develop a gutsy new strategy. For all his success developing the greatest trade in history, Pellegrini again was overlooked and didn't see much future at the hedge fund. On December 31, 2008, Pellegrini resigned to start his own fund to focus on currencies and larger economic trends, using $100 million or so of his own money to get it off the ground. Paulson wished him well.

Investors and competitors once scoffed at John Paulson. But he found newfound power, along with adulation and even envy, as a result of his big trade. Reaping about $6 billion over two years, the biggest sum of money ever made by a single person in the history of financial markets, along with $20 billion or so for his firm and its clients, tends to do that.

When news emerged in the summer of 2009 that Paulson & Co. had purchased $100 million worth of shares of CB Richard Ellis, shares of the real estate broker immediately surged 15 percent, leading to a quick $15 million profit, a sign of the Midas touch accorded to him. In August, news that Paulson was buying shares of Bank of America sent shares soaring and tongues wagging. *New York* magazine's online blog even introduced a periodic column called "If We Were Friends with John Paulson." It features snippets of imagined conversations between Paulson and a reporter who at one point asks Paulson: "Have you ever thought about adopting a child? Like, an adult one?"

Rather than celebrate, Paulson found that the trade meant more work. By the beginning of 2009, he managed $36 billion of clients' money. He and his firm quickly pocketed more than $400 million—including almost $70 million in one twenty-five-minute period—betting against shares of big British banks. Paulson appeared more tired than he had in years but at the same time he seemed energized by this new chapter in his career. He moved his firm to prime office space across from Radio City Music Hall, choosing soothing beige and white colors throughout the firm.

Paulson turned more protective of his private life, filing an application to beef up the hedges on the approach to his $41.3 million Southampton home as a security precaution.¹ He turned reticent about sharing seemingly innocuous information about his private life. Asked when he had begun collecting Calders, Paulson wouldn't say, other than to note that they were gouaches, a type of watercolor.

But in many other ways, Paulson hadn't changed at all—it was as if the trade hadn't taken place. At one point, a friend was shocked to bump into him in a supermarket in Southampton wheeling a shopping cart full of store-brand groceries. Paulson continues to arrive at his Manhattan office early, wearing a dark suit and a tie, and leaving around 6 p.m. for his short commute home. When it rains and he can't find a cab, Paulson still hops on a New York City bus.

"I only need transportation to go to work in the morning and when I come home," Paulson says, explaining why he doesn't have a car and driver. "It would be kind of a waste with nothing to do in between, as I rarely leave the office during the day."

Others who experienced the collapse of the housing market and the deepest economic downturn since World War II didn't have the luxury of choosing their method of transport. After many delays, the

Monteses, the home owners in Orange County who faced a skyrocketing interest rate on a house they no longer could afford, finally received a loan modification from their lender that lowered their payments. They cut out vacations and nights out, and pulled their daughters out of Catholic school, but still were left very stretched. In mid 2009, they were hoping for another loan modification under a plan unveiled by President Obama but weren't making much progress.

"We don't have much of a life," says Mario, whose wife now cuts his hair as well as her own. "We're one plumbing problem away from default."

JOHN PAULSON profited from one of the biggest financial bubbles in history. But another bubble inevitably awaits. Veteran investor Jeremy Grantham has identified twenty-eight bubbles in various global markets since 1920; the past decade alone has witnessed historic bubbles in Asian currencies, Internet stocks, real estate, and commodity prices, as if markets are becoming less efficient, not more so. Ever more furious competition among investors, and the growing ease with which they quickly can shift cash to almost any kind of market around the globe, may be partly responsible for the change.

Extremely low interest rates, a key ingredient in past bubbles, have the potential to inflate the next one. The appetite to lend likely has been sated for a while, but it won't be long before bankers convince themselves of the next easy way to score sure profits. Perhaps massive increases in public-sector borrowing, which likely will prove harder to reduce than they were to expand, will sow the seeds of the next financial bubble. Growth stemming from bank credit and government deficits seems more unstable than an expansion driven by innovation and rising productivity.

George Soros and others have encouraged regulators to step in to tame budding asset expansions. But it seems unlikely that any group of bankers, academics, or bureaucrats will be any better at predicting, or even identifying, future bubbles in time to help curtail them.

That so much trading today involves complex financial products in markets with little transparency makes it more challenging for professional investors, let alone individuals, who likely will find it hard to track arcane and yet crucial instruments such as distressed debt, credit-default swaps, and other derivatives that top traders increasingly focus on.

And yet, just as John Paulson and the group of investors who discovered how to profit from the housing collapse were largely outsiders to the mortgage and real estate game, amateurs may have the best opportunity to identify and profit from future bubbles. Financial pros increasingly form their views by watching the same business-television broadcasts and reading the same articles, creating an opening for those on the outside willing to challenge the conventional wisdom.

It may be no coincidence that the housing bubble burst around the time that products emerged to allow bearish renegades like John Paulson and others to bet against the real estate market. It would suggest that dissidents who dare to raise questions and wager against markets should be encouraged, rather than scorned.

B Y EARLY 2009, John Paulson itched to start buying investments again. He was never very comfortable as a short seller. Making money was his passion, not sticking with any particular dogma. As Paulson pored over the balance sheets of the financial companies that he had spent more than three years betting against, he concluded that they had fallen too far in price. Paulson ordered his traders to begin purchasing the debt of troubled companies, securities backed by home and commercial mortgages, shares of banks, and other investments.

It was a slow accumulation and well below the radar screen, but by August he owned a huge cache of about $20 billion of these investments, convinced that the economy had regained its footing. The step earned his firm about $3 billion in the first half of the year as financial markets began to show some life.

As Paulson sat in Andrew Hoine's nearby office one day, discussing how much was being spent by the United States and other nations to rescue areas of the economy crippled by the financial collapse, Paulson discovered his next target, one he was certain was as doomed to collapse as subprime mortgages once had been: the U.S. dollar.

Paulson made a simple calculation: The supply of dollars had expanded by 120 percent over several months. That surely would lead to a drop in its value, and an eventual surge in inflation.

"With all this spending, we're going to have massive inflation," Paulson told Hoine, arguing that almost every major currency was at risk, other than the Chinese yuan. "What's the only asset that will hold value? It's got to be gold."

Paulson never had even dabbled in gold, and had no currency experts on his team. Some of his investors were skeptical of his argument, noting a burst of inflation was unlikely with unemployment high, wages stagnant, and businesses running at a fraction of their potential capacity. Others said too many other investors already had flocked to gold. Some of Paulson's investors withdrew money from the fund, pushing his assets down to $28 billion or so.

Paulson acknowledged that his was a straightforward argument, but he paid the critics little heed and proceeded to buy more than $1 billion of shares of gold miners, or 12 percent of his largest fund. He also purchased billions of dollars of gold investments to back new classes of his funds denominated by gold and chose these classes for his own money.

Betting against the dollar would be his new trade.

"I couldn't be more confident," Paulson said in the summer of 2009. "Three or four years from now people will ask why they didn't buy gold earlier. Over time our currency will lose value and inflation will rise—that's our future."

His passion for yet another big trade was hard to mask.

"It's like Wimbledon," he says. "When you win one year, you don't quit; you want to win again."

afterword

The fact that an opinion has been widely held is no evidence whatever that
it is not utterly absurd; indeed, in view of the silliness of the majority of mankind,
a widespread belief is more likely to be foolish than sensible.
— Bertrand Russell

A FEW SAVVY INVESTORS—MOST WITH LITTLE RELATIVE EXPERI-
ence in real estate, derivatives, or mortgage investing—
anticipated a historic housing and financial collapse.
Their remarkable success begs an obvious question: Why did this unlikely group predict the crumbling of the housing market and the resulting pain felt around the globe, even as the experts were stunned by
the developments?

Top regulators, including Alan Greenspan, Ben Bernanke, Henry
Paulson, and Timothy Geithner, were caught flat-footed. Senior bankers
like Robert Rubin, Charles Prince, Stanley O'Neal, Richard Fuld, and
James Cayne oversaw firms that lost hundreds of billions of dollars from
mortgage holdings. Top analysts, traders, economists, and academics
expected housing to hold up. Real estate, mortgage, and derivative investors all missed the huge trade, as did so-called short sellers, investors
who go to sleep at night dreaming of calamities they can bet against.

Some blame the difficult period on overcompensated bankers and
the toxic products they created; others point the finger at cynical traders

who rolled the dice with their firms' money. These explanations are simplistic and overstated. Certainly, some Wall Street pros had concerns about housing and nonetheless peddled unsafe products, hoping to squeeze out one last, hefty bonus. Others embraced risky trades without worrying about the potential downside. But many more were shocked by the turn of events and squandered enormous wealth when subprime mortgages collapsed.

Why did the experts get it so wrong? And what can we learn from the episode?

The answers are varied. Products on Wall Street evolve, becoming more complicated with time, partly so hefty commissions can be charged and salesmen have something new to pitch customers. In the case of the housing market, residential mortgage-backed bonds begat collateralized debt obligations, leading to CDOs squared, and then synthetic CDOs. By the middle of the 2000s, top executives at global banks had few clues how dangerous these mortgage products had become, even as their own banks sold them to clients and retained huge pieces of them.

Rubin, chairman of the Citigroup board of directors' executive committee at the time of the housing bubble, testified before Congress in the spring of 2010 that until the fall of 2007 he didn't recall learning about CDO investments his bank was creating, owning, and selling. Sure, Rubin made $15 million a year at Citigroup. But examining these complex products wasn't what he was paid to do, he testified, partly because credit-rating companies deemed them supersafe.

"More senior level consideration of these particular positions was unnecessary because the positions were AAA-rated and appeared to bear de minimis risk of default," Rubin testified.

At the same hearing, Prince, who walked away with more than $100 million in compensation for his work as Citigroup's CEO during the housing bubble, added: "We believed that the top level would be immune to the problems. . . . Sitting here today, that belief looks unwise, but I think at the time Moody's was quoted as saying these problems would never reach the super-senior" slices of CDOs and other debt products.

Citigroup ended up losing $30 billion from CDOs, triggering a $45 billion federal bailout, the largest of any financial firm.

Within the boardrooms of global banks, Rubin and Prince were no exceptions. Most senior bankers were clueless about CDOs and other complicated mortgage products.

"If you find this confusing, you should," John Paulson told investors in 2010, referring to CDO investments. "Most people do. Even the people who participated in this market didn't understand it either."

Instead of mastering these products, senior bankers generally deferred to midlevel specialists. How did these pros get it so wrong? They often relied on top-notch grades placed on the investments by ratings companies. Others depended on sophisticated computer models suggesting that a national or international plunge for housing was unlikely—largely because such a downturn hadn't occurred in seven decades. The models couldn't have been more wrong.

Another key reason a widespread housing downturn seemed improbable: Few of the industry's experts had a memory of the early 1990s, when large swaths of the California, Texas, and Massachusetts real estate markets tumbled in value. Wall Street bankers, traders, and investors tend to make so much money that they retire early, or find other things to do, leaving the financial business to younger executives. At *The Wall Street Journal,* I go days without speaking with anyone who experienced the difficulties of 1998, when hedge-fund power Long Term Capital Management collapsed and almost brought down world markets. Those who remember the real estate troubles of the early 1990s are an even rarer breed. Too few bankers in 2005 judged a real estate collapse to be a realistic possibility because so few recalled previous housing difficulties.

Indeed, it's no coincidence the biggest winners of the downturn—John Paulson, Paolo Pellegrini, and Jeffrey Greene—were approaching fifty years of age. They retained vivid memories of past real estate problems. Youth was a detriment to pulling off the greatest trade ever and to preparing for the downturn.

It's also not an accident that many of those wracked by fears about the financial system in 2005 and 2006, such as Andrew Lahde and Michael Burry, didn't work at big banks, government agencies, or large companies. Those who climb to the top of big institutions, win elections, or are picked for important government posts tend to be optimists. They're leaders who inspire others, usually with an upbeat, can-do outlook. Placing one's feet on a desk, dimming the lights, and thinking hard about what could go wrong and how to prepare for it usually aren't steps that help an executive obtain a promotion. Ideas about how to top last quarter's profits, meet a short-term revenue goal, and stay a step ahead of rivals do.

On Wall Street, worrywarts tend to leave and work at hedge funds. Many of these individuals like to invest but don't entirely enjoy dealing with others, even their own clients. They get bored in meetings, have a hard time selling themselves to investors, and enjoy poking holes in bullish arguments. They may not be much fun to grab a beer with, but they're best suited to predict a coming disaster, as some did with the subprime collapse.

Wall Street talks a big game about the importance of taking a contrarian stance with investments. When it comes to a career in finance, however, there are few reasons to be a contrarian or to try to anticipate problems. Greg Lippmann took perhaps the most risk of any investor in pursuing the bearish housing wager. He was being paid millions of dollars annually by Deutsche Bank in 2005 when he first had concerns about subprime mortgages. If Lippmann had continued to make investments predicated on housing staying firm, he would have lost money, like others at his bank and on Wall Street. But he likely would have kept his well-paid job. All he had to do was trot out the well-worn excuses of the business. Sorry, boss, but the downturn was a hundred-year flood. Who could have predicted the perfect storm that damaged the global economy? By describing the collapse of the financial system as a natural disaster, rather than as a series of man-made errors, countless pros acted blameless and retained lucrative jobs.

Rather than take this route, Lippmann bought unpopular protection on subprime mortgages. He was teased and insulted. If real estate had remained strong, Lippmann likely would have been fired. His wager was profitable and he ended up making millions, but his decision wasn't the most rational one. Too much downside, not enough upside, most traders would say. Too often it makes little sense to make gutsy, unorthodox bets in business, or prepare for difficult times.

Another reason Wall Street does a poor job foreseeing meltdowns is few firms are very good at recruiting and promoting risk managers, or enabling them to examine the exposures of various parts of their global businesses. In early 2007, some traders thought their groups were facing danger, but they were sure colleagues elsewhere weren't embracing similar risks. Too often they were. The problem: There are too many silos within big financial firms and too few executives eager to share information and concerns.

Goldman Sachs's risk managers enjoyed a fuller picture of the risks of various trading groups, partly because traders work more closely together, helping to explain why Goldman became concerned about housing before rivals, though still late in the game.

Perhaps the biggest reason outsiders saw the approaching storm was they weren't mortgage or real estate practitioners. They didn't buy into the groupthink of those industries that the Federal Reserve or U.S. government wouldn't let housing collapse, and that derivative investments were scary and dangerous. Paulson, Pellegrini, Burry, and Greene didn't know much about derivatives, but they took the time to educate themselves.

Paulson also ignored concerns that buying insurance on mortgage bonds would enable competitors to score better short-term results. The excessive focus on near-term results handcuffed many executives who tried to prepare for the downturn.

There wasn't a single personality type required to pull off the greatest trade in history. Paulson, Lippmann, and Greene were upbeat, outgoing investors comfortable chatting up investors and grilling mortgage lenders. Pellegrini, Burry, and Lahde were downbeat and had difficulty communicating their dire outlooks, preferring late nights slumped over arcane housing data.

But those who anticipated the collapse all were outside of the mainstream. They shared a supreme conviction in their gloomy, unorthodox views, a historic perspective, and an ability to ignore immediate setbacks. Only by encouraging these contrarians within business and government can we hope to avoid future meltdowns.

SOME DISMISS PAULSON and the other prescient investors as flukes. In early 2010, former Fed Chairman Greenspan called them a "statistical illusion."

"Everybody missed it," he said. "Academia, the Federal Reserve, all regulators."

Fed Chairman Ben Bernanke said there was little that could have been done, anyway. "We had neither the mandate nor the tools to be the financial system's supercop," he said in 2010.

It's not encouraging that key officials haven't taken full responsibility for their mistakes. They ignored warnings about loose lending standards and failed to caution borrowers about the risks of aggressive mortgage products. A better tack would be to learn from the few investors who got it right and avoid an overreliance on industry experts.

Despite that, many of the financial reforms embraced to prevent future financial debacles depend on new agencies and savvy regulators spotting future troubles. It's not obvious why they will be more successful anticipating the next bubble than they were at predicting the last one. A better step would be to force large financial companies to set aside more cash as a buffer for the next brutal downturn, one that sadly may be inevitable in an age of financial bubbles.

AFTER PULLING OFF his historic coup, John Paulson set out to write a new chapter in his career. He turned bullish on the global economy in 2009, scoring a reported $2.3 billion in personal profits as markets turned higher, frustrating rivals who hoped he'd slip up, finally. Even as global financial markets crumbled in the summer of 2010, amid worries about various European countries and the United States, Paulson maintained a stubborn optimism, as if he was intent on shaking his image as an uber pessimist.

Paulson said it was a great time to buy a second house or help relatives purchase a home, predicting that housing prices in the United States would rise by as much as 12 percent in 2011 and that the economy would turn robust. He called the European debt crisis "manageable," even as his optimism led to trading losses in 2010.

"We are pretty excited by the opportunities in front of us," he told his clients, reassuring them. "If you don't own a home today, now is the time to buy one."

By the spring of 2010, investors had gained so much respect for Paulson that they had entrusted $33 billion in his hands, making Paulson & Company the second-largest hedge fund in the world. When he purchased a mere $44 million shares of Boyd Gaming Company, shares of the gambling company soared 12 percent, as other investors figured Paulson must be on to something.

But Paulson's tactics came under scrutiny in April 2010. That's when the Securities and Exchange Commission charged Goldman Sachs with civil fraud for its work with Pellegrini to create a $1 billion CDO, a deal that Paulson & Company bet against and scored $1 billion in profits. Goldman sold the deal in question, called Abacus 2007-AC1, to investors, including the big German bank IKB Deutsche Industriebank AG, which saw most of its $150 million Abacus investment evaporate.

It was just one of the series of deals that the Paulson team asked banks to create. The transactions led to huge losses for some of those very banks, such as Deutsche Bank, which didn't sell all of those products to investors and kept some on the bank's own books. But Goldman felt the biggest pain from the Paulson deals, emerging as the most despised banker in the world after the SEC levied its charges over the Abacus transaction.

Regulators suggested that unless new incriminating information arose, Paulson and his team wouldn't be charged with wrongdoing.

"Goldman was responsible for the representation to the investors, and Paulson was not," the SEC's head of enforcement, Robert Khuzami, told a group of lawyers and deal-makers.

Nonetheless, Paulson's involvement in the controversial transaction sparked a furious backlash in some quarters.

"He was involved in designing the security. For all we know right now, it was probably his idea," Simon Johnson, a well-known author and professor at the MIT Sloan School of Management told television host Bill Maher. "If he walks away without being charged, it shows how broken our system is."

Paulson even heard it from some outspoken moms. On a website popular in his Upper East Side neighborhood called UrbanBaby.com, a parenting message board where discussions normally center on strollers, diapers, and lactation consultants, some posters asked whether Paulson should remain on the board of the Spence School, a prestigious school for girls on the Upper East Side, and whether Paulson's profits from the housing bust were ethical. The question drew about seventy anonymous replies, some sounding off on the morality and utility of short-selling, credit default swaps, and hedge funds.

Paulson defended his actions to his investors, saying they were "appropriate and conducted in good faith. . . . We have always been forthright in expressing our opinions, and we never misrepresented our positions."

Paulson was no superstar investor at the time Goldman sold the CDO, he reminded investors.

"When we expressed our concerns about the mortgage markets, many of the most sophisticated investors in the world, who had analyzed the same publicly available data we had, were fully convinced that we were wrong, and more than willing to bet against us," he wrote to his clients.

Indeed, Paulson never sold any of the CDO investments under examination, including the Goldman CDO, to investors. Those who purchased Abacus were sophisticated institutions capable of examining the CDO's collateral, much as Paulson and Pellegrini did. As such, while Goldman withheld information from investors like IKB, such as the fact that Pellegrini played an important role in helping to create the controversial CDO, it's not clear they withheld *material* information.

By the late summer of 2010, Goldman had settled the charges, paying the SEC $550 million, and Paulson had largely put the controversy behind him. He turned his attention to his shiny new investment—gold. Paulson was so convinced that inflation would rise and that major currencies were set to fall that he and his firm plowed more than $5 billion into gold-related investments. That made Paulson the largest individual owner of gold in the world, with holdings that by some accounts topped those of Australia, Brazil, and Argentina. Paulson departed for London in the summer of that year intent on retaining his perch atop Wall Street upon his return.

As for Paolo Pellegrini, he watched the frenzy surrounding Paulson, Goldman, and the controversial Abacus transaction with mounting frustration. Early television reports in the spring of 2010 painted Pellegrini as a whistle-blower who had turned on Paulson and supplied key information to investigators. In truth, Pellegrini did little more than answer questions posed by government officials, telling them that he and Paulson did nothing wrong.

By early 2010, Pellegrini had little to do with Paulson or even the New York financial community. A year earlier, Pellegrini began splitting his time between Bermuda and New York, choosing to try to build his own hedge-fund empire by the calm, blue sea. Pellegrini scored big early trading gains, thanks to a more pessimistic outlook for global economies than his old boss Paulson. But Pellegrini only managed to raise about $50 million from investors for his new firm. And when a bearish wager against the U.S. dollar and Treasury bonds went awry in the summer of 2010 and his fund suffered losses of 11 percent, Pellegrini pulled the plug on his nascent firm and returned all of his clients' cash.

Building his own hedge-fund empire wouldn't be possible, Pellegrini concluded, regretfully. Managing his own money while enjoying Bermuda's low taxes, island setting, and opportunity to socialize with fellow financiers, such as New York City Mayor Michael Bloomberg, would have to suffice.

"Commuting to work with my outboard dinghy across Hamilton Harbor does facilitate a relaxed and productive setting for my Bermuda workdays," he said in an e-mail.

Andrew Lahde, from time to time, returns from his own island retreat to Los Angeles to meet investors, discuss business opportunities, and attend speeches about drug legalization. During the summer of 2010, he even contemplated starting a bank.

"After all, you can borrow from depositors and the Fed at 0.25 percent, then buy long Treasuries at 3.5 percent, and go to the beach," Lahde said in an e-mail message. "Of course, that would last only until rates rose and the value of your long bonds fell. But who in a capitalist economy cares about the next quarter if your bonus is tied to this quarter?"

In the end, though, he chose the island life, spending the entire winter by the sea as he dabbled in precious-metal investments and interests, including snorkeling, relaxing by the beach, and ogling women. Lahde even started a photography company "to pursue several of these interests simultaneously," he said in an e-mail.

"I have no motivation. I like not working. Stress is not fun," Lahde said, adding that he was trying to nurse himself back to health after "taking a beating" from two years of stress related to his big trade.

By the summer of 2010, Greg Lippmann finally tired of working for Deutsche Bank. After years of bluffing that he would bolt over disappointing bonuses, Lippmann told his bosses he was leaving to launch his own hedge fund. Like Paulson, however, questions surrounded Lippmann. He and Deutsche Bank weren't accused of any inappropriate actions. But some CDO-related transactions created by others at the bank came under investigation by federal authorities, presenting Lippmann with a potential challenge as he tried to round up clients.

Michael Burry spent months deciding what to do with the rest of his life, but he still had no concrete answer by the middle of 2010. Some of his bitterness had dissipated, thanks to belated public recognition for his early work detecting the financial bubble, recognition related to this book and one by author Michael Lewis. His trade didn't turn Burry into the next George Soros, but it did make him a wealthy man.

Burry even felt confident enough to publicly tangle with Alan Greenspan.

"As a nation, we cannot afford to live with Mr. Greenspan's way of thinking," wrote Michael Burry in an op-ed in the *New York Times* in April 2010. "The truth is, he should have seen what was coming and offered a sober, apolitical warning. Everyone would have listened; when he talked about the economy, the world hung on every single word."

But Burry remained gloomy about how his clients had treated him and how little had been learned from the dark period.

"I would say that I've lost a lot of faith in the human race, and that has yet to be restored," he said in an e-mail message. "That's what really hurts—not so much what was accorded to me, but the tremendous failure of American society. It rips my heart out to think we are veering so far from what made America great. It's remarkably sad on many levels."

Jeffrey Greene also decided to turn away from investing. Focusing on politics instead, he launched a quixotic effort to win the Democratic nomination for Senate from his new home in Palm Beach, Florida. Running as a Democrat and saying he was prepared to spend $40 million to win the seat, Greene met more than a few snickers. Some brought up his colorful past, including his friendships with boxer Mike Tyson and Heidi Fleiss, the Hollywood Madam, and Greene's escapades as an eligible bachelor, to suggest he wasn't a serious candidate. Fresh pictures of Greene chatting with troubled actress Lindsey Lohan in St. Barts didn't help his credibility.

But the heavy advertising spending and a serious mien helped convince some voters to ignore Greene's flashy past.

"Government has a very important purpose, and that's one of the reasons that I'm a Democrat," Greene told the *Miami Herald* editorial board, even though he hadn't registered as a Democrat until 2008. "To me, it's not about a safety net. It's about a trampoline. We need to create a chance for the people at the bottom to bounce back up."

By the summer of 2010, Greene was closing in on the Democratic front-runner opposing him. Once again, the experts were shocked.

acknowledgments

John Paulson spent more than fifty hours with me, discussing his trade, and for that I am appreciative. Many of the other protagonists in the story were just as generous with their time.

I'd also like to thank Robert Thomson, *The Wall Street Journal*'s managing editor; Nikhil Deogun, the paper's deputy managing editor; and Ken Brown, the editor of the paper's Money and Investing section, who gave their blessings for a leave to complete this book. Roger Scholl, my editor at Random House, and David McCormick, my agent at McCormick & Williams, provided expert insight and valued guidance, not to mention a snazzy title. I'm grateful for the invaluable counsel and critiques of colleagues, former colleagues, friends, and family members including Ezra Zuckerman Sivan, Hal Lux, Karen Richardson, Joanna Slater, Craig Karmin, Serena Ng, Richard Regis, Lynn Davidman, Avigaiyil Goldscheider, and Erin Arvedlund. William Lloyd and Janet Tavakoli made sure I kept mistakes to a minimum. And I'm indebted to Sarah Morgan and Shelly Banjo, two remarkable research assistants.

I couldn't have completed this project without the patience and support of my wife, Michelle, who somehow convinced me to keep going, as well as the love of Gabriel and Elijah, the best boys any father could ask for. I am eternally grateful for the unwavering encouragement and love of my mother and father. Their confidence in me is the backbone of whatever success I achieve.

When I was young and still impressionable, my father worked with me on my writing. Keep it as tight and simple as possible, he urged. Be creative. My work is an echo of his research and writing, his guidance as close as the keyboard in front of me. The greatest trade ever brought John Paulson billions of dollars. The opportunity to write about it gave me my own fortune—precious extra time with my father, of blessed memory.

notes

Chapter 1

1. Greenwich Associates, "In U.S. Fixed Income, Hedge Funds Are the Biggest Game in Town," August 30, 2007; Mark Jickling and Alison A. Raab, "Hedge Fund Failures," *Congressional Research Service Report for Congress*, December 4, 2006.
2. Dr. David DeBoskey, Charles W. Lamden School of Accountancy, San Diego State University College of Business Administration.
3. Michael J. de la Merced, "Culturally, Hedge Funds Go Public," *New York Times*, December 8, 2006.
4. Gregory Zuckerman and Henny Sender, "Exclusive Club: Ex-Trader Creates Hot Hedge Fund, and a Traffic Jam," *The Wall Street Journal*, January 12, 2005.
5. Gregory Zuckerman and Cassell Bryan-Low, "With the Market Up, Wall Street High Life Bounces Back, Too—Chartered Jets, a Wedding at Versailles and Fast Cars to Help Forget Bad Times," *The Wall Street Journal*, February 4, 2004.
6. Russ Alan Prince, Edward A. Renn, Arthur A. Bavelas, and Mindy F. Rosenthal, *Fortune's Fortress: A Primer on Wealth Preservation for Hedge Fund Professionals*, New York: MARHedge, 2007.
7. Gary Weiss, "The Man Who Made Too Much," *Portfolio*, February 2009.

Chapter 2

1. Benjamin Franklin, *The Way to Wealth*, 1758 (originally published as a preface to *Poor Richard's Almanac*).
2. Courtney Kane, "MasterCard Hopes to Become the Credit Card of Choice for Ordinary, Middle-class Consumers," *New York Times*, October 22, 1997.
3. Gregory Zuckerman, "Debtor Nation: Borrowing Levels Reach a Record, Sparking Debate," *The Wall Street Journal*, July 5, 2000.
4. Louise Story, "Home Equity Frenzy Was a Bank Ad Come True," *New York Times*, August 14, 2008.
5. Gretchen Morgenson and Geraldine Fabrikant, "Countrywide's Chief Salesman and Defender," *New York Times*, November 11, 2007.
6. Lew Sichelman, "Mozilo: End Downpayment Requirement," *National Mortgage News*, February 17, 2003.
7. James R. Hagerty, Ruth Simon, Michael Corkery, and Gregory Zuckerman, "Home

Stretch: At a Mortgage Lender, Rapid Rise, Faster Fall," *The Wall Street Journal,* March 12, 2007; John Gittelsohn and Mathew Padilla, "How New Century Ran Out of Money," *Orange County Register,* April 15, 2007.

8. Mark Zandi, chief economist and cofounder of Moody's Economy.com.

9. CNBC transcript; Interview: Angelo Mozilo of Countrywide Financial Discusses the Housing Market, CNBC: *Kudlow & Cramer,* December 23, 2004.

10. Carol Lloyd, "Impossible Loan Turns Dream Home into Nightmare," *San Francisco Chronicle,* April 15, 2007.

11. Peter S. Goodman and Gretchen Morgenson, "Saying Yes, WaMu Built Empire on Shaky Loans," *New York Times,* December 28, 2008.

Chapter 3

1. Gabriel Sherman, "New Kid in Town," *New York Observer,* April 11, 2004.

Chapter 4

1. Mark Pittman, "Subprime Securities Market Began as 'Group of 5' Over Chinese," *Bloomberg,* December 17, 2007.

Chapter 6

1. Christopher Reed, "The Damn'd South Sea," *Harvard Magazine,* May–June 1999.

2. James Grant, *Mr. Market Miscalculates: The Bubble Years and Behind,* Axios Press, Mount Jackson, Virginia: 2008.

3. "Jesse Livermore Ends Life in Hotel," *New York Times,* November 29, 1940.

4. Gregory Zuckerman, "Hedged Out: How the Soros Funds Lost Game of Chicken Against Tech Stocks," *The Wall Street Journal,* May 22, 2000.

5. Ezra Zuckerman, "Realists, Constructionists, and Lemmings Oh My! (Part 1)," post on OrgTheory.net blog, October 26, 2008. http://orgtheory.wordpress.com/2008/10/26/realists-constructionists-and-lemmings-oh-my-part-i/.

6. Aaron Lucchetti, "S&P Email: 'We Should Not Be Rating It,'" *The Wall Street Journal,* August 2, 2008.

7. Gregory Zuckerman, "A Bond Star's Plays Turn Riskier," *The Wall Street Journal,* August 23, 2006.

8. George Soros, *Soros on Soros,* New York: John Wiley, 1995.

Chapter 8

1. Devan Sipher and Mireya Navarro, "Mei Sze Chan and Jeff Greene," *New York Times,* November 4, 2007.

2. Michael Lewis, "The End," *Portfolio Magazine,* December 2008.

Chapter 9

1. Serena Ng and Carrick Mollenkamp, "Merrill Takes $8.4 Billion Credit Hit—It Plunged Into CDOs in '03, Hiring Pioneer of the Debt Securities," *The Wall Street Journal,* October 25, 2007.

2. Gary Gorton, "The Subprime Panic," working paper, Yale School of Management and National Bureau of Economic Research, September 30, 2008.

3. Serena Ng and Carrick Mollenkamp, "Wall Street Wizardry Amplified Credit Crisis," *The Wall Street Journal*, December 27, 2007.

Chapter 11

1. Kate Kelly, "Behind a Bear Analyst's Subprime Call," *The Wall Street Journal*, July 11, 2007.

2. Pierre Paulden, "TRADING—Trading on the Edge," *Institutional Investor—Americas*, June 13, 2007.

3. Vikas Bajai, "Prospering in an Implosion," *New York Times*, April 12, 2007.

4. Kate Kelly, "The Fall of Bear Stearns: Lost Opportunities Haunt Final Days of Bear Stearns—Executives Bickered Over Raising Cash, Cutting Mortgages," *The Wall Street Journal*, May 27, 2008.

Chapter 12

1. James R. Hagerty and Ken Gepfert, "Dream Homes Not Always Ideal: Some an Ordeal," *The Wall Street Journal*, September 2, 2007.

2. Jonathan Karp, "In Beverly Hills, a Meltdown Mogul Is Living Large," *The Wall Street Journal*, January 15, 2008; Devan Sipher and Mireya Navarro, "Mei Sze Chan and Jeff Greene," *New York Times*, November 4, 2007.

3. Henny Sender and Monica Langley, "Buyout Mogul: How Blackstone's Chief Became $7 Billion Man," *The Wall Street Journal*, June 13, 2007.

Chapter 14

1. Kate Kelly, "The Fall of Bear Stearns: Lost Opportunities Haunt Final Days of Bear Stearns—Executives Bickered Over Raising Cash, Cutting Mortgages," *The Wall Street Journal*, May 27, 2008.

2. Carrick Mollenkamp, Susanne Craig, Jeffrey McCracken, and Jon Hilsenrath, "The Two Faces of Lehman's Fall—Private Talks of Raising Capital Belied Firm's Public Optimism," *The Wall Street Journal*, October 6, 2008; Lawrence G. McDonald with Patrick Robinson, *A Colossal Failure of Common Sense—The Inside Story of the Collapse of Lehman Brothers*, New York: Crown Business, 2009.

3. See note 2 above.

4. Kate Kelly, "The Saga of Bear's Fund Chiefs—In a Jail Cell, One Asks, 'How Did We End Up in This Spot?,'" *The Wall Street Journal*, June 21, 2008.

Epilogue

1. Cityfile.com, "Security Precautions: John Paulson Beefs Up the Hedges," http://cityfile.com/dailyfile/4361, February 11, 2009.

index

about the author

GREGORY ZUCKERMAN is a senior writer at the *Wall Street Journal*, where he has been a reporter for twelve years.

GregoryZuckerman.com